Old Friends

Old Friends

VISITS WITH MY FAVORITE THOROUGHBREDS

Photos and Text by Eclipse Award-winning photographer

BARBARA D. LIVINGSTON

ECLIPSE PRESS

Lexington, Kentucky

Library of Congress Control Number: 2002101507

ISBN 1-58150-083-1

Printed in Hong Kong
First Edition: September 2002

Distributed to the trade by
National Book Network
4720-A Boston Way, Lanham, MD 20706
1.800.462.6420

ECLIPSE
PRESS

a division of The Blood-Horse, Inc.
PUBLISHERS SINCE 1916

Contents

Introduction

I was a wide-eyed girl of sixteen the first time I visited Kentucky. I had always loved Thoroughbreds but had seen only the horses that visited "my backyard," Saratoga. Kentucky was a wonderland to me.

I had read Joe Estes' stories in old issues of *The Blood-Horse* magazine and was riveted by his tales of retired Thoroughbreds and historic Kentucky farms. Estes transported me to another time in racing's grand history and brought horses like Whirlaway to life.

While in Kentucky, my mother and I went to farms such as Gainesway, Darby Dan, and Claiborne. But armed with our first "real" 35mm camera, we first drove through the famed front gates of Spendthrift Farm. It was 1977.

In Spendthrift's "Nashua Motel" courtyard, a groom pulled a twenty-five-year-old stallion from his stall for my waiting camera. The gentleman held the shank with attentive care, entertaining us with rich tales of the horse's lifetime and personality. From my childhood I had known this horse's name, as well as the statistics of his magnificent racetrack record. Yet the stories the groom told were at first hard to imagine, as the old stallion chewed indifferently on the shank.

But the old horse suddenly raised his head high and looked far past me, his brilliant eyes fixated on something beyond my scope. I snapped two quick shots, awestruck by his subdued power.

The great Nashua, of whom I have two mediocre photographs, died five years later at the age of thirty. Tears came easily when I read the obituary, imagining the loss that his loving groom, Clem Brooks, must have felt.

* * *

What began with awe in a teenage girl developed into a lifetime passion: visiting and recording older Thoroughbreds on film. What makes these older horses so special is difficult to put into words, and yet each animal is magic. Perhaps it is their lifetime of experience and their loss of the flightiness of youth. Perhaps it is part nostalgia, the love of what we remember from our own youths. Perhaps it is best expressed through stories…

Chinook Pass, 1983's champion sprinter, still attracts new fans to the sport through public appearances. The lovely Allegretta quietly continues to leave her mark on European classics through her descendants…

Like Nashua, some horses recorded in these pages blazed

MERRICK their names into record books. Even most casual fans are aware of Affirmed, Seattle Slew, and Spectacular Bid.

But other older horses are less conspicuous contributors to the breed, such as Coral Dance and Sans Supplement. Their names will most likely be enveloped by time, remaining familiar only to the most fervent pedigree historians.

Yet each has a story, and many have a person who has loved them as devotedly as Clem Brooks did Nashua.

* * *

For me, the benchmark of older Thoroughbreds is the gallant Merrick.

For Merrick, a name nearly lost now, his devoted person was J. Cal Milam. Milam purchased Merrick in 1906, when the horse was three years old. Over the years, Merrick won sixty-one races. Twice Merrick was claimed, and twice Milam bought him back.

In the Churchill Downs paddock before his 205th start, the eleven-year-old Merrick dipped his head gently against his devoted owner. Milam made his horse a promise: if he did not win that day, Merrick would never need wear a bridle again. Merrick lost and was retired to Milam's Merrick Place in Lexington, Kentucky, to live out his days.

As Merrick aged, his popularity increased. By the time Merrick passed away in March 1941, the beloved old-timer had attained the title of "the oldest Thoroughbred in the entire history of the race." He was thirty-eight.

In 2002 a stallion named Bargain Day jogs slowly to the corner of his California paddock where he socializes with a fellow stallion. Marilyn Rose, owner of Van Mar Farms where Bargain Day has held residence for more than thirty years, speaks proudly about how he helped her and her late husband in their farm's early years.

At the time of this writing, thirty-seven-year-old Bargain Day is fast approaching Merrick's American record.

I feel wonderfully honored to photograph Bargain Day and every other senior horse. But I cannot express the reasons why any more easily than I can explain what makes each horse so special me.

Perhaps what has so charmed me in these older Thoroughbreds becomes most clear through the writing, as I often used words such as "proud," "grace," and "dignified." These beautiful animals deserve no less. From Genuine Risk and Waya in their woolly winter best to Proud Birdie and Kris S. in their glossy summer beauty, each possessed a certain quality that only age could provide.

In their aged grace, all have held the hearts of the people who have loved them. And each has filled this photographer's heart with the same awe that the great Nashua did, a quarter of a century ago.

Barbara D. Livingston
Saratoga Springs, New York 2002

Affirmed

CH. H. 1975-2001, BY EXCLUSIVE NATIVE—WON'T TELL YOU,
BY CRAFTY ADMIRAL

The beautiful golden chestnut was considered by many to be the classiest Thoroughbred of all. Richard Stone Reeves has often written of Affirmed's class and grace, as have countless fans and horsemen. Even those with a penchant for the underdog, who preferred to dislike him because of a horse named Alydar, melted with just a glimpse at the golden chestnut. It was impossible not to respect him.

It was a warm morning in June 1998 when I drove into Jonabell. The sun had not yet risen but had made itself known by highlighting the horizon. I walked into the stallion barn where sounds of countless mornings were intermixing. Horses chomped on hay and swished tails, as grooms moved in busy order.

In one stall a light gray horse was plopped heavily in deep straw, his dappled coat luminescent against rich gold. His head was turned with pinned ears, his hind end aimed fully at the door. His head bobbed to the straw and then up again, as noises came from near and far.

A groom moved into the dozing horse's stall and pushed on his gray hindquarters. The lazy stallion swung his head around and told the groom it was too early. The groom pushed again, harder this time, and Holy Bull grudgingly rose.

Minutes later stallions were led to their paddocks, the sun as hesitant to rise as Holy Bull.

Virginia Rapids galloped in dizzy flight around his paddock, while Gold Legend stood quietly. Cherokee Run came next, his head down and mood quiet. Housebuster jogged to the far end of his plot and jogged back with his ears forward. "The Bull" was in no hurry to move outside, either.

All the while, the most beautiful stallion of all stood watching the morning unfold. Through the bars of the stall's back door, Affirmed's lovely profile was breathtaking. The twenty-three-year-old didn't move or make a sound.

Affirmed had not gone out because he was to breed that morning, and the groom asked whether he could pose the horse for me near the barn. Mesmerized by the charming stallion, I was happy to spend any time at all with him.

Affirmed made my heart melt again that 1998 day, as he had the first time I'd seen him at Saratoga twenty years earlier. He walked out with gentle dignity and stood the same way. And when we were finished with the photo session, Affirmed turned and walked back to his stall with the same relaxed style that had made him a favorite of countless thousands.

* * *

When Affirmed first headed postward on May 24, 1977, the Harbor View Farm runner was 14.30-1. But he ran like odds-on, romping by four and a half lengths.

The lovely chestnut next met a darker chestnut named Alydar, a colt with whom he'd be forever linked. The two colts clashed ten times on the track, and although Affirmed finished ahead on eight of those occasions, fans' hearts went out to Alydar for his determination and perseverance. Their Triple Crown battles are legendary. Affirmed swept the famed series, but Alydar's losses were by one and a half lengths, a neck, and a head.

Affirmed was an intelligent colt who moved with gentle grace. His mane and tail were braided before each race, and Harbor View's pink-white-and-black silks gave Affirmed an almost feminine look. Yet his composure and class were matched by a fierce competitive spirit that was undeniably masculine.

Affirmed was remarkable over three seasons, retiring in late 1979 after a powerful Jockey Club Gold Cup win over Spectacular Bid. Alydar had since been retired, and other steadfast campaigners such as Sirlad, Text, Tiller, and Coastal had replaced him in fruitless pursuit. As Patrick Robinson wrote in *Decade of Champions*: "…if there has ever been a more superlative example of stern, unrelenting courage in a thoroughbred horse, no one has yet made it public."

That courage resulted in a record of twenty-two wins, five seconds, and one third in twenty-nine starts. Affirmed set a track record of 1:58 3/5 in the Santa Anita Handicap, carried 132 pounds in victory, finished first in fifteen grade Is and earned $2,393,818.

* * *

He arrived at Spendthrift Farm when the famed stallion court known as the "Nashua Motel" was still in full swing. Nashua was twenty-seven, Gallant Man was twenty-five, and 1977 Triple Crown winner Seattle Slew had begun stud duties there the previous year.

Years passed, and Affirmed, gentle and quietly unassuming, was a favorite of Spendthrift tourists. When Spendthrift crumbled financially, Affirmed was moved to a most interesting location: Calumet Farm. There, he stood with — who else? — Alydar. The two chestnut descendants of Raise a Native resided in adjacent stalls, re-sparking memories of racing's most durable rivalry.

Alydar died in 1990 at the age of fifteen, as Calumet soon became embroiled in financial difficulties. Affirmed moved again, to Lexington's beautiful Jonabell Farm. There, the Triple Crown winner aged gracefully alongside a new group of stallions.

* * *

In October 2000 while in his paddock, Affirmed dislocated his left front pastern joint. Thus began a saga for the quiet fighter, later chronicled in a press release from the leading equine surgeon Larry Bramlage, who related that Affirmed "…began to overload the opposite forelimb. The condition was treated with a pastern arthrodesis. When he resumed exercise, he developed problems with the coffin bone joint and sesamoids related to his advancing age and his 26-year-old distal limb…"

Affirmed was sent to Rood and Riddle Equine Hospital on January 8, 2001, where his condition was studied closely. The breeding season would soon be underway, and Jonabell Farm contacted Affirmed shareholders to notify them that the grand stallion would miss at least the beginning of the season.

Twenty-three years had passed since Affirmed made history at Belmont Park, but the sturdy legs that had carried him to such heights had finally given way. Nothing more could be done for him, and on January 12, 2001, he was shipped back to his Jonabell home.

The golden chestnut stallion stepped off the van at Jonabell, his leg wrapped. He grazed in front of the barn for a while, happy to be home and content in the company of his caring, yet heavy-hearted, human companions.

Affirmed's last moments were spent outside, surrounded with love. Many tears were shed when the golden stallion was laid to rest later that day, a set of Harbor View silks interred with him.

No classier horse ever lived.

All Along

B. M. 1979, BY TARGOWICE—AGUJITA,
BY VIEUX MANOIR

imply put, All Along was awesome. And during the autumn of 1983, no Thoroughbred was better. She began the season in France with three losses, but came into her own on an October afternoon at Longchamp. First, she drove to victory in the Prix de l'Arc de Triomphe, then shipped to North America and just three races later left no doubt as to who was Horse of the Year.

After her Arc win, All Along ran three more races against colts, dominating each event. In Canada's Rothmans International, Walter Swinburn piloted her to an easy win over turf specialists Thunder Puddles and Majesty's Prince. She shipped to the States, and she again drew away from Thunder Puddles to win the Turf Classic by nearly nine lengths. Erins Isle, Late Act, and Chem languished in the beaten field.

By the time of the Washington, D.C., International, the bay filly was .40-1. Majesty's Prince (5.50-1) and Palikaraki (7.50-1) were given the only chance to beat her. She rewarded her backers with another rousing score, a fine

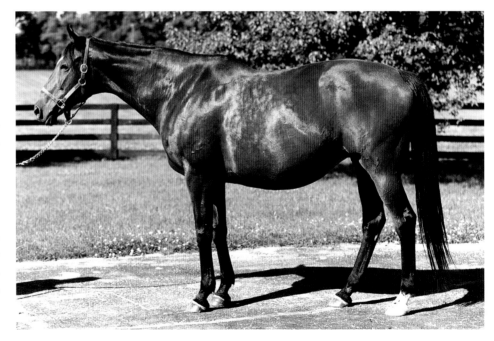

international cast sprawled out behind her.

That was all it took. The pretty filly, who went winless at four until October 2, had since dominated both sides of the Atlantic. She was named America's champion turf female and Horse of the Year, and champion older horse in France.

Even before October 1983, Daniel Wildenstein's All Along was good. She began her career in 1981 with a win, and came back in 1982 to race nine times. The Patrick Biancone-trainee won the group I Prix Vermeille, group II Prix Maurice de Nieuil, and group III Prix Penelope and ran a strong second in the Japan Cup to Half Iced.

But these good efforts were matched by equally convincing losses. In the 1982 Arc at 17-1, she weakened to finish fifteenth. By the time of the 1983 Arc, All Along had five straight losses and, as part of an entry, went off at 17.30-1.

Then came her remarkable win streak.

All Along raced again at five, globetrotting from New York to Longchamp to Woodbine to Hollywood, but she never won again. She was retired with $3,015,764 and nine wins in twenty-one starts.

All Along's first foal was a stakes winner. Named Along All, the Mill Reef colt won a French group II and earned $169,620. So far, he has been her best. Of her twelve foals of racing age, three are winners.

All Along was in foal to Three Chimneys' promising stallion Atticus in summer 2001. She is lovely, her beauty matched by her gentle disposition. She was tickled to be brought in from the Midway, Kentucky, paddock where she grazed with friends. Still awed by her racing performances, I was equally tickled to rub her face and say I'd touched All Along.

* * *

All Along produced a bay colt by Atticus on February 18, 2002, and was to be bred to War Chant.

Alleged

B. H. 1974-2000, BY HOIST THE FLAG—PRINCESS POUT,
BY PRINCE JOHN

*B*oth times I saw Alleged at Walmac International, he was standing the same way: on two legs. Alleged could be difficult, a horse who required two lead shanks and two grooms. Yet he was a beloved old stallion, and his fiery attitude made him all the more interesting. His groom had no fear of the big bay, dismissing any reports of attitude. "The only thing he doesn't like is the cold. Alleged hates the cold," he said.

Alleged was bred by June McKnight and born at Claiborne Farm, but he took the long route to Walmac. When a Robert Sangster partnership bought the two-year-old in California in 1976, Sangster took another look at his new purchase. He determined the horse's forelegs would be better suited to the less speed-oriented European tracks, and the horse was shipped overseas.

Alleged was one of the most popular European runners in the 1970s, accomplishing a feat only five horses have achieved: back-to-back wins in one of the world's most revered races, the Prix de l'Arc de Triomphe. More than twenty years earlier, Alleged's great-grandsire, Ribot, had accomplished the same.

In addition to dual Arc wins, Alleged blazed through nine wins in ten starts and earned $623,187. He was named champion three-year-old in both England and France in 1977, and the following year he was champion older horse in Europe.

Kentucky horseman William S. Farish bought into the colt in the winter of 1977-78, and Alleged was brought back to his native country after his second Arc. He entered stud at Walmac-Warnerton International Associates Farm.

He never topped a general sire list but was a tremendously successful stallion, cherished not just in America but in Europe as well. Among Alleged's seventeen international champions and two Eclipse Award winners were Miss Alleged, Flat Top, Sir Harry Lewis, and Law Society.

When I first saw the handsome champion at Walmac

in 1984, he was being bathed. It took maybe a minute or two before he decided to make the experience interesting by becoming — and staying — vertical. When he finally returned to earth, he seemed quite amused.

I visited again in 1999 on a sunny September morning when the twenty-five-year-old Alleged was brought out and led to a show area. This time it didn't take him a minute to take the weight off those forelegs. He went up immediately, stayed there for perhaps five seconds, then lightly touched down. For the next ten minutes or so, Alleged was a perfect gentleman. This time, I swear he was chuckling with childlike pride.

Walmac International, where Alleged stood his entire career, held the famed stallion in the highest esteem. After Alleged was pensioned in 1997, the farm dedicated its stallion brochure to the grand old horse. Eloquent words and photographs paid tribute to his greatness.

Alleged's forelegs had weathered two years of championship campaigning and twenty-six years of remarkable life. But the ravages of time finally humbled the stallion and on June 23, 2000, Alleged was euthanized and laid to rest in the Walmac cemetery.

The following week Walmac advertisements paid one more tribute, with a full-page photograph of Alleged's empty paddock. The simple words told the story: "Going the Distance. Alleged, 1974-2000. Champion racehorse and champion sire whose achievements in life stirred our hearts, and whose influence as a sire will continue to be a fitting tribute upon the breed."

Allegretta (GB)

CH. M. 1978, BY LOMBARD—ANATEVKA, BY ESPRESSO

*D*ear Barbara, We received your letter...regarding your desire to do another pictorial for *The Blood-Horse* on older Thoroughbreds. In fact, we do have one such mare...that you might be interested in for your project. Her name is Allegretta (GB) and she was born in 1978. Her produce record includes Urban Sea, winner of the Arc de Triomphe; King's Best, winner of the 2000 Guineas; and she is also the granddam of Anaba Bleue [sic], the recent winner of the French Derby."

The note was dated June 5, 2001, and by the time I visited in July, Allegretta's daughter Urban Sea had added another classic winner to the family's resume: Galileo. A few weeks later another daughter, Anzille, added a German group I winner, Anzillero.

* * *

When Allegretta was led out that sunny July morning, I knew she was one of the greatest broodmares I would ever see.

The Denali Stud crew had prepared her beautifully, and the long-headed chestnut mare's coat glowed. Her attitude glowed equally, a kind mixture of curiosity, patience, and pride. Her large almond-shaped eyes seemed somehow sad, and between her long body and face, she held the appearance of a nineteenth-century Troye painting. She strode out with long, elegant steps, sure-footed and surprisingly graceful for twenty-three.

A more willing model could not be found, and she lacked the nervous temperament that marked her racing career. While she started with two wins and a world of promise, her attitude became a deterrent, and she never won again. Sold at England's Tattersalls Sales in 1981 for $48,600, she was brought to America to race. Again she was not successful, and she was sold at the 1984 Keeneland November sales for $55,000.

Her stock has risen considerably. Urban Sea was her first hugely successful foal, winning the 1993 Prix de l'Arc de Triomphe and being named best older mare in

foal, Melikah, won the Pretty Polly Stakes and placed in both the group I Irish Oaks and Epsom Oaks.

Urban Sea's third foal is Galileo, the 2001 Epsom Derby and Irish Derby winner. A handsome bay colt with a stunning turn of foot, Galileo was retired in late 2001 to stand near his sire, Sadler's Wells, at Ireland's Coolmore Stud.

Allegretta's seventh foal, French group III winner Allez Les Trois, produced the wonderful Anabaa Blue, winner of the 2001 Prix du Jockey-Club or French Derby. Allegretta's eleventh foal, King's Best, won the 2000 Two Thousand Guineas over the grand Giant's Causeway. And Anzillero, out of Allegretta's second foal, Anzille, won Germany's group I WGZ Bank-Deutschland-Preis.

Allegretta is so far responsible for four classic winners, as well as an additional group I winner. It doesn't get much better than that.

* * *

Allegretta was bred to Woodman in 2001 but did not get in foal. She is in good hands, and the Denali staff is as enamored with this old mare as I. When asked about her attitude, broodmare manager Anthony Kennon thought for a moment. "She likes to be last at everything, especially being caught," he said. "She doesn't mind anything. She's a quiet, docile mare. She's just temperamental to catch."

After the session they led her to the paddock, where a small group of mares grazed on a far hillside. As they released her, Allegretta raised her head high and nickered. Her ears plopped forward on that long head. She jogged toward the group and then broke into a relaxed gallop. She moved easily toward her friends. A gray mare reached out to greet her, and then a bay.

The field was full of successful broodmares and mares with great blood or race records. But the chestnut mare with the long body and sad eyes stood out, as she would anywhere.

Europe. As a broodmare, Urban Sea has already been remarkable. Her first foal, Irish group III winner Urban Ocean, was highweight on the Irish Free Handicap at nine and a half to eleven furlongs at three. Her second

Angel Island

DK. B/BR. M. 1976, BY COUGAR II—WHO'S TO KNOW,
BY FLEET NASRULLAH

*A*ngel Island failed to make the cut for the 1977 Keeneland summer yearling sale, but Leslie Combs II was not disappointed to keep her at home. Spendthrift Farm had a policy of entering all of its yearlings in the sale, and those that didn't get selected were sold privately or kept for racing.

Angel Island's veins coursed with the blood of Myrtlewood, the grand dame and foundation mare of Spendthrift Farm. Angel Island's dam, Who's to Know, was a favorite of Mr. and Mrs. Combs. They chose to race Angel Island in their Spendthrift colors.

Angel Island rewarded them. In her third start she won her first stakes race, the Miss Collinsville at Nebraska's Fonner Park, and in doing so she became the first stakes winner for her popular sire, Cougar II. In two of her next three starts, she encountered the wonderful filly It's in the Air but was no match for that filly.

By the time Angel Island entered the grade II Alcibiades Stakes at Keeneland, she was dismissed at 8-1. A filly named Terlingua had shipped east weeks before, seemingly invincible until a shocking defeat in Belmont's grade I Frizette. Terlingua, a brilliantly fast sprinter by Secretariat, was odds-on in the Alcibiades. Angel Island, however, handed that filly her second straight defeat.

Angel Island won by six lengths over a sloppy track, with Terlingua four lengths ahead of the third-place finisher. It was Angel Island's crowning moment on the racetrack, although she added the grade III Golden Rod Stakes in her next start.

She raced ten times at age two, but for the next two seasons she raced sporadically due to various setbacks. She was retired with six wins in sixteen starts, four seconds, and three thirds.

* * *

While Terlingua gained international fame as the dam of Storm Cat, Angel Island was a wonderful dam as well. Her first foal, the filly Our Reverie, won the My Charmer Handicap and Bewitch Visitation Stakes. And Our Reverie herself produced Kentucky Cup Ladies Turf Handicap winner Silken.

Angel Island's third foal was her best known. Named Sharrood, this Caro colt placed in the group I Irish Two Thousand Guineas and in group II events in England and France before traveling to America. Here he added the grade II Eddie Read and Stars and Stripes handicaps. At ten, Sharrood was sold to Japan for stud duty.

Angel Island's next two foals were both stakes-placed, and her sixth foal, Island Escape, won two of eight races, including the Kentucky Breeders' Cup Stakes. Her 1992 colt, Jump the Shadow, was another stakes-placed performer. Angel Island's final foal, a Skip Trial colt named Jump Bail, was born in 1998 and is now a winner.

Angel Island, twenty-six in 2002, now spends her days with a large group of broodmares at Bridlewood Farm, relaxing in the glorious Ocala, Florida, sun. On occasion the mares break into spontaneous races, moving surreally around their expansive paddock. They gallop over hilltops and out of sight, the sound of their hoofbeats drumming through the warm air.

Every so often, when they pass the hillcrest on their return flight, the mare with the slight sway back and the white-flecked face is in the lead, her tail plumed behind her and her head held high.

Bargain Day

DK. B. H. 1965, BY PROVE IT—SPECIAL PRICE,
BY TOULOUSE LAUTREC

As many older horses do, he sometimes sleeps lying down. When he awakens, his legs sometimes remain asleep, resulting in his inability to rise. He lies there quite helpless, until a groom inevitably finds him and gives the old boy a hand. Pulling firmly on his tail, the groom waits as the horse jumps up.

The old stallion bows his neck, galloping in circles with a raised tail and a series of snorts, to leave no question of his prowess. Even if he might have his "senior moments," he is a grand stallion and king of all around him, and he wants to leave no doubt of that.

At age thirty-six, his reign has been a long one.

* * *

When I contacted Van Mar Farms in 2001 about seeing Bargain Day, the response was warm and inviting. As the July visit grew nearer, I worried whether Bargain Day would live till my arrival. After all, a thirty-six-year-old Thoroughbred is not just a rarity but also nearly a record-breaker.

It was a crisp California morning of sunshine and cool temperatures, a welcome departure from the heat wave of recent weeks. The farm was a relaxed mixture of dried grasses and expansive ranchland, with grazing horses dotting the golden landscape. Small bushes and trees provided greenery, and unusual flowers and plants grew near fence lines and pens. Although a far cry from the farms of Kentucky, a family element made this farm equally appealing.

We were whisked to the office, where coffee, doughnuts, and friendly conversation awaited. Several photos of Bargain Day were laid out on the desk. One was a composite win photo, more than thirty years old, showing a long-faced dark runner nosing out a competitor. E.E. Fogelson and his wife, actress Greer Garson Fogelson, smiled in the winner's circle. Another winner's circle portrait lay nearby. The calligraphy noted the important races, the 1970 Bing Crosby Handicap and the 1971 San Bernardino.

Another photo showed a young, thick, dark bay stallion with a Quarter Horse look. It was a faded color photo taken soon after Bargain Day's arrival at the farm. A proud young boy, perhaps ten years old, held the stallion's shank.

Then two more recent shots. One showed Bargain Day posing proudly in 2000 at the age of thirty-five at the farm's stallion show. The other showed him earlier that same day getting a bath, with a diminutive child holding the shank. This child, even younger than the boy in the other shot, was perhaps four.

We went outside, and the groom brought Bargain Day from his paddock. When he came into view, I instantly fell in love. His face was sweet with kind eyes; his mane was streaked with white; and his coat was in beautiful shape. As owner Marilyn Rose shared, "He's still sound. A bit swaybacked, but his legs are clean as a whistle."

His nameplate read "RAINBOW BLUES," and Marilyn apologized, smiling. "He's outlived his halter," she said, proudly.

We took a few photos, while learning more about Bargain Day. As with many equine seniors, when he chews grass, it sometimes clumps in his mouth and falls out. Although he has teeth, they are worn out, and he eats special pellets. He lives outside, as he doesn't care for the confinement of his stall. His hearing is nearly gone, not that he seems to care. His vision is clouded, but thirty years after looking for the finish wire, who cares?

Bargain Day got a bath that morning, and his handlers laughed at his annoyance with the chore. "This is ridiculous at thirty-six years old, having a bath," farm manager Mary Purrington said, voicing Bargain Day's intolerance. "He's taken on kind of an old-fart attitude."

Bargain Day soon found our photographic attempts boring. In an attempt to "wake him up," a young stallion was paraded in a paddock in front of Bargain Day. The

old stallion puffed up instantly, displaying his superiority. While there was something comical about watching the low-backed thirty-six-year-old bellow and posture, it was serious business to "Bargie." When they led the young stallion away, Bargain Day was darned pleased.

Bargain Day has had two close calls with death, Marilyn recalled. Many years ago he colicked and was driven to the vet. Along the way, however, the situation corrected itself, and he was brought right back home.

In the early 1990s the situation appeared much more bleak. He looked so sick and off-color they didn't dare ship him, and they placed Bargain Day in a paddock close to the office. In a nearby paddock several fillies played, in season and "strutting their stuff." Bargain Day was so enamored and desiring of the ladies' attentions that by the time the vet arrived, he was back to his old self.

BARGAIN DAY WINNING THE 1971 SAN BERNARDINO HANDICAP

As the years passed and Bargain Day woke up each morning, Marilyn Rose and her husband Van marveled at their aging stallion. Van told *California Thoroughbred*, "He's my best friend. He helped me get started in this business. We'll bury him right here on the farm when the time comes—unless, of course, he outlives me and Marilyn too."

Bargain Day has outlived Van, who died early in 2001, and now Marilyn is responsible for watching the old stallion. After all, Bargain Day did indeed help the Roses get started in the business, arriving at their new farm in 1972. "He was our first stallion," Marilyn said. "And believe me, we owe this ranch to him."

* * *

Bargain Day raced forty-three times, winning thirteen races and finishing second or third ten times. He won the 1970 Bing Crosby Handicap and Brentwood Claiming Stakes, the 1971 San Bernardino Handicap, and placed in four other stakes. In the Bing Crosby at Del Mar, Bargain Day set a seven and a half-furlong course record of 1:27 3/5.

With his race record, bloodlines (by Prove It), and good conformation, Californians were happy to breed to this stallion, and his offspring included twenty-four stakes winners. Among them were Elegant Bargain, who earned $466,012, and Hoedown's Day. The latter set a world record of 1:38 2/5 for one and one-sixteenth miles and ran in the 1981 Kentucky Derby. He finished twelfth, ahead of such upstarts as Tap Shoes and Cure the Blues.

Bargain Day has long since been pensioned, but he is still the self-proclaimed king of Van Mar Farms. He still gallops and displays his exuberance. Others from his crop, such as Dancer's Image and Forward Pass, were buried long ago.

When our shoot was finished, Bargie was put in his paddock, and he jogged smoothly to the far corner, blissfully unaware of the large hole dug nearby. The Roses had the hole dug many years back, when a sick Bargain Day caused them worry. Some day he will be buried there.

But for now, the horse moves to the corner where his friend, the young stallion Boomerang, waits. They have adjacent paddocks and, as Mary Purrington related, "The two of them just stand there and talk for hours."

Perhaps Bargain Day tells tales of a trainer named Charlie Whittingham, or of a time of movie stars and glamour at the racetrack. Or perhaps he speaks of an old stallion named Merrick, who died many decades ago at the oldest-recorded age for an American Thoroughbred, thirty-eight. Or maybe he just explains why his legs sometimes fall asleep beneath him. With each passing day, Bargain Day has a lifetime of stories to share.

* * *

In a note dated February 5, 2002, Marilyn Rose relates: "Bargain is doing fine. Looks like a hairy ape! Good thing you were here in July, not February!"

At age thirty-seven, Bargain Day is still going strong.

Basket Weave

DK. B/BR. H. 1981, BY BEST TURN—PASS THE BASKET,
BY BUCKPASSER

Shan*gri-la (noun) 1.) a remote, beautiful, imaginary place where life approaches perfection: utopia.

El Dorado Farms was magical, with overflowing flowerbeds and multi-colored pinwheels enjoying the summer breeze. Cats and dogs peered out from behind flowers then quickly wandered over to be admired. Horses seemed to smile as they poked heads over fence boards in a quest for attention, and the backdrop of Mount Rainier seemed ethereal in its grandness.

When I arrived, a woman stood up from gardening and came over with light feet and an even lighter smile. Introducing herself as Nina Hagen, she pointed to the flowers she was planting. It was the burial spot for Demons Begone, who had died just ten days earlier. Her voice broke unashamedly as she remembered him.

"He was the people's horse," she said, tears filling her eyes. "Basket Weave is going to be the same way. He made it the hard way. The people who believed in him never stopped believing in him."

No one believed in them more than Nina.

Basket Weave, often among Washington State's leading sires, has rewarded her in many ways. His most popular offspring, perhaps, is Enduring Knight. The Emerald Downs star won five of fourteen starts, finished on the board in four others, and earned $163,201. In her 2001 season opener, past the finish wire, Enduring Knight collapsed. She died of a ruptured artery in her lung.

Basket Weave's top earner, L.J. Express, based at Yakima Meadows, was a twelve-time stakes winner and earner of $306,230.

* * *

Nina and her husband, Ron, own this surreal haven. While Ron is a contractor and Nina oversees the running of the farm, Ron was busy helping on this day. As

we looked for a spot to pose Basket Weave, Ron was land-scaping, with a seemingly random pattern of boards and tools scattered about him.

"Slave driver," he smiled at Nina as we passed, and Nina smiled back. Several pets had been buried in the area Ron was tending, all having an eternal view of Mount Rainier and an eternal soft spot in the Hagens' hearts.

Nina couldn't resist the urge first to show off her other senior stallion, the beautiful Peterhof. He happily followed her out into the sunlight, the shank held loosely as he danced. She apologized for his slightly dirty coat, as she described the attributes of this handsome horse.

She then led him back to the barn, where Basket Weave was waiting in his stall. A good sprinter for Greentree Stable, Basket Weave didn't always visit the winner's circle. But he won two stakes races, the Bull Lea and Jaipur, and placed in many others. He won nine of fifty-three starts, with earnings of more than $350,000.

When Nina brought him outside, his near-black coat glowed brilliantly. Her nickname for Basket Weave is Weaver Dude, and it suits him and his surroundings well. I noted his large head, neck, and rippling muscles. He is a strong stallion with a young attitude, large dark eyes, and a proud countenance. But he minded Nina well, and again her hold on the shank was gentle. There was no need to force him. He was very happy to share this beautiful afternoon with friends.

We picked a spot that, while not perfect for sunlight, was impossible to resist. It can sometimes take long moments (or even hours) to persuade a horse to stand in a classic conformation pose. Nina backed Basket Weave up a time or two, and he quickly stepped into "the" pose. I clicked away as Basket Weave proudly played his role of equine model. Our shoot was over within minutes.

Other horses watched, enjoying the unusual show, and dogs sat comfortably in the grass. A cat stretched contentedly on the nearby porch, and the pinwheels continued their ceaseless Shangri-la spinning dance.

Nina proudly petted the grand horse. "This is the guy you wish could give you ten more years," she smiled. Looking around, I was certain that Weaver Dude wished the same thing.

Blue Ensign

GR. H. 1977-2001, BY HOIST THE FLAG—LAUGHTER,
BY BOLD RULER

he headline hit hard: Florida Stallion Blue Ensign Dead at 24. It wasn't that the death of a twenty-four-year-old stallion could be that surprising, but that three months earlier Blue Ensign had provided me quite a memorable morning. At the time he just seemed…so alive.

Blue Ensign was a successful racehorse, winning nine of twenty-eight starts. His biggest win was the grade III Woodlawn Stakes at Pimlico, but that and three other stakes wins were not his only selling points.

Blue Ensign's sire was the great Hoist the Flag, and his dam, Laughter, was out of the remarkable Shenanigans. In addition to Laughter, the beautiful gray Shenanigans was the dam of Ruffian, Icecapade, and Buckfinder.

Laughter herself produced five stakes winners, including Blue Ensign and Private Terms. Laughter's unraced daughter Laughing Look is the dam of stakes winners Coronado's Quest, Warning Glance, and Military Look.

Blue Ensign brought royal credentials to stud. He first stood at Comfort Acres Farm near Ocala, and although he moved several times, he stayed in the Ocala area. The big gray ended up at Sez Who Thoroughbreds, a stunning showplace of live oaks and Spanish moss.

It was at Sez Who where he dazzled me. Kim and Bonnie Heath, farm advisers, accompanied me and several farm hands who wanted to watch the grand stallion's photo shoot. They knew how lively and cantankerous he was, and everyone wanted to see the show.

Blue Ensign looked like an Arabian, with finely pricked ears and a tapered nose. Although he was nearly white, his eyes were circled with dark gray, and his brilliant coat was dappled. He carried his proud head very high and looked ready to enter a show ring.

He behaved well at first, although I didn't dare ask the groom to move the horse's legs. I sensed Blue Ensign was waiting for a better chance to strut his stuff. The stuffy atmosphere of a conformation shoot just wasn't "him."

After perhaps five minutes of standing fairly still, he'd had enough, and Kim Heath asked the groom if the horse was going to his paddock. He was.

Trying to think like Blue Ensign, we decided he'd find me most interesting near a spot personal to him. Kim pointed to the far corner of his paddock, where his favorite tract of sand beckoned. I stationed myself behind the fence, just beyond the sand.

Once free, Blue Ensign turned on his haunches and bolted toward me. He skidded to a halt just feet away, sand flying and his white mane and tail whipping. He circled at a lively jog, watching me and questioning my presence. Then he noticed a stallion in a far paddock and off

he went, thundering to the far corner. He again screeched to a stop, snorted, and galloped back to me.

He did this several times, the near-white stallion wowing everyone with his display of agility and vitality. He might have gone on like that all day, but we worried that he might hurt himself. We quietly walked away.

As we left, he remained on high alert, his tail waving and nostrils distended, looking for an excuse to explode. He was a picture of health.

* * *

Three months later on June 16, 2001, Blue Ensign underwent surgery to remove a non-cancerous fatty tumor from a spot near his small intestines. Bonnie Heath later related: "He was recovering great…He was screaming for mares an hour after the surgery."

But on June 24, the night before he was to return to the farm, he suffered severe complications. Bonnie Heath received the call that all horsemen dread. The grand old gray stallion was dead.

Brown Bess

DK. B/BR. M. 1982, BY PETRONE—CHICKADEE,
BY WINDY SANDS

*S*uzanne Pashayan relates a tale straight from a horse book by C.W. Anderson. She was only eleven when she dragged her father to a Del Mar horse sale in 1955. Although her father went to the track on occasion with friends, he wasn't what you'd call a racing fan. Still, they bought two Thoroughbred fillies at Del Mar, creating the name Calbourne Farm for their breeding stock and Calbourne Stable for racing.

The name's origin was simple. The girl from California knew of two famous horse farms in Kentucky: Calumet and Claiborne. She combined the names and added a "U" to make the combination a bit less obvious.

Her father's faith was not ill-placed. He helped his daughter fulfill a girl's dream, and Suzanne Pashayan is still in the racing business, nearly a half-century later.

Her best has been Brown Bess. Pashayan remembers buying Brown Bess' fourth dam, Duchess Doreen, for $4,700 at the 1962 Ridgewood Dispersal sale. From Duchess Doreen came Moog, and from Moog came Chickadee. Chickadee, to the cover of Petrone, produced Brown Bess.

"Chickadee had a lot of speed in her family — Noor, Nasrullah, Windy Sands, Hyperion — and Petrone was a distance horse," Pashayan explained. "He had speed, but he had that quality speed. He was also beautifully put together, with beautiful movement."

The result was a sassy little California-bred filly who would grow up, figuratively at least, to conquer the racing world.

She was not a quick developer and didn't win a stakes until May of her six-year-old season. But it was in her seventh year, 1989, that little Brown Bess showed the world what she could do.

At the height of her career, Brown Bess stood slightly under 15.1 hands and weighed a mere 850 pounds. But she towered on the California tracks in 1989, winning

BROWN BESS WITH HER 2001 CUTLESS REALITY COLT

five of nine races. In her one start against the boys, she finished third in the grade II Golden Gate Handicap. But Brown Bess showed her heels to most of the distaff turf set. She won the grade I Ramona and the grade III Countess Fager, Yerba Buena, and California Jockey Club handicaps.

Her crowning moment came in the grade I Yellow Ribbon Invitational at Santa Anita on November 12, 1989. Under Jack Kaenel, the little dark bay mare jumped out first at the break. Jack settled her back, and the first time past the packed grandstand Brown Bess nearly clipped heels.

Down the backstretch and around the far turn, Brown Bess moved past the field with shocking ease. She won by nearly two lengths, running the mile and a quarter in a new record, 1:57 3/5. The *Daily Racing Form chart* said, simply: "Hand ride."

Soon afterward, Suzanne Pashayan accepted the Eclipse Award for turf female for Brown Bess. At the time, Calbourne Farm/Stable consisted of one active broodmare, one retired mare (Chickadee), and one racehorse — Brown Bess.

* * *

Pashayan now boards her horses at Harris Farms in Northern California. Soon after Brown Bess was retired, the little lady was sent to Cardiff Stud for her first breeding. Brown Bess and her entire line, Pashayan related, are "tough as nails. None of them want anything to do with other horses, and they've all got an attitude."

People, therefore, were surprised when Brown Bess, upon returning to her Harris home, rediscovered a long-lost relative.

"When Brown Bess came back from Cardiff, they put her out in a field, and her dam, Chickadee, was out there standing off by herself. They recognized each other, and the two of them just ran off to the corner together."

* * *

Chickadee has since died, and Brown Bess is back to wandering her Harris fields alone. Some years, however, she has played the role of mother.

Brown Bess has had seven foals playing at her heels and pulling on her tail. When I visited her in July 2001 at California's Blooming Hills Farm, where she was being bred to Shanekite, her Cutlass Reality colt did all those irritating things that foals do. He was a bright bay, with a fuzzy black mane and a long, brilliant blaze. The flashy little sprite had a bold, daring nature.

Brown Bess, meanwhile, was one nervous lady. The dark bay mare was still small in height, but she had a strong body and moved beautifully. Nineteen years hadn't mellowed her attitude, and she was truly unhappy to have a paddock visitor. While the blazed-face junior crowded and buffeted me, Brown Bess circled at a safe distance and glowered.

Every few minutes she'd round the spunky colt up and he'd follow her, annoyed at being pulled from his new pals. After all, Mom could be a little less than entertaining at times.

Brown Bess was in foal for 2002 to Shanekite, a stallion referred to on Blooming Hills' web site as "A California Standard." Pashayan found his pedigree a solid match with her mare. For Shanekite, it was one more chance for success. He was pensioned after the 2001 breeding season.

Pashayan does not plan to breed Brown Bess again, and the mare will live out her days at Harris Farms, as did her dam.

* * *

While some might question Pashayan's choice to continue breeding in-state, she is resolute: "I never breed outside of California. I'm loyal to a fault. You need to support your local industry."

It's been more than a decade since Pashayan's loyalty to California paid off in spades, in the form of her diminutive dynamo. One thing every horsewoman knows, whether she is young in body or just in heart, is that hope springs eternal.

C.W. Anderson would be proud.

The Calumet Mares

C alumet Farm's famous equine cemetery was beautifully serene when I visited one May morning in 2001. The sun filtered through leaves as the last reminders of a foggy night drifted away and the grass glowed with dew and the brilliant green that accompanies spring. Two large rectangles of freshly laid grass were quite noticeable, neither plot yet identified with a marker. Beneath one patch of turf lay the remains of Gdynia, the dam of Danzig Connection; and beneath the other her friend, the great race mare and Eclipse Award winner De La Rose, was interred.

Henryk de Kwiatkowski, Calumet Farm's owner, provides his pensioned mares with a lifetime home. In the autumn of 2000, there were five oldtimers in the mares' field, including De La Rose and Gdynia.

When the difficult decision was made to put Gdynia down due to declining health, she was led from her paddock for a final time. As she was led away, her best friend De La Rose followed her along the fence line until she could go no farther. Despite caretakers' loving efforts to comfort De La Rose in her loss, she followed her friend into the cemetery within months.

* * *

Three mares remain in the retired Calumet band. Sabin, the most recognized name, was a popular race mare for de Kwiatkowski. She is certainly the most accomplished racehorse of the trio, the grade I Yellow Ribbon and Gamely handicaps being among her fourteen stakes victories. As a broodmare, she continued her prowess in producing two stakes winners, Al Sabin and Sabina, and the stakes-placed filly In Excelsis Deo.

Lulu Mon Amour won two of sixteen starts but gained more success as a broodmare, producing the stakes-winning filly Arbusha as well as Nicholas, a grade II stakes winner and current Calumet stallion. Wedding Reception, a stakes-placed runner herself, produced three stakes winners, Savina, Lech, and Crimson Guard, as well as a stakes-placed offspring.

During my visit on that May morning, two friends and

WEDDING RECEPTION
B. M. 1978,
BY ROUND TABLE—PRODANA NEVIESTA,
BY RENEGED

LULU MON AMOUR
B. M. 1980,
BY TOM ROLFE—SISTER SHU,
BY NASHUA

SABIN
CH. M. 1980,
BY LYPHARD—BEACONAIRE,
BY VAGUELY NOBLE

I traipsed out in their dew-covered field with a leather lead shank, a brush, and high hopes. Sabin is easy-going and enjoys human company. Lulu Mon Amour is pleasant as well, but Wedding Reception's reputation as an ornery old gal had preceded her. Our plans were to catch the two kind mares, clean them up, and stand them for official portraits. The best laid plans…

Wedding Reception quickly greeted us and swept a carrot out of a friend's hand. With that, she turned and rounded up the other mares, pushing them away. Grudgingly, Sabin and Lulu Mon Amour followed their leader, annoyed by their inability to visit. Each time we attempted to out-think Wedding Reception, the senior mare crowded the other two, forcing them away again.

This continued for perhaps twenty minutes, during which I contented myself with very informal portraits —

shots of muddy mares standing, pinning their ears, or jogging away. I finally conceded defeat and sat down in the grass to take a few last photographs.

The mares slowly came to me, intrigued by my apparent disinterest. Within moments, I was brushing Sabin gently, taking care not to spook the trio as I scrubbed the layer of dried mud from the lovely chestnut. Sabin thoroughly enjoyed the attention. She lowered her head as the brush moved over her body and removed the patches of famous Calumet dirt.

Wedding Reception and Lulu Mon Amour watched quietly for moments and then moved forward, setting the group back in motion. Sabin also moved on, but this time she led the way in proud fashion. Wedding Reception provided no challenge, and Sabin, at least for the moment, had become the group's leader.

With this cue, I said my goodbyes to the departing mares and left the field, as the equine trio moved slowly up the hill. They didn't look back as I shuffled to my car, and as they reached the crest, far from me now, they were nearly silhouettes against the backlit sky.

As I turned to take a last look, the lead mare, Sabin, carefully lowered herself to her knees and then to the ground. I watched as she slowly rolled once, twice, a third time before gently climbing back to her feet, seeming to have forgotten I had ever been there.

But as she shook herself, Sabin looked back our way for a long deliberate moment, undoubtedly proud of her fresh coating of dirt. Then she lowered her head to graze again, at least for the moment the leader of Calumet's retired broodmare band.

Chinook Pass

DK. B/BR. G. 1979, BY NATIVE BORN—YU TURN, BY TURN-TO

*I*n July 2001, the Hallin family's back pasture appeared not unlike other horse lovers' homes across America. Four happy horses wandered the large paddock, with an old goat to keep them company. Jill Hallin's equine family included an Appaloosa, an Arabian, and a compact, calm bay gelding with the look of a Quarter Horse. The goat, named Ribbon, had the run of the place, but stayed close to the bay.

While the scene itself was not extraordinary, the bay gelding certainly was. Named Chinook Pass, this Thoroughbred set a five-furlong world record in 1982. He earned the only Eclipse Award ever given a Washington-bred and in 2000 was crowned Washington Horse of the Century.

Unlike most old racing geldings that disappear from the public's consciousness, Chinook Pass is still very much a public figure. He has performed at race-tracks, appeared at a hotel dinner, and even helped thwart a crime.

* * *

Ed Purvis bred Chinook Pass in the name of his Hi Yu Stables. By the Native Dancer stallion Native Born and out of Yu Turn, by Turn-to, Chinook Pass was foaled and raised at Dewaine Moore's Rainier Stables in Enumclaw, Washington.

Chinook Pass won at first asking, June 20, 1981, at Longacres, but he was disqualified and placed second that day. He would more than make up for that loss.

Chinook Pass ran hard and fast during a three-year racing campaign, defeating rivals from Del Mar to Turf Paradise, from Santa Anita to Hollywood Park. And yet it is Longacres with which he is associated, as he set a five-furlong world record there of :55 1/5.

He also displayed his blazing speed at other tracks that year, equaling Hollywood Park's five-furlong mark (:56) in the Meteor Handicap and setting Santa Anita's six-fur-

long mark (1:07 3/5) in the Palos Verdes Handicap.

Chinook Pass was not rewarded for those three superb efforts with 1982's Eclipse Award, however. In his only graded stakes attempt, the Longacres Mile, he finished second. The brilliant filly Gold Beauty was named champion sprinter.

In 1983 Chinook Pass won five of seven starts, including the grade II Longacres Mile by six lengths in 1:35 3/5. That graded stakes win and victories in the Bing Crosby, San Simeon, Sierra Madre, and Potrero Grande handicaps were enough to convince Eclipse Award voters this time around. Chinook Pass was named 1983 champion sprinter.

But Chinook Pass' hard-driving style and determination had taken their toll. He came out of the Longacres

Mile with a fractured splint bone, and weighing that injury against two earlier bowed tendons, the decision was made to retire him. With a record of twenty-five starts, sixteen wins, four seconds, and a third, and $480,073 in earnings, Chinook Pass went home to Rainier Stables.

* * *

In 1987 Ed and Dewaine decided to put Chinook Pass back into training, and he was sent to nearby Donida Farm.

Donida Farm was well known for its use of the Aqua-Tred, an equine treadmill immersed in water. Hundreds of horses went through the routine every year, but farm manager Jill Davis knew immediately that Chinook Pass was unique. And while Chinook Pass' comeback never came to fruition, Jill was definitely smitten. She spoke often with Dewaine, always mentioning her fondness for Chinook.

Jill changed jobs in 1988, and her new position had a perk: an empty stall to fill. Dewaine happily agreed to let Jill care for Chinook Pass, as he saw the two were a perfect match. Jill became Chinook's caregiver and best friend.

Within several years, with Jill's help, a new Washington State tradition began: Chinook Pass Day at Longacres. Considering Chinook Pass' intelligence and proud bearing, Jill taught him dressage, and he easily took to this new challenge. Jill enjoyed the chance to show that racehorses could have productive retirements, and the fans welcomed the chance to see their old hero. For several seasons, he displayed his technique to the Longacres' crowd.

But while Chinook Pass was thriving, Longacres was not. Rumor was the track was to be sold, and in 1991 Seattle's SeaFair Torchlight Parade became a forum for a group trying to save the foundering track.

The event attracts hundreds of thousands to Seattle, culminating in a tumultuous nighttime parade. Jill rode Chinook Pass at the event, and Longacres patrons, employees, trainers, and friends gathered to rally for their cause.

Chinook Pass even got his first look at an overhead train, which he definitely found interesting.

But their attempts, and those of others, were in vain. On September 21, 1992, Longacres held racing for the last time. Chinook Pass was paraded one final time past the grandstand where, a decade earlier, a crowd had watched him set his world mark.

Jill's husband, Curtis, suffering from cancer, was hospi-

talized and unable to watch the final day's activities at the track he so loved. As Jill remembered, "After the appearance I was presented with a picture of Chinook, the big one in our living room. I actually took that up to the hospital that night, and Curtis was very aware of the tribute to Chinook…A lot of racetrackers came up to tell him about the last day. It was an emotional time, but he was a great fan of Chinook's, and a huge support in me having him." Curtis died two days later.

Years have passed, Jill has since remarried, and Chinook Pass is as popular today as when he was running. When the Tacoma Dome hosted an All-Breeds Extravaganza, Chinook Pass proudly represented the Thoroughbred. When racing returned to Washington in 1996 with the opening of Emerald Downs, Chinook Pass was there. When Ron Crockett was honored for his work in Washington racing, Chinook Pass was led willingly into the Red Lion Hotel and to the head table. During Emerald Downs' opening week in 2000, Chinook Pass and Jill made an appearance, and Chinook participated in a photo session with one of his riders, Laffit Pincay Jr.

Laffit remembered the gelding fondly: "I think that Chinook Pass is the fastest horse that I ever rode or saw. It was just a pleasure riding him." That's no small praise from the world's winningest jockey, who has ridden many fast horses in more than nine thousand career wins.

Also in 2000, Chinook Pass was awarded an honor even more memorable than an Eclipse Award: he was voted Washington Horse of the Century.

In 2001, Chinook Pass appeared in downtown Seattle in celebration of Emerald Downs' season opening. Jill and Chinook were enjoying the activities when Jill noticed a man jogging toward them being followed by a police bicycle. A police officer herself, Jill recognized the man was trying to escape inconspicuously, and she quietly backed Chinook Pass up. By the time the man looked up, he found himself face to face with what Laffit Pincay once called "the fastest hind end around." The crook was caught, both by surprise and by the law.

When I arrived at the Hallin household in July 2001, it was nearly evening, but Jill saddled a willing Chinook Pass and showed me some of his moves in an open garden. When Jill finished Chinook's routine, she patiently posed him for a variety of photos. The twenty-two-year-old bay gelding seemed half his age, still looking every bit a sprinter.

Ribbon watched the photo session, waiting for his friend to be served dinner. Ribbon and Chinook had been buddies for many years, and Chinook gladly shared meals with the friendly goat. Jill had raised Ribbon, and when he was just a kid, Jill held him in her lap at feeding time. Now, more than a decade later and in full adult form, Ribbon still tried to climb onto her lap when she offered it, although without entirely successful results.

We finally finished, and Chinook seemed quite content when Jill filled his feed tub. He lowered his head, and Ribbon dove in as well. When we left the beautiful scene, the sun was setting behind the tall pines of the Hallins' backyard.

Several weeks later, Ribbon began to show signs of illness, and Jill summoned the vet. At the age of eleven, Ribbon was a senior, and he was suffering from acute kidney failure. While Jill and her family had provided him a lifetime of love, they could not help him this time. He had to be put down.

Chinook Pass was morose for days, mourning the loss of his friend and dinner companion. But he eventually stopped looking for Ribbon and now seems content with his equine friends.

Longacres exists only in memory now, and Chinook Pass' world record has since been broken. Regardless, Washington is much the richer state for Chinook Pass' existence, and for the willingness of Dewaine Moore and Jill Hallin to share their treasure.

Chris Evert

CH. M. 1971-2001, BY SWOON'S SON—MISS CARMIE,
BY T. V. LARK

W hen the lovely Six Crowns was pensioned in 2001, it marked the end of an era for the Rosen family — and all of racing. Carl Rosen had campaigned the tremendously popular filly Chris Evert, and after Carl's death in 1983, the family continued racing under the name Carl Rosen & Associates.

Chris Evert produced five foals, all fillies, for the Rosens, and the family kept them for breeding when their race careers were over. Six Crowns was her best, but each member of Chris Evert's quintet was successful.

* * *

Chris Evert was named for the tennis star, who promoted Carl Rosen's sportswear fashions. The equine version was a large filly by Swoon's Son, and as a two-year-old she won four of five starts. But it was at three that the racing world took note of her, as she blazed through the Filly Triple Crown. Chris Evert (the person) even appeared in the winner's circle with Chris Evert (the horse), which made the filly even more popular. This was on the heels of Secretariat's Triple Crown win, when the outside world was still watching horse racing with much interest.

After her Triple Crown score, she represented the East Coast in a match race staged at Hollywood Park. Her opponent was the brilliant mare of the West, Miss Musket. But it was not the race that people had hoped for. Miss Musket ducked in near the break, and as Chris Evert's lead increased, Miss Musket was eventually eased. Chris Evert's final margin of victory was listed as fifty lengths.

Once retired Chris Evert was bred to Secretariat — the "other" Triple Crown winner — and the result was a filly named, not coincidentally, Six Crowns.

While not a top-level racehorse, Six Crowns was Chris Evert's crowning achievement as a broodmare. Six Crowns achieved immortality as the dam of Chief's Crown. Another Six Crowns' foal, a near-black filly named Classic Crown, was a multiple grade I winner.

Chris Evert's second foal, Tournament Star, was

stakes-placed, and her third foal, Wimbledon Star, was a stakes winner.

Chris Evert's fourth filly, Nijinsky Star, produced three stakes winners, including the durable grade I-placed Hometown Queen. Chris Evert's final foal, Center Court Star, continued the Rosens' tennis-themed names. While she was not a star on the track, Center Court Star produced two stakes winners and a stakes-placed runner.

Chris Evert's half sister, stakes-winning All Rainbows, made even bigger headlines by producing the 1988 Kentucky Derby-winning filly Winning Colors.

* * *

When I visited Chris Evert in 1998, the old chestnut mare resided with a band of mares and preferred the company of horses to humans. Getting her to show interest was no simple task, but after countless minutes her ears popped forward to watch a dog pass by. She then proceeded to tug at her shank, wanting so very much to be back in her paddock.

The twenty-seven-year-old mare looked her age, her body thin and her eyes tired. Three Chimneys had provided a caring home for her pensioned years, and the grooms were proud of the old champion. Chris Evert's long, lopping ears and unusual blaze were always her trademark. But in her old age, her eyes had become quite unusual, as if ringed with eyeliner.

Despite the old mare's aloof nature, the groom knew the chestnut mare's true soft spot: Chris Evert loved to be scratched beneath her belly. Before being returned to her paddock, the caregiver found the perfect spot and began scratching her briskly.

Chris Evert instantly lost all sense of decorum. Her head drooped low, tucking under her belly. Her eyes became dreamy, and her lip quivered strongly. Suddenly, she was quite happy to have been cleaned up and brought out, and she was in no hurry to return to the field.

* * *

Chris Evert was euthanized due to the effects of old age on January 8, 2001. The thirty-year-old was laid to rest in Three Chimneys' broodmare cemetery. She was the eighth mare so honored. The farm sent out a heartfelt press release noting the great mare's passing.

Christmas Past

GR. M. 1979, BY GREY DAWN II—YULE LOG,
BY BOLD RULER

gden Phipps was well known for breeding top-quality Thoroughbreds. His daughter Cynthia

has bred many top-notch runners herself, but perhaps none better than Christmas Past.

When Christmas Past reached the races in 1981, she was a long, sizable, dark gray filly with a slim face and much breadth between her large eyes. Her beautiful face made her easily recognizable.

Racing in Cynthia Phipps' purple-and-gold colors, she broke her maiden in the second start of her three-year-old year, and two stakes wins followed. She took the Poinsettia Stakes at Hialeah by six lengths, with the talented Larida and Smart Heiress in her wake. In the Bonnie Miss at .40-1, she scored easily again by three lengths.

She wasn't quite ready for grade I competition by the Acorn Stakes, and she struggled home fifth behind the erratic, but interesting, Cupecoy's Joy. Christmas Past improved in the Mother Goose, failing to catch Cupecoy's Joy by less than a length. In the Coaching Club American Oaks, she finally beat her new rival by a widening six lengths.

In the Gazelle, again at odds-on, the big gray ran fourth in her first attempt against older distaffers. But just eleven days later she vanquished some of those same foes by five easy lengths in the Ruffian. The formidable Love Sign ran third, more than seven lengths back.

Angel Penna Jr. tried Christmas Past against the boys in the Jockey Club Gold Cup, and she lay near the pace before weakening to finish third. It was the final start of 1982 for Christmas Past, and the striking iron gray was tucked away for the season.

Christmas Past, with a record of six wins in eleven starts, was honored with the Eclipse Award for three-year-old filly.

Christmas Past raced only twice at four, winning both starts. In the Gulfstream Park Handicap in February, she got up by a neck to defeat top male competitors such as Crafty Prospector and Rivalero.

"She's perfect," Penna said when her retirement was announced a week later. "She's sound; she feels great, but the weights she would have to carry the rest of the year would be very difficult for her, especially against the fil-

lies. What does she have left to prove? Cynthia Phipps is a breeder; if we went on with Christmas Past we had little to gain and a lot to lose."

Christmas Past headed home to Claiborne Farm in Paris, Kentucky, where the Phipps family keeps most of their mares.

The beautiful gray carried beautiful bloodlines to the breeding shed. Her dam, Yule Log, was out of Plum Cake. Plum Cake was a daughter of Real Delight, a famous member of the Calumet dynasty. Plum Cake's daughter Sweet Tooth, dam of both Alydar and Our Mims, will have an impact on the breed for generations.

But Christmas Past's record since 1984 is a bit disheartening. She has not yet been fortunate as a broodmare, with barren years, slipped foals, and offspring that did not live long enough to be named. But of her six foals to make it to the track, she has had one wonderful runner thus far.

Christmas List, a lanky, dark gray filly, won four of eleven starts for trainer Shug McGaughey and earned more than $125,000. With her long body and Cynthia Phipps' silks, Christmas List rekindled memories of Mom.

Christmas Past, in 2001, was still an active producer at twenty-two. A handsome mare, her body is still long and lean and her coat is now nearly white. Her large eyes are still set unusually far apart, and her finely tapered head is still beautiful. As she was on the racetrack, she is still a sight to behold.

* * *

In 2002, Christmas Past produced a colt by Out of Place. After the colt is weaned, Christmas Past was to be pensioned to live out her life at Claiborne.

Coral Dance
and Smart Heiress

She's blind in one eye and can't see out of the other," groom Karen Thomas said of Smart Heiress, as we walked into the paddock.

The senior mare's infirmity was visible as she raised her head and cocked it slightly, listening as we approached. Smart Heiress, a multiple stakes winner and producer, has been steadily losing her vision over the past few years. The Offutt-Cole Farm staff watches her closely. Now nearly blind, the lovely light chestnut mare relies on her pasture companion for guidance.

That companion is the wonderful Coral Dance, a 1978 Green Dancer mare. Slim and well proportioned, her dark bay coat blazes with dapples.

The day was oppressive at the Midway, Kentucky, farm, but Coral Dance didn't seem to mind. She watched us through kind eyes for a few moments, then moved closer to Smart Heiress.

Coral Dance raced for two seasons in her native France. She won one of five starts and placed in three others, including a second in the group I Prix Marcel Boussac and third in the group III Prix d'Aumale. She was brought to America at four, where she won two of eight starts and earned $32,020.

As a producer, she's been extraordinary. Her son Pennekamp won the group I English Two Thousand Guineas and Generous Dewhurst Stakes, Black Minnaloushe won the group I Irish Two Thousand Guineas, and Nasr El Arab was a major grade I winner in America.

Success was expected of Smart Heiress, as her dam, Smartaire, had already produced several well-known runners by the time Smart Heiress was born. In 1975 Smartaire produced Quadratic, a popular stakes winner. The next year she foaled another major stakes-winning colt, Smarten, and the following year she produced

CORAL DANCE
DK. B/BR. M. 1978-2001, BY GREEN
DANCER—CARVINIA, BY DIATOME

SMART HEIRESS
CH. M. 1979, BY VAGUELY NOBLE—
SMARTAIRE, BY QUIBU

Smart Angle. Smart Angle not only won four grade Is, but was the Eclipse Award-winning champion two-year-old filly in 1979.

Smart Heiress was born in 1979, the same year her dam received the highest award for producers: Broodmare of the Year. While Smart Heiress did not achieve the recognition on the track that her half siblings did, she earned more than $150,000 and won six of twenty-one starts, including three minor stakes races.

Smartaire's other accomplished runners carried their success to the farm. Smarten and Quadratic became popular sires, and among Smart Angle's offspring was a speedy colt named Houston.

When Smart Heiress retired, she made her mark quickly. Her first foal, Homebuilder, was a major stakes winner and racing millionaire during a long, popular campaign. Smart Heiress also produced Aztec Empire, another graded stakes winner who earned more than $300,000.

Smart Heiress is in good condition for twenty-two, but the chestnut mare moves around carefully. She has a thick, muscular body with a strong hind end, and her face is marked with a distinctive blaze that spills down into her nostrils. Her clouded vision has changed her mobility, and she seems dependent on her friendship with Coral Dance. When Coral Dance moves around the paddock, Smart Heiress follows, careful to stay close by.

In return, Coral Dance seems to understand her friend's impairment, and she pays special attention to Smart Heiress. The graceful dark bay mare grazes carefully, often lifting her head to watch her friend. When my movements with a clicking camera were a bit too foreign for them, Coral Dance placed herself between me and Smart Heiress, and gently herded her friend a safe distance away.

While they have not been together long, they have become best buddies in their senior years.

Karen Thomas is fond of the mares and is proud of their special bond. "Coral Dance is Smart Heiress' eyes," she said. When they run in the paddock, Coral Dance kind of guides her. We'll never separate them."

* * *

Sadly, while Offutt-Cole might not have separated the mares, nature did. The lovely Coral Dance, 23, succumbed to Cushing's Disease on December 14, 2001.

Smart Heiress was given a new pasture mate, Brilliant Melody, but it is difficult to replace a friend. Smart Heiress and Brilliant Melody get along well, but while Smart Heiress almost always stayed close to Coral Dance, the nearly blind mare often strays far from Brilliant Melody.

On March 27, 2002, Smart Heiress produced a chestnut colt by More Than Ready.

Cormorant

B. H. 1974, BY HIS MAJESTY—SONG SPARROW, BY TUDOR MINSTREL

C ormorant emerged from the stallion barn, prancing and grandly arching his neck. If ever a horse "breathed fire" it was he, and twenty-seven years had done nothing to diminish the flame. He stopped and stood for a mere moment, arrogantly surveying the lands for a challenger. When none could be found, he decided to argue with the man at the end of the shank.

Cormorant could not be persuaded to stand still until he caught a glimpse of a mare through a barn window some fifty feet away, behind a running pickup truck. While she was just barely visible, it was all the stallion needed. He stood unmoving for minutes, enchanted with the view.

"I used to go to the barn laughing, wondering what kind of antics he'd have on display that morning," trainer J.P. Simpson remembered. "He was entertainment in extreme. He was like a jazz band. He could hit some high notes."

Now retired, eighty-two-year-old Simpson spoke of Cormorant as if he had trained him last week rather than a quarter century ago. "He was a character that demanded your attention," he vividly recalled. "He was the most notorious one in that regard I ever had. His enthusiasm and energy would go on display every day, sometimes two or three times a day."

Simpson brightened at the mere mention of Cormorant, fondly remembering his time with the high-spirited son of His Majesty. "I'd have to have two hotwalkers for him. The first would take three or four turns, and then his alternate would take over. He'd go three or four turns, and then the first one would pick it back up. Cormorant was squealing and kicking and dragging them all over the place."

One thing that Simpson still wishes however, is that Cormorant had been born another year. "I'm just sorry I had to run into Seattle Slew. Most other years Cormorant would have been three-year-old champion or even Horse of the Year."

Simpson remembers watching a televised race ten minutes after Cormorant had won the 1977 Bay Shore and said worrying. "Devastating! I don't think we will want to go where he is," Simpson thought at the time. "He" was Seattle Slew, and he had just won Hialeah's Flamingo Stakes. But Simpson and Cormorant did not avoid him for long.

By winning the Bay Shore, Cormorant enhanced his already lofty reputation. He had now won six of seven starts, including a win over Royal Ski in the Marlboro Nursery Stakes, and Laurel clockers were used to putting a bullet next to his name. There were those who thought Cormorant would be the one to dethrone the quickly rising star, Seattle Slew.

Cormorant's next start was the Gotham Stakes, a race for which Seattle Slew had originally been considered. Slew's connections decided against running, and Cormorant took full advantage of the easier company. He won the mile and one-sixteenth event in an impressive 1:43 3/5, just three-fifths of a second off the track mark.

In his spare time Cormorant amused himself by trying to rip off his leg bandages and buffeting the crew around. Danny Wright, Simpson's stable rider for seventeen years and Cormorant's only jockey, galloped and worked Cormorant at first. "I got to the point where I couldn't gallop him because he was so high strung," Danny remembered. "He would hear my footsteps coming down the shed row and start banging against the wall. He thought I was coming to work him. He would actually recognize my footsteps — he was that intelligent."

While being prepared for the Kentucky Derby, Cormorant came down with a fever, postponing a meeting with Seattle Slew, who won easily. But Cormorant was waiting for him at the Preakness.

Cormorant sprung to the lead, and Seattle Slew raced near his throatlatch. After a quarter in :22 3/5 and a half in :45 3/5, Danny Wright felt very confident on Cormorant. He was stunned when, with a half-mile to go, Jean Cruguet

turned and asked him matter-of-factly, "Where do you think you're going, jock?" as he and Seattle Slew roared past.

Cormorant had simply met one of the greatest Thoroughbreds of the century, and when Seattle Slew was shipped to Belmont, Simpson shipped Cormorant elsewhere. The colt won the grade I Jersey Derby and finished second in the Ohio Derby.

On July 5, 1977, while working at Laurel, Cormorant suffered a slab fracture of his right knee. After undergoing surgery, he was retired to stud where another chance at greatness awaited him.

After two years in Virginia, a syndicate headed by Tom Martin moved Cormorant to New York's Schoenborn Bros. Farm for the 1980 breeding season. Cormorant's sire, His Majesty, was by Ribot, a stallion known for his internal fire. His dam was by the lovely Tudor Minstrel, and Cormorant himself was a strong, handsome grade-I winning stallion. He was well received.

A veterinarian named Jerry Bilinski began working with the stallion and was immediately smitten. When Cormorant couldn't tolerate seeing other stallions while in his paddock, Jerry had a ten-foot-high closed-board fence erected. A window was cut in one end so Cormorant could view the road without seeing adjoining paddocks.

When Cormorant was first let out, Jerry stood outside and listened as the horse circled the enclosure. Within minutes, however, Jerry was humbled when a set of front hooves appeared over the fence. Cormorant was simply testing his constraints and showing his disapproval, but he soon calmed down and poked his head through the window. "I couldn't believe it," Jerry laughed, still impressed twenty years later.

Cormorant moved several times as syndicates and farms came and went; yet, he remained in the Empire State. For entertainment he enjoyed attacking anything placed in the paddock: buckets, tires, and even a goat. Cormorant wasn't dangerous, but he had a strong lively streak that the farm crews respected.

Cormorant led New York's sire list for five years, and in 1994 he not only led the state list but also reached the national top ten.

CORMORANT AT AGE TWENTY IN 1994, THE YEAR HIS SON, GO FOR GIN, WON THE KENTUCKY DERBY.

That year his son Go for Gin won American racing's most famous race, the Kentucky Derby, but he was not Cormorant's first nationally recognized runner. His daughter Saratoga Dew earned the Eclipse Award for three-year-old fillies in 1992, and another filly, Grecian Flight, was a grade I winner who earned $1,320,215.

Jerry Bilinski received the news that Go for Gin had won the Kentucky Derby while Cormorant was breeding late one afternoon. "There's a word for that feeling," he remembered. "Bittersweet. I had a horse where it was difficult to breed, and now there'd be more interest than ever."

The difficulty to which Jerry referred was not with the stallion's interest, but with Cormorant's waning fertility. Jerry, who had since taken over the stallion's management, worked hard with him. He bought mares that had already produced Cormorant foals, the horse underwent countless fertility tests, and he bred Cormorant at odd times — even late at night — when the moment was right. But it was all in vain, and Cormorant produced few foals after 1994.

One of his finest runners was also one of his last. Gander, a rangy gray New York-bred, was born in 1996 and has earned well over a million dollars. Cormorant's shareholders still receive bonus awards due largely to Gander's exploits, and there is even an Internet fan club called the Gander Gang.

Cormorant passed his stubborn streak on to many of his offspring, and most colts were gelded. A few weren't, and Cormorant is emerging as a successful sire of sires. Scarlet Ibis is a popular New York sire, as are Mighty Magee and Raffie's Majesty. Go for Gin, standing at Kentucky's Claiborne Farm, is already the sire of grade I winner Albert the Great.

Jerry was finally forced to pension his old friend, and Cormorant now leads a relaxed life at Bilinski's Waldorf Farm. Jerry still puts Cormorant in his stallion advertisements, the regal horse's portrait above the others with the word "Pensioned" beneath.

Cormorant no longer has a ten-foot-high paddock fence, but as he still can't stand to see other stallions outdoors, he is let out when the other stallions are brought in.

Across the aisle from Cormorant, his son Mighty Magee carries on the family name. Yet there is no family attachment for Cormorant. When Mighty Magee was brought out for portraits, Cormorant could be heard complaining in his usual fashion: the staccato banging of a steel-shod hooves against metal stall rungs, as Cormorant methodically "voiced" his disapproval during the entire fifteen-minute session.

When Cormorant was led out for photos, Jerry asked to watch. He proudly noted how good the horse looked and how full of fire Cormorant still is. I asked Jerry if he'd like to be photographed with Cormorant and, as the saying goes, I didn't have to ask twice. Jerry beamed like a schoolboy with his first prom date.

Seattle Slew's days have come to an end and countless thousands have mourned his passing. Many will recall his blazing wins and times they saw the dark bay colt. Stories of his greatness will grace newspapers and magazines.

When Cormorant breathes his last, far fewer will notice. But for those fortunate enough to have been entertained by him, the loss will be profound.

Cozzene

GR. H. 1980, BY CARO—RIDE THE TRAILS,
BY PRINCE JOHN

I remember the first time I photographed Cozzene. He was in a post parade at Saratoga with the popular gelding Win, who passed me first. The Barachois gelding's head hung low, his bright red blinkers obscuring his plain bay head. Both ears flopped slightly as he ambled along. Then came Cozzene.

His mane had recently been braided, and it flowed in silvery waves, the red-and-white silks accentuating his beauty. The gray Caro horse bounced during the post parade, tugging on the reins and looking squarely at my camera. He knew that I was photographing him. I was certain of it.

I photographed him again months later in the Breeders' Cup winner's circle, having known when he first stared at me at Saratoga that he would end up there. Cozzene glowed like a vision through the gloom of that cold, dark Aqueduct day.

He retired after that 1985 Breeders' Cup, with a record of ten wins in twenty-four starts and earnings of $978,152. He was unplaced only four times, and after trainer John Nerud sent him to the turf, Cozzene was truly at home.

Cozzene entered stud at Lexington's Gainesway Farm in 1986, and the next year Cozzene's Prince was born. In a seven-year campaign, this durable colt earned more than $1.2 million and became a Canadian champion. Other wonderful Cozzene runners followed soon and often. Star of Cozzene earned more than two million dollars and was a multiple grade I winner. Hasten To Add, a Canadian champion, was a beautiful gray turf specialist. Running Stag was a multiple graded stakes winner whose globetrotting earned him more than a million dollars.

Although Cozzene lived comfortably at Gainesway, a world away from that of the Breeders' Cup, his impact on the event continued. In 1994 his dark gray son Tikkanen stormed home in the Breeders' Cup Turf. In 1996 his son Alphabet Soup, a lighter gray, surprised the racing world by defeating Cigar in the Breeders' Cup Classic. Cozzene thus, at the relatively young age of sixteen, became the first and only Breeders' Cup winner to sire two individual Breeders' Cup winners on two different surfaces.

In 1996, assisted by Alphabet Soup's earnings, Cozzene led America's sire list.

Cozzene's runners have kept his name near the top of the general sire list, and he is perhaps more popular now than ever. He has sired more than fifty stakes winners, and his yearlings occasionally top the one-million-dollar mark at auction.

Cozzene leads a peaceful life of quiet grandeur, and I was honored to have another chance to photograph him in June 2001. Cozzene was twenty-one, and as with other Gainesway stallions, he was led to his paddock soon after 7 a.m. Stallion manager Marion Gross greeted me with a wide smile and a comfortable handshake, and Cozzene emerged from his beautiful European-style barn. Gross asked what I wanted the stallion to do, and Cozzene complied pleasantly with each request. The term is perhaps overused, but Cozzene was a model of "true class." He never pinned his ears, struck out, or even fidgeted.

Gross spoke proudly of Cozzene's class and professionalism as a groom moved him to several attractive backdrops. Within ten minutes, we were done. Cozzene was let loose in his paddock, and he strode out comfortably through the grass like a monarch.

The morning was warm with the waning dew of night, and sunlight had yet to reach the grass. As he walked away through the rich pasture dotted with small white flowers, Cozzene looked squarely at my camera. He knew that I was photographing him. I was certain of it.

Creme Fraiche

B. G. 1982, BY RICH CREAM—LIKELY EXCHANGE,
BY TERRIBLE TIGER

*I*t was a blustery April morning, frost lying thick on any surface not fortunate enough to be touched by sun. Flowers poked daring heads upward, and the grass was sweet with the promise of spring.

Brushwood Stable features a stunning old stone barn, its stalls consisting of seemingly timeless wood and timeless dreams. In a far stall a new arrival stretched his white-stockinged legs. By Storm Cat, this three-day-old chestnut was a full brother to High Yield. His mother, Scoop the Gold, occasionally dipped her head to nuzzle him as she watched a large gelding getting a bath in the wash room.

"He hasn't had a bath in ten years," farm manager Brooks Adams said, probably joking. Regardless, it was obvious Creme Fraiche did not often have this much hands-on attention, as he fussed a bit. To keep him amused, the groom held out a yellow brush, which Creme Fraiche quickly swept away. He juggled it in his teeth for several moments before dropping it, and the groom picked it back up. Again, he waved it and Creme Fraiche whisked it away, bobbing his head for a moment in proud conquest.

The visit to Creme Fraiche's Pennsylvania home came with a humorous disclaimer from office manager Mona Phillips: "He looks like a big, furry broodmare." His winter coat was thick, and he certainly is heavier than when he was racing. But Creme Fraiche earned his retirement, running sixty-four times in a six-year campaign. He deserves a cushy life, and owner Betty Moran is happy to provide it.

Creme Fraiche's woolly coat dried slowly, and by the time he was brought outside, the wind was bitter. He had not often visited this side of the barn, and the damp gelding was definitely not happy to be away from other horses. He called out and then fussed some more.

He stood long enough for a quick portrait before a grand blossoming magnolia tree, then decided he was truly unhappy with his current situation. He danced in circles, protesting with voice and body, and we conceded. It was time to return him to his paddock.

Creme Fraiche's paddock was a long walk from that

stunning barn, perhaps a quarter mile down the golden hill, past a cornfield. Adams had the not-so-pleasant task of walking the freshly irritated gelding through the numbing breeze, around the expansive corn.

In his paddock, two geldings awaited their friend, watching the cornfield where they had seen him disappear. Tostadero and Glenbarra, both successful old stakes performers, paced the fenceline nervously and called out in their vigil. When Creme Fraiche finally appeared, the two geldings became almost frantic in their delight.

Creme Fraiche was greeted in the paddock with a warm round of nickers, jostles, and nose touching, and the trio wandered a short way. I was certain Creme Fraiche was telling his buddies of the awful time he had experienced, of that irritating man with the cold water, and of that woman who clicked. Creme Fraiche stood unmoving, but undoubtedly apologizing as the other two snuffed at his coat for long moments, trying to make sense of his fresh flowery scent.

Finally content that it was still indeed their friend, the two other geldings relaxed and they soon dropped their heads to graze. When we left them, the grazing trio was just slowly wandering from sight.

* * *

The list of races Creme Fraiche won is remarkable. He's most remembered for being one of Woody Stephens' five consecutive Belmont Stakes winners and the only gelding to win that classic. Yet he also won the grade I Meadowlands Cup, Super Derby, American Derby, and Jerome; the grade II Paterson, Donn, and W.L. McKnight handicaps; two runnings of the Tropical Park Handicap in the same year; and back-to-back runnings of the grade I Jockey Club Gold Cup. In doing so, this gelding earned $4,024,727, and he is still the third-highest earning gelding of all time, behind John Henry and Best Pal.

Dahlia

CH. M. 1970-2001, BY VAGUELY NOBLE—CHARMING ALIBI,
BY HONEYS ALIBI

ahlia accomplished something that no other horse has ever done: she won stakes races in five countries. That is a remarkable achievement, but she was a remarkable racehorse.

The races Dahlia won are among the best the world had to offer, from the group I Irish Oaks to America's grade I Man o' War, from the grade II Canadian International to Longchamp's group I Prix Saint-Alary. She won back-to-back runnings of both the group I Benson & Hedges Gold Cup and group I King George VI & Queen Elizabeth Stakes.

Dahlia was England's Horse of the Year twice, as well as champion older mare. She was also Ireland's champion three-year-old in 1973 and in 1974 was voted champion grass horse in America. She raced through 1976 for owner Nelson Bunker Hunt, and her earnings of $1,427,354 marked another record: she was the first distaff millionaire.

Retired to Hunt's Bluegrass Farm in Lexington, Kentucky, Dahlia was as remarkable a broodmare as she had been a racehorse. In 1981 her first stakes winner was born, and Dahar became not just a grade I winner in two countries, but a millionaire as well.

Other stakes winners followed. Rivlia, a 1982 foal, won the grade I San Luis Rey Stakes and earned $1,005,041, and the 1984 foal Delegant took the grade I San Juan Capistrano Handicap and earned $623,941. Dahlia's 1987 foal, Wajd, won a grade II stakes and is a good producer herself, being the dam of two stakes winners.

In 1988, when Hunt dispersed his stock, Dahlia was purchased for $1.1 million by Allen Paulson. Dahlia never missed a beat, and for Brookside Farm she produced grade I winner Dahlia's Dreamer in 1989. Her final stakes winner, grade II Jersey Derby winner Llandaff, was born in 1990, and in 1996, at the senior age of twenty-six, Dahlia's final foal was born.

Not only a champion racemare, Dahlia also became one of the greatest broodmares of the twentieth century, producing six graded stakes winners, two millionaires, and two stakes-placed runners.

When this beautiful mare posed in 1998, farm manager Ted Carr escorted me to the broodmare barn where the groom was preparing Dahlia. In the stall next to Dahlia's, Dahlia's Dreamer stood quietly, looking nothing like the handful she was at the racetrack. It was early, just before eight o'clock, and the fog was still lifting sleepily from the farm's rolling valleys.

Dahlia's legs were stiff as they brought her out. The twenty-eight-year-old mare suffered from arthritis, and the groom circled her slowly several times as she loosened up. The impairment could not hide her grace, however, and the dew-coated grass provided her a kind footing.

When the groom slowed Dahlia to a gentle halt, she immediately stood in a near-perfect conformation pose. It seemed she knew what we wanted, and she raised her famous blazed head high, looking in the correct direction. I wondered what caught her interest, but there was nothing obvious. I had photographed another old chestnut mare once, long ago, who almost instantly assumed the same noble pose. Her name was Shuvee.

* * *

Allen Paulson has since passed away, and his beautiful Brookside Farm has been sold. Dahlia passed away as well, on April 6, 2001, at age thirty-one. Her body was interred at Brookside, where she had spent her last thirteen years.

Dahlia was a Kentucky-bred member of the amazing foal crop of 1970, which included such giants as Forego and Secretariat. Most of those campaigners are long gone, and in the past few years Mr. Prospector and Our Native have joined them.

But perhaps no star shone more brightly than Dahlia, the lovely globetrotting mare.

Dance Forth

GR. M. 1978, BY DANCING COUNT—FOURTH DIMENSION, BY TIME TESTED

We've lived a charmed life as far as horses go, but Dance Forth was where it all began," said Tom Bowman. A respected Maryland veterinarian and horse breeder, Bowman was a relative newcomer to racing when he bought a share in a stallion named Dancing Count. Bowman was a soccer coach at Chestertown's Washington College for two decades, and he began a veterinary practice in 1973 at nearby Thornmar Farm. He alternated between loves: coaching soccer in the fall and tending to broodmares in the spring.

Bowman leased a mare named Fourth Dimension and bred her to Dancing Count. The resulting foal was a lovely gray filly. Bowman's wife and daughters all took dance lessons, and combined with the names of the filly's parents, Bowman decided upon the name Dance Forth.

When Dance Forth sold as a two-year-old in 1980 for $24,500, Bowman recalled, "That was huge. Frankly, that probably more than doubled my income."

Bud Delp trained Dance Forth for Nancy Bayard, and the filly got off to a strong start, winning three of her first four races. In her fourth start, Dance Forth won the $20,000 Bicker Stakes at the Fair Grounds in New Orleans. Tom Bowman, in his first attempt, was now breeder of a stakes winner.

Dance Forth, the first horse Bowman bred and sold at auction, and his first to win a stakes, became the namesake of his Chestertown farm.

Dance Forth raced three seasons, winning five of nineteen starts, including the Twixt and Gala Lil handicaps, and running third in the Boiling Springs and Majorette. With earnings of $68,494, Dance Forth was retired.

Bowman lost track of her for a few years, but rediscovered Dance Forth when he began doing veterinary

work for Allaire du Pont's Woodstock Farm. Mrs. Bayard boarded her horses at Woodstock, and Bowman helped tend to the lovely mare.

Of Dance Forth's eleven foals to race, all were winners and two won stakes. Balotra, a 1987 filly by Oh Say, earned more than $300,000 and won two stakes races, including the grade III Sixty Sails Handicap. Mudra, a 1993 Private Terms gelding, won two stakes and earned $158,726.

Dance Forth struggled through a difficult delivery of a Concern filly in 1997, and Mrs. Bayard decided to pension her. Some time later Bowman noticed that the gray mare was happy and healthy, recovered fully from the delivery.

Still holding a soft spot in his heart for his first stakes winner, Bowman called Mrs. Bayard to see if she might part with Dance Forth. He believed the mare might still be able to produce a healthy foal. Bowman hoped for a Dance Forth filly, so that her blood would continue at Dance Forth Farm.

Mrs. Bayard gave the mare to Bowman, and in 1999 Dance Forth produced a healthy Valley Crossing filly. Named Almighty Hannah, the gray filly was not the most correct, and she did not race. Instead, Dance Forth's daughter will be bred in 2002 to continue the family line.

Dance Forth Farm specializes in foaling. So, Dance Forth and her daughter live at Bowman's second farm, Roland. The fields at Roland are expansive and comfortable. Nearby farms include the historic properties of Northview and Woodstock.

Dance Forth, a sweetheart of a mare who loves to be visited and coddled, has a lifetime home at Roland. The only exception, Bowman said, would be "if someone needed a gentle old mare to baby-sit a sick horse or something, if she could contribute to somebody else the way she contributed to us."

Bowman continued: "In a world where most things are driven by financial considerations, this is just a happy little story where we allowed sentiment to be involved somewhat. Dance Forth is a reminder that sometimes the horse is more important than the four feet it stands on."

Danzig

B. H. 1977, BY NORTHERN DANCER—PAS DE NOM,
BY ADMIRAL'S VOYAGE

*E*veryone on the farm says I have him spoiled rotten," said Jerry Richardson of twenty-five-year-old Danzig, the groom's Southern drawl laced with a smile. "I had a group of people out the other day looking at him, and he reached out and licked my nose.

"He licks on me all the time when I'm grooming him. I've been grooming him coming on six years now; and me and him, we have no trouble. He's my boy. He's my baby, really."

Danzig is an impressive baby indeed. His 168 stakes winners rank him second only to Mr. Prospector among North American stallions, and that number is likely to rise.

Joe Brocklebank, a former jockey and now a successful bloodstock agent, remembered Danzig's early days well. "I was working horses for Woody (Stephens). I'd just met Woody, and he was giving me a chance to work the young horses."

Joe took the unraced Danzig to the track with another Stephens trainee. It was the first time Danzig breezed, and without effort the powerful colt worked seconds quicker than Stephens had requested. Joe knew then that

Danzig was special, and he told Woody he would throttle the colt's speed in the mornings.

Joe had several good reasons to keep the thick Northern Dancer colt under wraps. The colt already had a troublesome problem, a sore knee since early training in Aiken, South Carolina. Also, Joe hoped to ride the colt in the afternoon. The fewer people who knew how special Danzig was, the greater Joe's chances.

Joe worked Danzig perhaps twenty times before the colt's first start, and twenty-two years later, the memory remained vivid. "He was always extremely intelligent. I don't remember him doing anything wrong. Schooling in the gate, the other horses were still in the gate, and he'd clear them by far coming out of it. He was just naturally fast."

Joe earned the first mount. It was June 25, 1979, at Belmont Park.

"When he ran, I think he was number two. I remember the horse next to him broke through the gate. Then a horse in the five or six hole flipped in the gate. And Danzig was just standing there, like he was saying, 'What's wrong with these guys?'

"He was in front leaving the gate, and he stayed there. It could have been the feature race, against older horses, and he would have won."

Despite a brilliant performance, Danzig did not start again that season. His knee was X-rayed before the race and again afterward. There were changes, and surgery was performed to remove bone chips. Those were the days before arthroscopic surgery, and Danzig was put away until May 1980.

With regular stable rider Eddie Maple now in the irons, Danzig won his return by seven and a half lengths. Two weeks later he won again, by five and three-quarters lengths. But then his knee forced his retirement. *The Blood-Horse* ran a mere one paragraph note about his retirement to stud, in its July 26, 1980, issue.

When Danzig arrived at Claiborne Farm for the 1981 season, he sported an impressive sprinter's physique, an undefeated record, and promising bloodlines. His initial stud fee was $20,000.

Danzig's sire was the best in the world, and his dam was a minor stakes winner by Admiral's Voyage. Danzig's female line is solidly dotted with black type, although not necessarily the stuff of legend. His third dam was England's three-year-old filly champion, Steady Aim. And Steady Aim's dam, Quick Arrow, was an unraced half sister to the successful Chrysler II.

Marshall Jenney and William Farish III bred Danzig. Jenney undoubtedly had high hopes when Danzig was born at his Derry Meeting Farm in Pennsylvania. So did Henryk de Kwiatkowski, who purchased Danzig as a yearling at the Saratoga sale of 1978. But even Jenney, with his positive nature and eternally high hopes, could not have foreseen what Pas de Nom's little bay colt would become when he was born on February 12, 1977.

It's difficult to dream that high.

Any questions about Danzig's ability as a sire were squelched with his first crop. Nine of his thirty-four foals won stakes. His crop earnings were an incredible $5,505,743, and his earnings per starter averaged $203,916. A member of that crop, Chief's Crown, dominated the first Breeders' Cup race ever, the 1984 Breeders' Cup Juvenile, and was named champion two-year-old.

His first crop was no fluke. Danzig has produced outstanding runners every year since, and on three occasions — 1991, 1992, and 1993 — he has led America's general sire list.

Danzig is a handsome bay stallion, 15.3 hands high, and his thick body looks quite similar to Northern Dancer's. His jowls and neck are thick, coupled with a powerful shoulder and hind end. His rich bay coat is seemingly always sprinkled with dapples.

But in the mid-1980s, Danzig began sporting an unusual look.

Much of Kentucky received a facelift when Queen Elizabeth II visited in 1984, and Claiborne was no excep-

DANZIG AND JERRY RICHARDSON

tion. White and yellow paint was applied, bushes were trimmed, leather was cleaned, and fences were painted with creosote.

"He likes to try to rub his halter off sometimes," said Jerry, his groom. "Well, he got a splinter in his eye. He's pretty much blind in that eye now, but he still sees a little bit. Not much, but he sees shapes and light."

Danzig's right eye took on a surreal appearance, not unlike another famous stallion — old Lexington, the "Blind Hero of Woodburn." Danzig's eye, combined with his reputation for being tough, merely enhances the sire's mystique.

But his eye is not the only thing about the stallion that seems surreal. His numbers are unbelievable and appear to be misprints. As of May 2002, Danzig was the sire of 168 stakes winners and twenty champions. The championships are spread around the world: United States, England, Japan, Canada, Spain, France, United Arab Emirates, and Ireland.

Danzig's 1989 crop earned $9,508,872, more than the crops of many sires' entire careers. Eight of his crops surpassed the five-million-dollar mark. Eighteen percent of his foals have won stakes races, as have 24 percent of his starters. Danzig's average earnings index is currently the highest in the country, 4.63. The legendary Seattle Slew, with 4.19, is second.

Ninety-five of his offspring are graded stakes winners, and an unbelievable forty-four have won grade Is. Danzig's grade I winners include Pine Bluff, Lure, Dispute, War Chant, Agnes World, and Versailles Treaty, but with 168 stakes winners from which to choose, the list seems endless.

When I saw Danzig in 1986, the groom warned me to stay back from the fence. While Danzig looked harmless enough, grazing in seemingly random fashion, the groom knew the horse enjoyed the opportunity to bolt toward perceived invaders. What looked like a smallish horse enjoying the afternoon sun was really a strong nine-year-old stallion waiting for a chance to remind me of his power. I stayed back.

Fifteen years later, in 2001, Jerry proudly brought Danzig out. The bay stallion stood calmly, and Jerry reached back to scratch Danzig's broad hind end. The horse's ears flicked back and forth, as euphoria slowly set in on his famous face. Stories about the horse's attitude were hard to imagine.

Jerry dismissed stories of Danzig's reputation. "We don't put a whole lot of faith in him when he's loose," Jerry said. "If he's in his paddock, we still leave him alone. He's still territorial, but not like he used to be. He's good to work with.

"He's mellowed out a lot with age. Now, I think you could open his stall and he'd walk right out to his paddock by himself, he's so used to it," Jerry said, laughing.

Just in case, however, Danzig is not left to his own devices. The twenty-five-year-old stallion is led carefully from his stall each day.

Even his stall is awe-inspiring. Claiborne leaves the old nameplates on the stall doors when its grand horses pass on. Danzig's brass nameplate glows, the names REVIEWER and AMBIORIX on either side. Given a few moments to dream, a visitor can envision the handsome Reviewer being led down the lane or Ambiorix quietly chewing hay in the stall. For horsemen Claiborne is a sacred place of new and old dreams.

At such a magic place, Danzig is still a favorite with tourists and visiting horsemen. As Jerry said, placing Danzig in some pretty grand company: "He's one of the main attractions — besides Mr. Prospector's and Secretariat's graves."

That's pretty grand company, indeed.

The Dowagers of Darby Dan

L exington's Old Frankfort Pike is a magic country road, winding past crumbling stone walls and lands rich in tradition. Entry signs announce such farms as Three Chimneys, Hopewell, and Mare Haven.

No land is more steeped in tradition than that of Darby Dan. The old stone pillars and long, tree-lined driveway send one back to another time, when E.R. Bradley himself lived here on a farm called Idle Hour. Bubbling Over stood here, and Black Toney, and Behave Yourself.

Since John Galbreath purchased the property in 1957 and renamed it Darby Dan, stallions such as Ribot, Graustark, and Roberto have made it their home. Also, Darby Dan has always been known for its quality brood-mare band, and top race mares from Love You by Heart to Soaring Softly graze over its acres of bluegrass.

Two older mares live here as well, both of whom have made their mark on the breed: Wings of Grace and Kelley's Day.

The mares have marked differences as well as similarities. Their body types are very dissimilar. Wings of Grace is long, willowy, and elegant, while Kelley's Day is a thick, low-headed, shorter mare. Yet both stride out beautifully and are kind and patient with their handlers. Both have bright eyes and a wise attitude. And each took an open-minded interest in her role of playing model.

Kelley's Day is by Darby Dan stallion Graustark, out of the wonderful Hasty Road mare, Golden Trail. In 2001, Golden Trail gained added recognition as the fifth dam of Kentucky Derby winner Monarchos, but she was already well-known. She had produced three stakes winners in Gleaming Light, Java Moon, and Sylvan Place and a stakes-placed filly in Kelley's Day.

Kelley's Day's biggest contribution to racing was through her son, Brian's Time. He was a two-time grade I winner and a racing millionaire. Since moving to Japan, he has also become a top sire, and every year his name ranks high on that country's sire list.

Wings of Grace is out of the Darby Dan mare Far Beyond, a half sister to major stakes winner Mehmet and to stakes winner Miss Swapsco, foundation of a line that includes Glorious Song, Devil's Bag, and Saint Ballado, etc. Far Beyond, in addition to producing the graded stakes-winning Wings of Grace, was also the dam of a minor stakes winner. One of Far Beyond's other fillies, stakes-placed Battle Creek Girl, has produced stakes winners Tricky Creek, Parade Ground, Wavering Girl, Speed Dialer, Everhope, and Parade Leader.

The lovely Wings of Grace is herself the dam of two grade I winners. Her 1987 foal Plenty of Grace won five graded stakes including the grade I Yellow Ribbon Invitational. Eight years later, Wings of Grace's twelfth foal arrived, a chestnut filly who grew to be long and willowy like her mother. Soaring Softly, a high-strung filly, blossomed on the turf at age four, when she ripped through seven wins in eight starts. Her final start was a powerful win in the 1999 Breeders' Cup Filly & Mare Turf.

As Darby Dan's John Phillips related to *The Blood-Horse* after Soaring Softly's Breeders' Cup: "She'll be in

WINGS OF GRACE
B. M. 1978, BY KEY TO THE MINT—
FAR BEYOND, BY NIJINSKY II

the Darby Dan broodmare band, as was her mother before her, and her mother before her, and her mother before her."

Soaring Softly has been retired, and it is now her turn to shine as a broodmare.

Wings of Grace and Kelley's Day each have more chances for posterity. Wings of Grace's final foal, an Arch colt, was born in 2001. Kelley's Day currently has two successful racehorses in training, Storm Day and Ellie's Moment, and in 2000 she produced a Kris S. filly named Day's Sunset.

Wings of Grace and Kelley's Day are heartwarming examples of the old axiom: "Blessed are the broodmares." Each had a good, but not overly impressive, race record. Each has wonderful blood and a proud, kind attitude. And each has contributed admirably to the breed.

KELLEY'S DAY
B. M. 1977, BY GRAUSTARK—
GOLDEN TRAIL, BY HASTY ROAD

Deputed Testamony

B. H. 1980, BY TRAFFIC COP—PROOF REQUESTED, BY PROVE IT

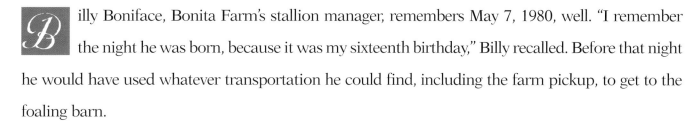

Billy Boniface, Bonita Farm's stallion manager, remembers May 7, 1980, well. "I remember the night he was born, because it was my sixteenth birthday," Billy recalled. Before that night he would have used whatever transportation he could find, including the farm pickup, to get to the foaling barn.

That evening, when he received the call that Proof Requested was in labor, he drove his new, used Jeep. "It was my first legal drive to the barn," he laughed.

The Boniface family could not know what impact the new bay colt with the white-striped face would have on their life. Proof Requested had raced four times in two years, winning once and earning $1,797. While most of her foals were winners, none were exceptional.

The Boniface family had brought two stallions from Kentucky, Cabildo and Traffic Cop, to stand the 1979 season at their farm. The bay colt, born in 1980, was from Traffic Cop's first Maryland crop. Named Deputed Testamony, he would become both his dam's and sire's best runner.

Deputed Testamony was born, raised, and broken at Bonita Farm in Darlington, Maryland. Billy's father, Bill, trained the handsome bay colt, and Deputed Testamony, nicknamed D.T., raced off the farm in typical Boniface fashion.

Every Maryland breeder dreams of one day winning the state's crowning classic, the Preakness Stakes. Over a muddy surface on a dreary day in 1983, Deputed Testamony blazed his way home, and the Boniface family converged in the winner's circle. It was a grand day for the state, as a beaming Maryland-bred family accepted the Woodlawn Vase for its Maryland-bred runner.

Deputed Testamony won eleven of twenty starts in his three-year campaign, including the Preakness, Haskell Invitational, and five other stakes races. He set a mile track record of 1:36 1/5 at the Meadowlands at age two and another track record at four at Pimlico. That mile and one-sixteenth mark of 1:40 4/5 still stands today.

Deputed Testamony earned $674,329, far more than Proof Requested's other eight foals combined.

When Deputed Testamony broke a bone in his foot in 1984, his role changed from racehorse to stallion.

The next year, the Boniface family moved Deputed Testamony and its other horses nearby to a new Bonita Farm, a more expansive, beautiful piece of open Maryland countryside with limitless potential. Deputed Testamony was partly responsible for the move.

"He was a huge part of it," Billy said of their Preakness winner. "He gave us some national exposure, really put us on the map. It gave us a whole new client base."

Deputed Testamony stood alongside Traffic Cop.

When Traffic Cop died, he was buried near the front of the property. Proof Requested, Deputed Testamony's dam, is buried at his side.

* * *

Bonita Farm is a thriving Thoroughbred farm, and the morning I visited in December 2001 was a busy one. Morning sets moved quietly from the training barn to the track, as horses from earlier sets grazed. In the nearby stud barn Billy greeted me warmly and spoke of Deputed Testamony's accomplishments. The twenty-one-year-old stallion was tucked comfortably in his expansive stall.

Billy brought Deputed Testamony outside, and they stopped on the beautiful cobblestone walkway. Several

Boniface family members helped as the stallion posed proudly, glancing from person to person as they called out to him.

Billy led D.T. to his paddock, down a long, scenic road with open land on either side. Five-plank fencing enclosed the large paddocks.

Billy took Deputed Testamony to the far, lower end of his paddock, knowing the stallion would turn and run to his favorite corner. Deputed Testamony, usually a gentleman, didn't care for this game and reared gracefully.

The stallion's coat, a mix of unusual curls and countless rich brown tones, glowed brilliantly. His lovely face showed no malice — only eagerness to be set free. A strong stallion of good bone with a professional attitude, Deputed Testamony longed to run.

Billy unclasped the shank, and Deputed Testamony bolted up his hill toward the corner, where a stallion waited in an adja-

cent paddock. D.T. moved with driving, youthful strides, his ears forward. Valley Crossing waited, and when D.T. reached him, the two set off in a relaxed match race.

After several minutes of mock competition, the two stallions settled down. Deputed Testamony dropped his head to graze. Just beyond his paddock, a beautiful old church, appropriately named Harmony Church, stood proudly. With its oversized steeple and timeless old cemetery as backdrop, Deputed Testamony spends his days in a Norman Rockwell scene.

As with many older stallions, Deputed Testamony is no longer fashionable, and only ten mares visited his court in 2001. His 2002 stud fee, $2,500, is one-tenth that of his 1985 fee, but Deputed Testamony still has faithful followers. And well he should.

He has sired five Maryland Million winners, and six of his runners have earned more than $400,000. Churchbell Chimes, his leading earner, won seven stakes and earned $577,844. Testing, Winsox, Reputed Testamony, Under Oath, and Testafly were other popular Mid-Atlantic-based stakes winners.

Now retired from training, Bill Boniface still believes in his old Preakness winner. "His offspring, they're just as game as a racehorse comes. At any price range, they'll give you all they've got, like he did."

Deputy Minister

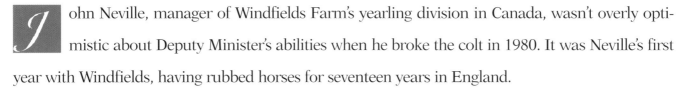

DK. B/BR. H. 1979, BY VICE REGENT—MINT COPY,
BY BUNTY'S FLIGHT

*J*ohn Neville, manager of Windfields Farm's yearling division in Canada, wasn't overly optimistic about Deputy Minister's abilities when he broke the colt in 1980. It was Neville's first year with Windfields, having rubbed horses for seventeen years in England.

"He was a tough horse, a headstrong horse," Neville remembered twenty-two years later, his voice softened with an English accent. "He was a Vice Regent, and they could be tough. He would send you a telegram when he was going to do something, a signal that he was going to explode."

But the handsome Canadian-bred colt had not only ability but also intelligence. He sent many telegrams as he exploded upon the racing scene in 1981.

Deputy Minister had such promise that his ownership changed three times in his freshman year. No one backed off, but additional owners jumped on the handsome colt's back, each hoping for a Triple Crown ride.

After Deputy Minister's fourth win in as many starts for owner/breeder Centurion Farms, Kinghaven Farms came aboard as half-partner. Deputy Minister won four of his next five starts, including the Young America and Laurel Futurity, and Centurion and Kinghaven each sold half-interest to Robert Brennan's Due Process Stable.

Deputy Minister was voted Canada's 1981 Horse of the Year and two-year-old champion colt in both Canada and the United States.

But the owners' classic dreams were crushed when Deputy Minister ran badly in the Bahamas Stakes and a subsequent Hialeah allowance race. X-rays revealed a slight fracture in a sesamoid, and for a time his racing future was in doubt.

That autumn Deputy Minister returned with a Woodbine allowance score, then finished off the board in Aqueduct's Sport Page Handicap. Robert Brennan bought out his partners "at a much lower price than the first time," Due Process racing manager John Perrotta recalled. Deputy Minister headed to Florida, to trainer Reynaldo Nobles.

Under Nobles' patient hand, the four-year-old Deputy Minister won the Donn and Tom Fool, both grade II

events, and the Gulfstream Sprint Championship Handicap. He placed in the grade I Vosburgh Stakes and grade II Stuyvesant Handicap, then he wrapped up his career with a second in the grade I Meadowlands Cup.

Before the Cup, Deputy Minister had been partially sold again, this time to E.P. Taylor's Windfields Farm. He was retired to Windfields' Maryland division to stand alongside the aging Northern Dancer.

Deputy Minister's female line did not seem a recipe for greatness. Perrotta recalled that the horse's dam, Mint Copy, was a $6,500 claim. She went on to win eleven races in her five years on track, earning $53,945. Her sire, Bunty's Flight, produced only three stakes winners in fifteen crops.

It's back to the fourth generation before major names are found on the female side, but they are good ones: Bimelech and Polynesian.

Vice Regent, on the other hand, had classic blood. His sire, Northern Dancer, is still considered by many the greatest sire in history. On Vice Regent's female side, several nice names emerge, including Windfields himself.

Deputy Minister, whose first foals were born in 1985, was responsible for two major champions, and four Eclipse Awards, before the end of the decade.

Open Mind, from Deputy Minister's second crop, won the Breeders' Cup Juvenile Fillies in 1988. She earned the Eclipse Award for two-year-old fillies, then came back to take three-year-old filly honors the following year.

Deputy Minister's next crop included the ill-fated Go for Wand. The brilliant filly also won the Breeders' Cup Juvenile Fillies and garnered back-to-back Eclipse Awards.

By the time two-year-old Open Mind thundered home in the Breeders' Cup, Windfields Farm closed its Maryland operation. Deputy Minister needed a new home, and in

Versailles, Kentucky, a farm needed a new stallion. It was a perfect fit.

Fred Seitz grew up on historic Brookdale Farm in Lincroft, New Jersey. His father was a carpenter at the farm, a hallowed place where famed Thoroughbreds such as Regret and Twenty Grand spent relaxing days.

Brookdale Farm in New Jersey was sold when Seitz was in college, but he never forgot those early days. In 1983 he began a new Brookdale Farm in Versailles. Seitz had one stallion, Greinton, when Deputy Minister and fellow Windfields stallion Imperial Falcon were shipped to him.

Deputy Minister has held court at Seitz' beautiful Brookdale Farm ever since. His champion two-year-old colt Dehere wowed crowds in 1993 with devastating wins. Diva's Debut and Hello Seattle earned Canadian championships. Eloquent Minister was champion three-year-old filly in Ireland.

Awesome Again won the Breeders' Cup Classic. Touch Gold squelched Silver Charm's Triple Crown bid in the Belmont Stakes. Keeper Hill dominated the Kentucky Oaks. Deputy Commander won a riveting Travers. Turf specialist Flag Down earned nearly $1.7 million. Millionaire Mr Purple took the Santa Anita Handicap; Clear Mandate the Spinster; Salt Lake, the Hopeful.

By March 2002 Deputy Minister had sired sixty-nine stakes winners, including international performers of the highest caliber. He has twice been America's leading sire, in 1997 and 1998. His $150,000 stud fee seems a bargain. In 2001, the average price for his yearlings that sold at auction was $425,192.

Seitz is understandably proud of the twenty-three-year-old stallion. "He's aged extremely well. He's never been mean, but he's always been 'all man.' He's a handful, in a masculine way.

"He's one of the best breeding stallions in Kentucky, between his vigor and his vitality. He's usually a one-jump stallion, and he's always ready. He's still a marvel."

When stallion manager Victor Espinoza, Deputy Minister's longtime groom, brought his charge out in 1999, I was stunned. Deputy Minister has a classic look and stands 16.2 1/2 hands. He doesn't have the compact appearance of so many from that line, but he sports a wonderful sloping shoulder, wise eyes, and proud countenance. Deputy Minister is elegance.

He displayed aloof disregard for my photographic attempts, refusing to provide the classic "look of eagles." As with most stallions, Deputy Minister was usually presented showing his near side. Victor suggested he could aim the horse toward the right.

Victor knew his stallion. Deputy Minister perked up at the change in routine. Seconds later, I had my portrait.

Robert Brennan sold his equine interests more than a decade ago, and Windfields is now the largest shareholder in Deputy Minister. Windfields' only other stallion also stands at Brookdale. Silver Deputy, out of a Mr. Prospector mare, is the sire of seven champions, including Silverbulletday. He stands at the bustling Brookdale Farm alongside his sire, Deputy Minister.

"Deputy Minister has been a godsend to Brookdale." Seitz said. "He really put us on the map in the stallion business, and in other aspects of the business as well… He's a star."

.

The Ladies of Derry Meeting

*T*he horses at Derry Meeting were on full alert. Their tails were high, some flipped in anxious salute. Heads strained, and pricked ear tips nearly touched. All eyes peered into the distance, searching beyond their viewscape. Occasionally, a mare snorted a warning.

Derry Meeting workers also watched, their trucks idling as they stood together by a farm road out in the cold. They, too, were concentrating, riveted by the unseen.

Suddenly, deer bolted across a broodmare field, scattering with uncertainty and nervousness, necks craning backward. Mares shuffled in the deer's wake, then froze again to listen.

It was a stunning December day at the Pennsylvania farm, with clear skies and frigid wind chills — a perfect day for foxhunting, unless you were the fox. Baying hounds could be heard in the distance. The hunt was moving closer.

Derry Meeting Farm is a beautiful place of tradition, begun in 1967 by horseman Marshall Jenney. If it had been nothing more than the birthplace of Storm Cat and Danzig, it would already be priceless. But it has been much more. For decades, it's been the source of top-quality performers at racetracks around the world. Many of those performers were Derry Meeting's own, while others were George Strawbridge's Augustin Stable runners.

Strawbridge and Jenney had a friendship and work rela-tionship that lasted more than thirty years. They went to school together and even rode against each other in amateur steeplechase races. Jenney, a big man known for his humor and good nature, died in November 2000. Worries that Derry Meeting might be sold were quickly squelched, as Marshall's wife, Bettina, took over. Under her gentle guidance, Derry Meeting has continued its winning ways.

Many Strawbridge runners spend early days building strength and confidence on Derry Meeting property, and many Strawbridge mares find their way back to Derry Meeting soil when their racing days are through.

Among them is Annie Edge. Only twenty-one in December 2001, she looked the part of an equine senior citizen. Her temple was marked with white, white hairs flecked her woolly chestnut body, and a small white patch was splashed across her near side.

She and another pensioned mare, the sturdy bay First Approach, share a field. Both mares, wonderful runners and producers, definitely preferred not to be bothered or fussed with. I did both.

Annie Edge raced in England in 1983. Strawbridge sent a promising filly named Silverdip "across the pond," and a colt named Salieri beat her. When Salieri then lost to a chestnut filly named Annie Edge, Strawbridge later told *The Blood-Horse*: "I thought she must be a pretty good filly, so we bought her."

Annie Edge was good, winning England's Kiveton Park Stakes and running third in the group I Irish One Thousand Guineas. She came to America and continued to win, annexing the grade II New York Handicap, and three additional stakes.

As a broodmare, Annie Edge was darned good, too. Among her four stakes winners was Selkirk, one of Strawbridge's best runners. Racing primarily in England, Selkirk won the group I Queen Elizabeth II Stakes and

FIRST APPROACH
B. M. 1978,
BY NORTHERN FLING—FAST APPROACH,
BY FIRST LANDING

ANNIE EDGE (IRE)
CH. M. 1980,
BY NEBBIOLO—FRIENDLY COURT,
BY BE FRIENDLY

three group II events. He earned nearly one million dollars.

First Approach, a rich bay with a large star and classic look, won the grade I Flower Bowl, grade II Queen Charlotte, and four other stakes. She earned $332,898 in four years for Augustin Stable and Strawbridge's trainer, Jonathan Sheppard.

Perhaps First Approach's most popular stakes winner is the mare Alice Springs, who began her career in France. In the United States, she won five stakes and earned more than $700,000. Tribal Crown, another stakes winner, earned $82,555. First Approach also produced grade I steeplechase winner Irish Approach, who earned $333,802.

On another part of the farm, Heartbreak was grazing on a far hill with another group of mares that included

HEARTBREAK
CH. M. 1981,
BY STAGE DOOR JOHNNY—
ROYAL FOLLY, BY TOM FOOL

on filly Moccasin, champion Ridan, and stakes-placed Thong, the granddam of influential sire, Nureyev.

Trebor's Choice has been a successful broodmare, as eight of her nine foals to race are winners. Her best, Fitz, was a two-time stakes-winning Waquoit colt who earned $221,943. Another Waquoit—Trebor's Choice offspring, stakes-placed Rippleton Road, earned $202,948.

Heartbreak posed with grandeur and self-confidence, and minutes later she was returned to the field. She waited

her best buddy, Trebor's Choice. Farm manager Bob Goodyear and his son, Bob Jr., trekked up the large hill with lead shanks, and returned moments later leading the beautiful duo.

Heartbreak, a rich chestnut with a wide blaze and stockings, has the robust look of her sire, Stage Door Johnny. While she wasn't a notable racehorse, winning one of five starts, she's been a crackerjack mother. She was also a world traveler.

At four, Heartbreak spent time in Ireland. In 1991 at age ten, fresh on the heels of her son Thirty Six Red's exploits, she was sent to Japan. Her daughter Corrazona won the 1994 grade I Beverly Hills Handicap, and the next year Heartbreak returned to America.

Trebor's Choice, Heartbreak's favorite pasture mate, is a nervous but exquisite gray Damascus mare owned by Derry Meeting Farm. Her dam, Star Strewn, was out of multiple stakes winner Staretta, whose dam, Gambetta, produced the champion filly Gamely. Gambetta is one of Rough Shod II's least known offspring, but there is a good reason for that. Among her half siblings are Horse of the Year and champi-

TREBOR'S CHOICE
GR. M. 1982-2002, BY DAMASCUS—
STAR STREWN, BY NATIVE DANCER

dutifully near the fence for Trebor's Choice, who was not so happy to suddenly be a solo act. Trebor's Choice tolerated us for a minute or two, then fretted and danced. We conceded and returned her to her friend.

The two mares compared notes for a second or two, then bolted back up the hill to the broodmare band. The heavy chestnut, Heartbreak, led the way, with the lovely gray Trebor's Choice very content to stay just behind.

Then there is Reiko. At twenty-three, this Strawbridge mare shares a paddock with several promising younger mares, including Sweet Bunny and Alice Springs. Reiko is a gorgeous rich bay mare with worlds of class. She was a

REIKO (FR)
B. M. 1979, BY TARGOWICE— BERONAIRE, BY RIBERO

stakes winner in France before moving to America at age four. The next year, 1984, she set a track record at Atlantic City, completing a mile in 1:37.

Her first foal was born two years later. Named Turgeon, the Caro colt won two group Is, four group IIs, and placed in numerous others. His international earnings topped $700,000.

Reiko's next foal, stakes winner Greenville, earned more than $200,000. Her 1988 arrival, Suva, is dam of group II stakes winner Surgeon.

But it was Reiko's fifth foal who provided Strawbridge perhaps his greatest American success to date. Tikkanen, a dark gray Cozzene colt, topped his career with a dominating win in the 1994 Breeders' Cup Turf. He was later sold for stud duty in Japan.

Derry Meeting Farm is a haven of dreams fulfilled and dreams still to come. With each new Derry Meeting arrival, hope begins anew as strongly as it did when Storm Cat and Danzig took their first uncertain steps.

And for the pensioners, such as Annie Edge and First Approach, their efforts have been rewarded with a lifetime home, overflowing with respect and love.

* * *

The 2002 foaling season was unkind to two Derry Meeting producers. On February 9, 2002, Heartbreak produced a dead foal. In March, when the lovely Trebor's Choice went into labor, complications set in. Despite the staff's best efforts, both Trebor's Choice and her foal were lost on March 7, 2002.

Yet their bloodlines carry on…

First Approach's final foal is a 2000 Runaway Groom filly named Soloing. Reiko's final foal is an unnamed two-year-old gray filly by Cozzene. Heartbreak's most recent, the Seeking the Gold colt Heart Seeker, is two. Annie Edge's final foal is a two-year-old Danzig colt named Rimrod. And Trebor's Choice's final foal is a three-year-old colt by Irish River named Macgillicuddy.

Dr. Blum

CH. H. 1977, BY DR. FAGER—DUE DILLY, BY SIR GAYLORD

*T*he day was cold, and winds pushed the year's final surrendering leaves in odd dances as I wound my way up to Sugar Maple Farm's stallion barn. The inside of the expansive barn felt warm, the thick wooden walls absorbing gentle sounds of stallions shuffling through straw and settling in from their day outside.

In the first stall, stallion manager Luis Hernandez put the final touch on Dr. Blum, running a soft cloth along the chestnut stallion's neck and side. He clasped the shank onto Dr. Blum's halter, pushed the door open, and brought the horse into an adjacent courtyard.

Dr. Blum pranced from the barn, bowing his sleek neck and tugging at Luis. He glowed a brilliant burnt sienna when the sun emerged from the clouds and splashed across his coat. His feet were light and carefree as he danced through rustling leaves, and he occasionally humored himself by nipping at Luis. "He just feels good," Luis said, easily holding the shank.

Dr. Blum was quick enough to nip successfully had he desired, but he obviously didn't care to. The beautiful stallion was just full of life — happy to be outside and enjoying the day. His large eyes watched everything with wonder, absorbing the familiar view as if he'd never seen it before. Even at twenty-four, Dr. Blum was refined in appearance with a strong, agile body. He didn't look 16.2 hands high as his last stallion pages listed, but perhaps it was because his body was put together so well.

Dr. Blum is from the final crop of the great Dr. Fager, and his dam, Due Dilly, descended from the remarkable mare Hildene. Due Dilly was victorious in her only start, and in addition to Dr. Blum, she produced Peter Pan Stakes winner Spirit Level and five-time stakes winner Ring of Light.

A popular New York-based runner, Dr. Blum had a fondness for Aqueduct's inner-track six-furlong events. In his two-year campaign, he won the Coaltown and Pegasus stakes, Sporting Plate and Toboggan handicaps, and the

ner Richard R., who earned more than $300,000; and multiple stakes winner Detox. He also sired the Mexican champion sprinter, Someday Jack.

Many of his foals sported doctor-related names. Medicine Woman, The Mad Doctor, Bedside Manner, Brainstorm Dr., Dr Brook, D'youville Nurse, Dr.'s Nurse, Dr. Fisher, Delightful Doctor, Dr. Goode, Dr. Margaret, and Trust Me I'ma Dr. all won or placed in stakes.

While Dr. Blum never sired a "breakthrough" horse, he was popularly received throughout his career, often ranking among New York's leaders.

While many older stallions suffer from a lack of fertility, Dr. Blum suffered instead from something more unusual — lack of interest. Breeding sessions became tedious affairs, sometimes lasting an hour and a half or more. Eventually, even that much time was not enough. Dr. Blum sired five foals in 1998, and the next year only four. After the 1998 breeding season, Dr. Blum was pensioned.

He is still a farm favorite, and Luis, who has been with the horse for four years now, is proud to tend to such a professional stallion. Dr. Blum lives in the same style as in his breeding days, taken out and brought in at the same time as his fellow stallions.

"He is very sweet," Luis said quietly, while watching the golden stallion settle back into his stall after his playful courtyard jaunt. "He never does anything wrong."

Paumonok Handicap over the speedy Clever Trick.

He entered stud in 1982 with nine wins in twenty-three starts and earnings of $253,520. His first crop included minor stakes winners Dr. Bee Jay and Dr.'s Nurse, and in nearly every crop since, he's sired a tough competitor or stakes winner. Among his best were eleven-time stakes winner Nurse Dopey, who earned $456,362; grade II win-

Dr. Patches

CH. G. 1974, BY DR. FAGER—EXPECTANCY, BY INTENTIONALLY

arch 16, 2001. The afternoon waned as the man walked into the paddock. No longer young, he moved slowly with a burden much greater than the feed bucket he was carrying.

Behind him, an aged chestnut gelding with a sun-bleached winter coat and tired manner followed. The man emptied the bucket's contents into a worn tub on the ground and turned. He petted the horse with a seemingly unconscious motion as the old gelding dipped his head down to his dinner.

Leaving the paddock, the man walked to a small house not far from where the horse dined. He went inside and took a quick look out the window to watch his friend.

The day's last sun glowed with sudden brilliance on the gelding's chestnut coat, as shadows from Spanish moss played delicately across his long, sloping back. The afternoon would soon be evening; then evening, night.

One more day had passed, with Dr. Patches safe at his childhood home.

* * *

Dr. Patches is still best known for defeating the seemingly invincible Seattle Slew one night at the Meadowlands. But the old gelding has more formidable foes now: progress and time. This time the gallant chestnut is in a battle he cannot win.

Dr. Patches was a popular sprinter for many reasons: his looks, name, bloodlines, and connections. Interestingly, only three of his seventeen wins came in stakes events, and his only stakes sprint victory was the seven-furlong Vosburgh. His other stakes wins were the grade III Paterson at a mile and one-eighth and the Meadowlands Cup at a mile and a quarter.

But he did win six of eleven starts in 1978 and that combined with his conquering of the Triple Crown winner was enough for him to be named co-champion sprinter along with J. O. Tobin. It was a fitting tribute to his sire, Tartan Farm's legendary stallion Dr. Fager, who had died two years earlier at the age of twelve.

Racing fan Michael Amoruso recalled Dr. Patches with fondness. "The race I remember best, I believe, was one of his first after being named champion. Can't even remember if he won. Angel (Cordero) was always very

DR. PATCHES WITH BRYAN HOWLETT

vocal, and he liked to sing when he mounted his horse. I think that the horses liked it, and it unnerved his opponents. He was very animated with Patches. That's what he called him.

"He kept saying 'You are the champion,' 'you're the champ,' over and over, while he stroked the big horse's neck. Dr. Patches brightened noticeably at the attention."

That race was the Met Mile, and Patches finished second that day to State Dinner. All told, Dr. Patches won seventeen of forty-seven starts and earned more than $700,000 before being retired and returned to his home, Tartan Farm.

Dr. Patches still lives on the famous Ocala property where he was raised, although he bears little resemblance to the blazing sprinter he once was. His legs seem uncomfortable as he shifts his weight from side to side, and his feet, which have never been totally sound, are failing him. He is a large horse with strong bones standing nearly seventeen hands, and on one leg is an odd patch of white.

His chestnut coat is a mixture of gold and red, and he has a knowing eye, encircled with dark hair. The result gives an appearance of eye shadow, with light-colored lashes for accentuation.

Dr. Patches is aloof and pretends not to care when

visitors occasionally stop along the roadside to visit. But once he does wander over, he will stay all day if he is scratched on his rump. He also has an odd fondness for nibbling on shoelaces and shoes, and he seems to prefer men to women.

Tartan Farm has been sold, and Dr. Patches is the only horse left on the property. Tartan's general manager, Bryan Howlett, takes loving care of his charge. Bryan has been with this farm, and this horse, for more than two decades. He visits Patches daily at feed times, and the blacksmith comes on a regular basis. Bryan worries about his longtime friend and what will become of him when the farm is developed. Bryan has no plans for his own future either.

Dr. Patches resides in a paddock in front of Bryan's house, and the horse sometimes wanders up the fence line to the home. Dr. Patches likes watching Bryan through the windows, and Bryan enjoys watching Dr. Patches through the same windows. The two friends are a link to a magic place, which soon will exist only in memory.

Tartan's trophy collection has been catalogued and moved, and soon the beautiful barns and training track will be lost forever as a development company begins bulldozing. There is talk that Dr. Patches might be donated to the Florida division of the Thoroughbred Retirement Foundation, but his future is uncertain.

There is room for him in the Tartan/Mockingbird Farm cemetery. The cemetery, which rests on Mockingbird Farm property, was once part of Tartan. In 2002, Eugene Melnyk bought the lands; and the cemetery, at least for now, seems safe from development.

Dr. Patches' sire lies in the cemetery, as does Dr. Fager's sister Ta Wee and their dam Aspidistra. Other Tartan greats of the past rest there as well, the horseshoe-shaped cemetery overlooking a large pond known as Lake Ta Wee. It would be a fitting final resting place for Dr. Fager's champion son.

Time will tell what will become of Dr. Patches. Until then, Bryan tends to his needs, and Dr. Patches waits, occasionally galloping across his paddock in a heavy-footed gait. But usually the big chestnut gelding passes his days quietly near the stallion barn in which his great sire resided, on the magic land where he was raised.

Fanfreluche and Optimistic Gal

hey socialized, raised children together, even quarreled. In their old age, the two gals became best friends. One was an extrovert, a lady who enjoyed visiting and exploring. The other, shy and not particularly friendly, let her outgoing friend lead as she stayed in the background.

They led grand lives. Each was a star athlete many moons ago, and both were good mothers. One even survived a kidnapping of international proportions. For years, the two ladies lived side by side.

Watching them grazing far off in a field on Old Frankfort Pike in Midway, Kentucky, they looked merely like two old brown horses. Yet they were so much more.

Fanfreluche was a handsome bay daughter of Northern Dancer, out of the stakes-winning Ciboulette. She won eleven of twenty-one starts in her two years on the track, finishing off the board just twice. For owner Jean-Louis Levesque, she won the Natalma, Princess Elizabeth, and Alabama stakes and the Quebec Derby, and finished second in the Queen's Plate. When

Fanfreluche galloped home in the Manitoba Centennial Derby, Queen Elizabeth II was part of the appreciative audience.

Fanfreluche's accomplishments earned her the crown as Canada's Horse of the Year in 1970. That same year, she shared U.S. champion three-year-old filly honors with Office Queen. While preparing for her return at four, she ruptured a tendon sheath and was retired.

Fanfreluche had already produced two babies by the time her friend-to-be Optimistic Gal was born in 1973. A long, rangy unmarked bay, Optimistic Gal raced two years in Diana Firestone's colors. She won thirteen of her twenty-one starts, including six grade Is. Six years after Fanfreluche invaded Saratoga to take the Alabama,

FANFRELUCHE
B. M. 1967-1999,
BY NORTHERN DANCER—CIBOULETTE,
BY CHOP CHOP

Optimistic Gal won the same event. She also took the Delaware Handicap and the Matron, Frizette, Selima, and Spinster stakes, earning $686,861.

Despite an outstanding career, a championship eluded the lovely filly, and she was retired in late 1976.

Fanfreluche was a wonderful broodmare from the outset. Her first foal, L'Enjoleur, was a grade I winner. Just four years after Fanfreluche left racing, L'Enjoleur was named Canadian champion two-year-old colt and Horse of the Year. The next year he was both champion three-year-old colt and, again, Horse of the Year.

Fanfreluche's second foal, L'Extravagante, ran third in the Canadian Oaks. Her third foal, Grand Luxe, won ten of twenty-five races, including three stakes.

Her fourth, La Voyageuse, earned more than $500,000, winning twenty-six of fifty-six starts, including the Canadian Oaks and twelve other stakes. She was Canada's champion three-year-old filly in 1978.

That same year her half brother Medaille d'Or, Fanfreluche's fifth foal, won the Coronation Futurity on his way to the two-year-old colt championship. With two championship offspring in the same season, Fanfreluche was named 1978 Sovereign Award winner for Canada's Broodmare of the Year.

The year before, however, Fanfreluche had been on a most unusual adventure, the stuff of mystery novels.

On June 25, 1977, the staff at Claiborne Farm, where Fanfreluche was boarded, made a terrifying discovery: Fanfreluche had been stolen from her paddock. The crime, reported initially to the police, was quickly turned over to the FBI.

OPTIMISTIC GAL
B. M. 1973-1999, BY SIR IVOR—
HOPES AHEAD, BY TRAFFIC JUDGE

FANFRELUCHE (LEFT) AND OPTIMISTIC GAL

No doubt about it, Fanfreluche was very valuable. Theories for the theft swirled around three possible motives. Ransom was the most obvious, but weeks passed and no demands came.

Fanfreluche was in foal to Secretariat, and perhaps the motive was to use the foal as a ringer. It could either outrun its pedigree in a gambling coup or even be used for breeding.

The third option, the least likely, was political revenge. Fanfreluche's owner, Jean-Louis Levesque, was an important industrialist who had political influence.

The FBI released Fanfreluche's identification photos to racetracks, farms, and newswires. Fanfreluche's markings, including her star, two hind socks, coronet spots, and even tattoo number became common knowledge among horsemen. But month after month passed, with no sign of the kidnapped mare.

Then, as suddenly as it had begun, it was over. On December 8, 1977, the racing world breathed a tremendous sigh of relief at the news: Fanfreluche had been found.

How or why she ended up 150 miles from Claiborne in Tompkinsville, Kentucky, is still a mystery. Local residents Larry and Sandra McPherson received a call from a friend in early July that one of their horses was loose. They went to investigate and found a stout bay mare wandering along the roadside.

She had rope burns along her left hind leg and behind one ear, with scratches along her broad back. She wore no halter, but when they caught her she followed them willingly back to their house.

The McPhersons asked around town whether anyone was missing a horse. Even when they heard about a missing prized racehorse way off in Paris, Kentucky, it didn't dawn on them that the mare they'd found could be Fanfreluche. The years far from the track had taken away her racy look.

They named her Brandy and kept her in a lumber shed behind their mobile home. They rode her several times, as Sandra later told *The Blood-Horse*. "She rides rough when she's going slow, and she's hard to hold back sometimes."

It wasn't until late autumn that they realized she was in foal, and soon afterward, on December 8, they were visited by the FBI, which had received a tip. Claiborne Farm president Seth Hancock accompanied agents to the McPherson home. Seth entered the shed and viewed the woolly, heavy mare. He checked her coronet spots and her lip tattoo and made a positive identification. Fanfreluche was taken back to Claiborne.

The December 12, 1977, *Blood-Horse* cover showed Fanfreluche looking happy and healthy, and heavy with foal. The headline brought smiles: A Christmas Present: Fanfreluche Home Safe at Claiborne.

Her 1978 foal was named Sain Et Sauf, French for "safe and sound." He wasn't one of her best racehorses, winning just three races and eventually being sold to India for stud duty. But Sain Et Sauf was undoubtedly her most welcome.

Fanfreluche was sold in 1978 to Bertram Firestone, and she produced one more outstanding racehorse. D'Accord, a grade II winner who earned $163,368, later became a successful New York sire.

Optimistic Gal's offspring were, by comparison, unremarkable. Eleven of her babies were winners, however, and she is the second dam of several stakes winners.

When Bert and Diana Firestone purchased Big Sink Farm in Midway, Kentucky, Fanfreluche and Optimistic Gal came together.

Butch Murrell was a groom at Big Sink Farm, and he still works on the property, which is now owned by Three Chimneys Farm. He began rubbing horses long ago at King Ranch, working with such greats as Bee Mac and

Middleground. Butch easily recalled other wonderful horses he groomed, names like Genuine Risk and Law Society, and top yearlings he took to auction.

"I've got over forty years with horses," Butch said, his voice rich with a gentle Southern accent. "I worked at Big Sink Farm for twenty-eight years. There were three owners during that time. I started here (on Big Sink property) in 1966. You know, you work with the mares, go to the breeding shed, work with the yearlings.

"I took care of both mares, Fanfreluche and Optimistic Gal. They were different.

"Fanfreluche, she was just a sweet mare. You could do anything around her, and she never had any problem getting along with any of the other mares. She raised good babies, and she raised them well. Anything else I could say about her, it would all be good.

"Optimistic Gal, she was okay. She would make a mistake sometimes, when she was mad at another mare. She'd go to bite her, and she'd bite you instead. Other than that, she was fine, but she had a bit of an attitude, especially when you'd rub her. The fillies, they were more like her. But the colts were okay."

When I visited Big Sink Farm in May 1998, Optimistic Gal was twenty-five years old and Fanfreluche thirty-one. Both were long since pensioned, still living on the tremendous piece of property adjacent to Three Chimneys. A groom accompanied me to the paddock, but said that catching Optimistic Gal was probably out of the question. He was right.

Far away, two mares grazed in the warm afternoon sun. Both showed signs of age, and the unmarked bay's head popped up as she heard us approach. Her long, sweeping tail, which would have otherwise swept the ground, was cut in European fashion.

Fanfreluche came to us readily, her head low and streaked with white reminders of age. She asked to be rubbed, but as I moved to touch her face her grumpy friend interjected. Optimistic Gal pinned her ears and gave her best cutting-horse imitation. Fanfreluche seemed to shrug and moved off to confer with her friend.

They touched noses, the two senior citizens comparing notes about risk and reward. Oddly, the mare who'd been kidnapped two decades earlier trusted me. The risk of visiting was worth the reward of a kind word or gentle touch.

For Optimistic Gal, who spent years denying her name, the risk was definitely not worth it. She never did come close.

She eventually persuaded Fanfreluche to accompany her to a far corner of the paddock, and the two mares walked away slowly in tandem. They were beautiful, those old gals, their tails swishing gently, their bodies tired from their long lives' efforts.

The two gals lived together side by side, and the year after I saw them they died together. In mid-July 1999, the lovely Optimistic Gal passed away, and she was buried on the farm.

Within a matter of days, her life's effort became too much for Franfreluche. At age thirty-two, Canada's 1970 Horse of the Year, who'd shared time with royalty and kidnappers, finally breathed her last. The great mare was buried next to her ornery old companion.

Big Sink Farm's Barry Robinette found a lovely stone, had a metal plaque made, and placed the stone over Fanfreluche's final resting place. He had hopes of finding a matching stone for Optimistic Gal, but before he could, the farm was sold and he changed jobs. Optimistic Gal's grave, to Fanfreluche's left, is still unmarked.

Flatterer

DK. B/BR. G. 1979, BY MO BAY—HORIZONTAL, BY NADE

His sire was an intelligent, hard-knocking stallion, a useful sort, eventually sold to the Brazilian National Stud. His dam, an inexpensive claiming horse, was sold to Jonathan Sheppard for four thousand dollars. The foal of those two less-than-great horses became one of the greatest steeplechase horses America has ever known.

Flatterer did things no other horse in this volume did: won at three miles, carried 176 pounds to victory, earned Eclipse Awards in four consecutive years, won ribbons for dressage, and even attended a wedding. But before anyone knew just how special he was, the dark bay son of Mo Bay ran in twelve claiming races.

Racing for George Harris and breeders/owners William Pape and Jonathan Sheppard, Flatterer broke his maiden at Keystone Park (now Philadelphia Park) in March 1982. After a year of uninspired flat racing, Jonathan tried him over the jumps in April 1983. Flatterer scored handily under John Cushman on a rainy April day in Atlanta, and his glory days were under way.

From that race through the end of 1986, Flatterer won seventeen races and earned four straight Eclipse Awards. The dark bay runner, who stood a shade over sixteen hands, jumped beautifully and possessed remarkable acceleration.

In April 1986 Flatterer won the Atlanta Cup by two lengths under 173 pounds, setting a course record. The seven-year-old gelding then set a mark no other American steeplechase horse has since approached.

Flatterer ran in the National Hunt Cup in Radnor, Pennsylvania, under the incredible impost of 176 pounds. The great Neji had once raced under 176 pounds and had three times tried 175. But no American horse had ever won under such weight, and Flatterer conceded between twenty-six and forty pounds to his rivals.

Under many lead weights and Jerry Fishback, Flatterer took the lead at the twelfth of fourteen fences and pulled away, scoring by seven easy lengths. Flatterer's mystique grew.

Flatterer's camp received an invitation to France's premier jumping race, the Grande Course de Haies d'Auteuil. French horsemen were eager to see the famed American runner, and the racing paper, *Paris-Turf*, described Flatterer as "Un Champion, Pas Un Touriste" (A Champion, Not a Tourist). On a day when the temperature reached ninety-six degrees, Flatterer ran a strong second to Le Rheusois.

Flatterer returned to America and romped in his two remaining 1986 starts, including his fourth straight Colonial Cup. Under 162 pounds, Flatterer pulled away with bravado to win by seventeen lengths. Naturally, he romped in Eclipse Award voting as well, earning his fourth straight statuette.

Flatterer was eight when he faced the starters in 1987. He began the year with another visit to Europe, running a determined second in England's two-mile Champion Hurdle. Back in America, he ran third under a record impost of 178 pounds in Middleburg's Sport Council Handicap, then won the Iroquois, coasting home by four lengths under 168.

The Breeders' Cup Steeplechase on October 31 was the next, and loftier, goal.

After five months off with a slightly torn sesamoidal ligament, Flatterer came back in a Great Meadows allowance on October 17. Winning easily by six lengths in the flat event, Flatterer set a new course record but reaggravated an ankle injury.

Always a careful horseman, Sheppard watched his beloved champion closely. Flatterer had never been the soundest horse and had on several occasions been laid up with injuries. But he moved soundly in the days prior to the race, and when the flag dropped for the 1987 Breeders' Cup Steeplechase, the gallant Flatterer — at .80-1 — was in the field.

He raced well through the seventh fence, but at the eighth, jockey Richard Dunwoody suddenly steered Flatterer from the course and pulled the competitive gelding to a halt. Dunwoody jumped off, as Flatterer circled him slowly. As the large crowd watched in worried silence, Sheppard assistants Graham Motion and Betsy Wells walked the lame champion from the course.

Flatterer had suffered a badly bowed tendon. His racing days were over.

Including flat races, Flatterer won twenty-four of fifty-

FLATTERER (LEFT) AND HIS PASTURE MATES

one starts, finishing second or third in twelve more. But of his twenty-four steeplechase events, Flatterer won sixteen and recorded five seconds, one third, and one DNF (did not finish). His earnings totaled $538,708.

Flatterer spent a few years in retirement but soon began a second career. "Basically you have these retired horses, and you think you're going to ride them, and hack around on them, but you don't," Sheppard said. "It just didn't seem right that, when (Flatterer) got right again, he should just stand around in a field somewhere stamping at flies."

Flatterer was loaned for several years to Lesa Williams, a respected dressage rider. She taught the intelligent gelding dressage, and although his long black ears were often pinned, he cooperated. "He did well in quite a lot of shows," Sheppard said, recounting Flatterer's rise through the dressage ranks. "I can count sixteen ribbons just in the office here."

Nowadays, Flatterer lives at William Pape's My Way Farm in Unionville, Pennsylvania, with several friends to help him stamp at flies. Pape is understandably proud to give his four-time champion a lifetime home.

Flatterer does have his limits, however. When Pape got married at his farm several years ago, farm manager Jeff Stanton cleaned Flatterer up for the occasion and brought him over to join the festivities. Flatterer stood willingly for a photo with the bride and groom. But when they tried to add the entire wedding group, Flatterer decided that the party was definitely over. "He didn't want anything to do with that," Stanton recalled, smiling.

"We don't put them down," Pape said of his band of pensioners. "They're like family." The extended family includes the multiple stakes-winning mares Lonely Balladier (twenty-three in 2001), stakes-producer Martie's Delighted (twenty-four), and Flatterer's half brother, Polar Parallel (twenty).

Polar Parallel was no slouch himself, earning $337,325 and winning the Atlanta Cup. But the two half brothers are surprisingly different in appearance and nature. Polar Parallel, a high-headed chestnut with a blaze face, is a spirited prankster.

When I visited in December 2001, Flatterer had little interest in me. Nevertheless, he cooperated and stood for photos, his head low and attitude relaxed. Jeff had the old boy cleaned beautifully, and his winter coat was nearly black. Small red points highlighted Flatterer's muzzle and flank, and he appeared much younger than his twenty-two years.

When released into his field, Flatterer was in no hurry to rejoin his friends, who were suddenly fascinated by him. They approached eagerly and took turns sniffing, as Flatterer ignored them.

"He's all cleaned up. He doesn't want anything to do with them, the dirty bums. 'Go home and take a shower, and then I'll talk to you,' " Pape said, laughing.

Flatterer shuffled away from the trio, and Polar Parallel chased him playfully. Flatterer pinned his ears and moved farther away, and Polar Parallel took the hint. The horses quickly settled back down to graze.

What made Flatterer one of steeplechasing's all-time greats? Neither William Pape nor Jonathan Sheppard has a definitive answer.

"He doesn't look special," Pape said, watching his champion. "He just acts special. He's a freak, frankly."

Jonathan Sheppard, while not sure why Flatterer was special, certainly knows what was most special about his great runner. "I could never say that, in all of the races that he ran, that he ran anything other than his best.

"I could never say that about any other horse. Every horse has some reason to not do well on some day, like he doesn't like the track, or he got a bad ride. But not him. He always, always gave his best."

Freetex

B. H. 1969-1999, BY VERTEX—FREEDOM AT LAST, BY NEEDLES

f all the equine pensioners I've had the privilege to photograph, none is more special than my beloved Freetex. Sometimes a horse makes an impression through his race record or attitude, or his striking physical appearance.

Freetex was different. What made him so special is perhaps impalpable, but when he died early on September 7, 1999, I was heartbroken.

When I visited Ocala in March of 1998, I picked up a Florida farm directory. I noticed a name at M.J. Stavola Farms that rang a faint bell: Freetex. I remembered he had raced in Riva Ridge's Kentucky Derby, the first Derby that I tape-recorded. I was just eleven then, but I still remember playing it repeatedly. I knew Freetex's name from that tape, but I couldn't remember where he had finished or anything else he'd done.

Doubting he was alive at age twenty-nine, I called the farm. I was delighted when the secretary said he was and even more delighted when she said I could see him. I drove right over.

A gentleman named Bob Gilpin met me and as it was feed time, I followed him to Freetex's paddock. We drove through the expansive farm, making a right turn, a left,

another right. And there, at the end of a small drive, I saw him. There were no other horses in sight, and Freetex had the run of a large pasture. Several years earlier, Bob related, Freetex had a goat friend. But when the goat passed away, it had not been replaced, and Freetex was now a solo act.

It was a dark day with rain on the air, and I could barely make out his features under the imposing trees. I walked closer, and he attained form. He was an unmarked bay, with a long, sun-bleached mane and tattered nylon halter. His feet were shod, he was clean, and he was obviously well-tended. He had the strong look of a horse who'd seen many battles but who was tired of the fight.

Bob snapped a lead shank on Freetex's halter, and Freetex tried his best to back away. To add to his distrust, I grabbed scissors and aimed for his face, snipping tatters from his halter. His nervousness showed plainly as I backed away and raised my camera.

His curiosity took over, and his fear soon subsided. I took one shot, two...Bob straightened the old boy's mane a bit, and I snapped another. Freetex eyed me another moment and then his patience was through. He shook his long head, snorted, and pushed against Bob. Bob undid the shank, and Freetex moved quickly back to his corner under the trees, where his feed tub waited.

When I got home, I looked up Freetex's record. His victories included the Gotham Stakes, Ohio Derby, Heritage Stakes, and Kindergarten Stakes. Yet in his greatest victory, the 1972 Monmouth Invitational over 3-10 favorite Riva Ridge, Freetex was barely noticed. Riva Ridge became embroiled in controversy after the race when tests determined he had perhaps been drugged. Freetex's crowning moment was dismissed.

Riva Ridge went on to a very successful four-year-old campaign, in which he set a world record and earned an Eclipse Award. Freetex slowly slipped toward obscurity.

* * *

I visited Freetex again in November that year, and Bob had him primped. Freetex's mane was trimmed, his leather halter quite clean, and his eyes burned brilliantly with the look of a horse who'd received much recent attention. He posed proudly although somewhat nervously, and I took four quick rolls. Yet the perfect shot still eluded me.

I stopped at the barn office on the way out, and Bob and his wife, Joyce, showed me win photos of horses they'd helped raise there. Belong to Me, Virginia Rapids, Classy Mirage, and Missy's Mirage stared back at me in eight-by-ten-inch form, all carrying jockeys in the Stavola family's yellow-and-black silks. It was a very impressive graduate list for a farm with a low profile.

Freetex was their first "big horse," and through the years he had stood at stud first in New Jersey and then Florida. When he was pensioned, owner Mike Stavola made a promise that Freetex would always have a home there.

I visited again in March 1999, and Bob agreed to meet me early. Bob mentioned that on occasion, Freetex would gallop up to meet him in the morning, and I hoped to capture this on film. While Bob usually fed Freetex at 5:30, he waited for me, and I used the sunrise as an excuse to wait until 7:00. I hoped for a photo of this wonderful old stallion galloping up through tall trees, the sun streaming through his long mane, his nostrils flared…

What greeted us instead was an annoyed old horse, pacing back and forth beneath the trees. He moved through the shadows, scolding Bob with his eyes. We were late, and he was not one bit happy about it. Nor was he happy that Bob had brought a visitor.

He backed up as Bob set the feed, looking back across his pasture, and for a moment the sun glowed brilliantly over his aged face. I took two quick frames, but then Freetex moved to his bucket. "He didn't expect to get his picture taken now. All he wants to do is eat," Bob said apologetically. Freetex dipped his head into the bucket, and we retreated. I took a last look through the rearview mirror and saw a silhouette, head lowered, under those trees.

I went back to New York and processed my film. In that quick moment, when Freetex had gazed toward the sun, I finally got my perfect portrait of him there.

I would not see Freetex again.

Freetex received a new set of shoes on Monday, September 6, and contentedly ate his fourteen quarts. Bob had recently helped the thirty-year-old through a sickness, and Freetex seemed to be doing well.

But when Bob went to the paddock on Tuesday morning, Freetex was not waiting for him. Sometime during the night, early on September 7, Freetex had passed away without a struggle. It was a quiet end for this gallant old horse who had tried his best to earn a place in the history books.

Broken-hearted, Bob could not bear to go to the still bay stallion, and he instead went for assistance. But he did make a difficult phone call to Freetex's biggest fan, a horse photographer more than a thousand miles away in New York, so she would not first learn the news on a daily page.

The farm office has a new plaque: "Freetex — 1969-1999 — The Start of a New Era." Outside, Classy Mirage grazes with her latest arrival and Belong to Me's dam relaxes in the sun.

Up past the office and the broodmare barn, down that winding road and at the end of a small drive, stand a line of tall trees, imposing in their grandeur. There, buried beneath the trees that afforded such comfort to an old horse, my equine hero lies

forever at rest.

Mike Stavola had made good on his word. Freetex would always have a home there.

The Greentree Gashouse Gang

I n 1984 a group of geldings wandered a vast paddock at Greentree Stud in Lexington, Kentucky. They were current members of the so-called Gashouse Gang. For almost a half-century, Greentree had let its good performers live out their lives on its land. The original Gashouse Gang members — Cherry Pie, Easter Hero, Twenty Grand, and Jolly Roger — had long since been interred in the famed Greentree Cemetery, yet the tradition had continued.

There were five or six geldings there in 1984, including the older Cyrano, Weatherwise, and Eurasia. They grazed down in a back paddock, crossing a small stream to come back at feedtime. Two younger horses grazed among them, names much more familiar to me: Bowl Game, the 1979 Eclipse Award-winning turf champion, and Cast Party, winner of the 1982 Laurel Futurity. Open Call, who had recently finished his racing campaign, was in a nearby paddock awaiting induction into the ranks.

When Greentree Farm was sold in 1989, the personnel at Gainesway, the flanking farm that had bought the property, tended to the three surviving Gashouse Gang members. In the mid-1990s, Bowl Game, Cast Party, and Open Call were given to the Thoroughbred Retirement Foundation and moved to a farm in Virginia.

For Open Call it was not a long transition, as he died soon after arrival. When The Jockey Club was contacted in 1998 for information about Cast Party, he was listed as deceased. But he is still very much alive and there, on the vast lands of their beautiful Virginia home, Cast Party and Bowl Game reside, grazing in a band of some twenty-three geldings.

Bowl Game looks little like the amazing champion who took to the turf back in 1978. He was still a maiden in February of his four-year-old year when trainer Jack Gaver moved him to the grass and was rewarded with a wonderful campaign. In the next year and a half, Bowl Game won such races as the Gulfstream Park Handicap, Pan American Handicap, Turf Classic, Washington, D.C., International, and Man o' War Handicap, and he was crowned champion turf horse in 1979.

These days, Bowl Game is the least social of the

Virginia geldings, and he grows the woolliest coat in the winters. Although he keeps company with the other horses, he prefers to keep a distance from people. He had no desire to be held or cleaned up for portraits.

Cast Party, however, was a different story. While not the racehorse that Bowl Game was, he was a grade I winner by virtue of his 1982 Laurel Futurity conquest. He also won the Golden Grass Stakes, finished third in the Cowdin, and earned $219,466 during a campaign in

CAST PARTY
GR. G. 1980, BY CARO—
CASTING CALL,
BY STAGE DOOR JOHNNY

BOWL GAME
B. G. 1974, BY TOM ROLFE—
AROUND THE ROSES,
BY ROUND TABLE

classic Greentree watermelon-pink silks. But his lovely dished face and body still look young, his actions are comfortable, and he seems very content with his friends. And contrary to Bowl Game's opinion, he enjoys human companionship equally to the company of his equine friends.

Bowl Game and Cast Party don't seem great buddies, but one can't help but wonder whether they remember their sunny days together back at their Greentree home, telling stories with the old-timers and crossing that trickling stream as they sauntered back up to the shed at feed time.

This is probably the final stop for these last two members of the Gashouse Gang, and it is doubtful that their bodies will ever rest in the famous Greentree cemetery. Yet, they seem happy here, wandering virtually unnoticed among other Thoroughbred Retirement Foundation geldings: former claimers and allowance horses, horses with bad ankles and knees, and scars quite visible to the eye.

which he won four of eleven races.

Cast Party's coat is no longer the deep gray that some racetrackers remember driving to the wire, carrying the

Here, they are all equal.

Gato Del Sol

GR. H. 1979, BY COUGAR II—PEACEFULLY, BY JACINTO

*A*t Stone Farm one afternoon in October 1999, several stallions relaxed in their paddocks. As late afternoon light splashed the autumn leaves with a golden brilliance that enhanced already grand colors, a near-white horse grazed with lithe grace. His tail was cut in European fashion, and his face and body were long and elegant like the subject of a Stubbs' painting.

Gato Del Sol heard me approach and raised his head slowly. He watched me for a long moment, seeming to debate a visit, then dipped his head gently back down to the rich, sunlit grass. His coat reflected a startling mixture of white overlaid with gold, and the serenity of the moment was profound.

It was a world away from the screams of more than 140,000 fans on a sunny day seventeen years earlier at Churchill Downs when a darker gray Gato Del Sol won the race most cherished and longest remembered.

One of racing's most heart-warming stories of 1999 was the return of Gato Del Sol to American soil. Influenced by the ill-fated Exceller, Staci and Arthur Hancock purchased their gray Kentucky Derby winner back from his German owner, and Gato Del Sol came home to Stone Farm.

When Gato Del Sol won the Derby, Kentuckians were proud of the colt and the Hancocks. But Kentuckians were not the only ones with reason to cheer; Californians did as well.

Gato Del Sol's sire was the Stone Farm stallion Cougar II, an immensely popular California campaigner in the early 1970s. The Chilean-bred Cougar was an elegant rich bay who bowed his neck grandly, his thick mane and tail whipping wildly when he ran. Fans loved this determined horse, and he seemed to love them as well. During post parades, Cougar would often stop and gaze for moments at the crowd until his rider finally coaxed him back into action.

While Gato Del Sol won several other stakes races, he never matched his brilliance of that sunny afternoon in

slaughterhouse death of champion Exceller in Sweden, contacted the German farm where Gato Del Sol was residing. Spending $25,000 of their Menifee's recent winnings, the Hancocks repurchased their first Kentucky Derby winner. In late August 1999, he stepped off the van at Stone Farm.

A bit underweight, Gato Del Sol seemed happy to be home. He took up residence in the stallion barn near two old friends, Northern Baby and Halo. He quickly put his weight back on, although he was never a big stallion; and his tail, which sported the European cut, grew out and now sweeps the ground.

Nowadays, he receives frequent visitors who admired him as a racehorse, who like Kentucky Derby winners, or who just found his homecoming story inspirational. Gato is a kind, curious horse who usually approaches visitors with keen interest.

May 1982. He entered stud at Stone Farm, where he stood alongside his sire, Cougar II. But Gato Del Sol was not much of a sire, and, when a German breeder offered the Hancocks $100,000 for their Kentucky Derby winner, they accepted.

Seven years later Staci, worried by recent stories of the

On occasion Staci, when visiting with her old friend, sweeps her hand across his long back and jokingly contemplates riding him. He would undoubtedly enjoy that, too, but he deserves his leisurely life. Here on the land where Gato Del Sol was raised, and where his gallant sire Cougar II is buried, his future seems secure.

Genuine Risk

CH. M. 1977, BY EXCLUSIVE NATIVE—VIRTUOUS,
BY GALLANT MAN

She will always be one of racing's most popular distaff stars by sheer virtue of being the second filly to win the Kentucky Derby. With her distinctive golden chestnut coat and brilliant blazed face flashing, Genuine Risk captured the nation's heart during her Triple Crown campaign.

Sadly however, Genuine Risk continued to make headlines after her retirement not because of what she accomplished, but because of what she could not.

She was a tall, handsome filly who raced for owner Diana Firestone and trainer LeRoy Jolley. Slim, with an elegant look and knowing eye, Genuine Risk carried herself with high-stepping pride. While she ran third to the popular Plugged Nickle in her first effort against colts, the 1980 Wood Memorial, she turned the tables on a much more important day — at Churchill Downs on the first Saturday in May.

Genuine Risk made countless fans, many of them female, when she stormed home at 13-1 to win the Kentucky Derby. In the Preakness, as the 2-1 favorite, the gallant filly became embroiled in one of racing's hottest controversies.

As long as people discuss racing, they will debate whether Angel Cordero intentionally steered Codex wide in the Preakness' final turn and whether his whip grazed Genuine Risk's fine head. What's not debated is that Codex and Cordero stopped Genuine Risk in the midst of her strong run (she came home second to that pair), and the 1980 Preakness became part of racing lore.

In the Belmont, Genuine Risk gamely finished second behind longshot Temperence Hill. Codex was far back, eased with a career-ending injury. With a win and two seconds, Genuine Risk's record in the Triple Crown races has never been equaled by any other filly.

She retired in 1981, and the next year Genuine Risk was bred to the great Secretariat. It was the first mating of Kentucky Derby winners, both immensely popular chestnuts splashed with white, and the nation watched intently. But that mating ended with sadness as Genuine Risk delivered a stillborn foal. It was just the beginning of the heartbreak for her many fans.

After a decade of failed attempts, Genuine Risk finally delivered a healthy Rahy colt in 1993. The colt was a bold,

flashy chestnut with three white stockings and a blaze, and pictures of the proud mama and her baby graced magazines and newspapers nationwide. Appropriately, the Firestones named him Genuine Reward, one of the hundreds of names suggested by enchanted fans.

After two more barren years, Genuine Risk produced a Chief Honcho colt. Named Count Our Blessing, this colt was also a chestnut with a blaze. But neither foal inherited his famous mother's talent nor her determination, and neither ever raced.

Finally, in 2000, Diana and Bert Firestone announced Genuine Risk's retirement. She had more than earned it, and she was to live out her life on the farm where she received her early training. Genuine Risk made one more trip, back to Newstead Farm in beautiful Upperville, Virginia.

Her attendants now are long-time Newstead employees who knew an eager Genuine Risk when she was first broken to saddle. They accompanied the willowy chestnut on her van ride to Churchill Downs; they remember the way she proudly pranced on the way to the post; and they still firmly believe in her superiority to a dark bay colt named Codex.

Despite a slight sway to her back and an enlarged left knee from her racing days, Genuine Risk moves well for a senior citizen. When lifting her feet for portraits, there was the telltale cracking that accompanies arthritis, and yet she didn't flinch or complain. She has a gentle manner and seems content in her daily routine.

Genuine Risk spends her time in vast paddocks, often gazing for countless moments toward the distant, beautiful Blue Ridge Mountains. Seeing her far off in her paddock as she turns her head and flashes that famous blaze, a fan becomes lost in memories, enchanted once more.

Glowing Tribute

B. M. 1973, BY GRAUSTARK—ADMIRING,
BY HAIL TO REASON

*I*f racing historians ever determine the most influential broodmares of the twentieth century, Glowing Tribute will rank high on the list. She was expected to be a good producer from the outset, but has far outshone those high expectations. She has produced a Kentucky Derby winner, but he is just one of seven stakes winners from this grand mare. And her sons and daughters are proudly carrying on the line.

Glowing Tribute descends from the blue hen mare La Troienne and has a pedigree laced with remarkable female ancestors. Her second dam, Searching, was a stakes winner whose first three foals were amazing. Affectionately came first, followed by full sisters Admiring and Priceless Gem. All three fillies were stakes winners themselves, and Priceless Gem was the only horse — male or female — to hand Buckpasser defeat in a two-year-old stakes.

Affectionately won twenty-eight of fifty-two starts and earned honors as champion two-year-old filly of 1962 and champion sprinter and older mare of 1965. From only four named foals, Affectionately produced 1970 Horse of the Year Personality. Among Priceless Gem's foals were the great race mare Allez France and the outstanding producer Lady Winborne, dam of five stakes winners. And yet, it was the third mare, Admiring, who produced the filly that will probably have the most lasting influence on the breed: Glowing Tribute.

Paul Mellon bred Glowing Tribute and raced her in the famous gray-and-yellow Rokeby Stable silks. In a three-year campaign, Glowing Tribute raced twenty-four times, winning nine. Among those wins were the Diana Handicap and back-to-back runnings of the Sheepshead Bay Handicap, both popular grade II turf events. It was not to be her only influence on the Diana. While she was a valuable race mare who earned more than $230,000 on the track, as a broodmare her value increased dramatically.

When Glowing Tribute's foals hit the track, they came out running, as the saying goes. Her first offspring was turf specialist Hero's Honor (by Northern Dancer), who won two grade I races on his way to earning nearly $500,000. Her next foal, the filly Wild Applause (also by Northern Dancer), duplicated her mother's feat of winning the Diana Handicap. She earned more than $240,000, and as a broodmare, produced the popular stallion Eastern Echo, multiple graded stakes winner Roar, and graded stakes winner Blare of Trumpets.

Next for Glowing Tribute was the winning Mr. Prospector filly Glowing Prospect. Victoria Cross, by Spectacular Bid, was born in 1983, and although she never raced, she is the dam of stakes winner England Expects and 2001 multiple group I winner Mozart. Glowing Honor (by Seattle Slew) was Glowing Tribute's next foal, and she won two renewals of the family's favorite stakes race, the Diana Handicap, on her way to earning $296,450.

Seattle Glow, another Seattle Slew, was born in 1986 and became a minor stakes winner. Crowning Tribute (Chief's Crown) followed, and though he won four races, his best stakes effort was a fourth in the Champagne. Then came Sea Hero.

Sea Hero, by Polish Navy, earned nearly three million dollars and became a racing hero when he won the 1993 Kentucky Derby for his popular owner-and-trainer team, Paul Mellon and Mack Miller. While Mack often said that he couldn't figure out what made Sea Hero tick, he did manage to condition the unpredictable colt to impressive wins in the Champagne Stakes, Kentucky Derby, and Travers Stakes.

Glowing Tribute produced four foals after Sea Hero, and two became stakes winners. Coronation Cup (by Chief's Crown) earned $172,179 and won the Nijana Stakes on the turf, and Mackie (by Summer Squall) earned more than $164,000 and captured the Busher Stakes.

Paul Mellon, in his estate planning, dispersed his breeding stock at Keeneland in November 1992. Once again Glowing Tribute "did him proud," as did several of her fillies. Then nineteen, Glowing Tribute, whose son Sea Hero was still six months from winning the Kentucky Derby, sold for $460,000 in foal to Summer Squall (the resulting foal would be stakes-winning Mackie). Glowing Honor, in foal to Easy Goer, brought $1.1 million. Wild Applause, in foal to Forty Niner, sold for $1.05 million; and Victoria Cross, in foal to Slew o' Gold, brought $550,000.

These days, Glowing Tribute lives a quiet life on Offutt-Cole Farm near Midway, Kentucky. When her best friend Prospector's Fire died in the spring of 2000, Glowing Tribute sank into depression and lost weight. Her caregiver Karen Thomas relates, "They were like Siamese twins." But when the sad mare was placed in a field with three other fine old broodmares, her attitude and appetite improved.

Her current pasture mates are the mares Embellished (twenty-one years old), Taba (twenty-eight, the dam of Turkoman), and My Turbulent Miss (twenty-five, the dam of four stakes winners including Prized and Exploit). "There are four A personalities who have somehow managed to get along," Karen said proudly as she led me into the paddock.

Glowing Tribute isn't an outgoing, friendly mare nor is she easy to catch, so I photographed her "on the move." In her racing days she was a cribber (as was her dam, Admiring) and the fence line suggests that she still is. While the other three mares watched with some interest and what appeared to be good humor at my visit, Glowing Tribute kept her distance as she circled with slight annoyance.

But while she moves with her elegant head low and in an aloof manner, her regal bearing is unmistakable. It is the movement of a true queen, descended from royalty and a producer of royalty.

She is truly a grand dame.

Halo

DK. B/BR. H. 1969-2000, BY HAIL TO REASON—COSMAH,
BY COSMIC BOMB

*I*f ever an American Thoroughbred caused the heart to race, it is Halo, the source of countless tales of equine mischief. On a recent visit to Arthur and Staci Hancock's Stone Farm, I was accompanied into each stallion's paddock to take photographs, except for one: Halo's. His paddock is strictly off-limits, as Halo, even at age thirty-one, has a strange interest in crowding and occasionally climbing onto visitors. And while it definitely seems to entertain Halo, it's just bad public relations.

I stood outside the fence as Halo relaxed in his paddock. He is a grand horse to watch, seemingly indifferent and yet somehow very intense. His dark bay coat looks black as night. As the afternoon light softened into a golden evening, he grazed methodically as he wandered the paddock. Gato Del Sol and Northern Baby grazed nearby, occasionally watching Halo, and yet he seemed not to notice them. His back is deeply swayed now, and his ears flop forward awkwardly from his poll. Somehow, however, these things only add to his mystique.

Halo slipped from the public eye over the years as he quietly resided in a back stall of the stallion barn. But when Gato Del Sol returned to the States from Germany, fans flocked to Stone Farm, and Halo was "rediscov-ered." Photographs of Halo appeared on personal web sites, and fans mentioned visits with him on fan forums. Some referred to him as a "crusty old guy," and the name fits him well.

Even during his racing days, Halo had a reputation for being tough. He was a grade I winner, but he's had a much greater impact since his retirement, siring such runners as Kentucky Derby winner Sunny's Halo, Canadian Horse of the Year Glorious Song, champion two-year-old Devil's Bag, Goodbye Halo, Saint Ballado, and Strodes Creek. His foals won on dirt and turf, going short or long, with a turn of foot and an ability to go a distance.

One feels reverence in Halo's presence. Here is not just a solid racehorse and two-time leading American sire, but also sire of the greatest horse in Japanese stud history, Sunday Silence.

Even at his advanced age, Halo can be deceptively quick and a handful for his groom. You get the feeling that he is constantly plotting something, while grazing or standing quietly. And while he no longer wears the metal muzzle that dangled from his halters for years, he is still a horse to be greatly respected.

Halo does have his quirks, however. While he seems to fear no person or horse, odd things intimidate him. When the stallion manager moved his paddock feed tub from the ground onto a fence post, for instance, Halo eyed that bucket suspiciously for four days before finally deciding it was safe to approach.

Halo has always been identifiable by his eyes: frightening, rich, cold eyes that he passed on to many of his offspring, including Devil's Bag, Sunday Silence, and Lively One. In turn, those sires have passed those same eyes on to many of their offspring. Even looking at photos of Devil's Bag's foals Diablo, Devilish Erica, and the lovely, ill-fated Devil's Cup, with their cold eyes glowing, can be disconcerting.

Yet it is not just the physical traits of those eyes that are so intimidating: Halo's head rarely moves when he watches you. His head remains stationary, his eyes alone following you in cat-like fashion.

Behind those eyes are stories that have perhaps been slightly glorified over the years, but this grand black stallion has etched himself a unique and eternal spot in the racing annals, not only in America but also around the world.

* * *

Halo died several weeks after this piece was written, on November 28, 2000. Staci Hancock sent an e-mail, simply titled "Halo": "Barbara, Just wanted you to know…HALO died this am. He was his regular ole grumpy self yesterday and feeling just fine…just one month from being 32! It looks like a heart attack, but we aren't going to put him through finding out. He will be buried today at the stud barn…just knew that you would want to know. Sorry about the sad news… Staci"

Horatius

CH. H. 1975, BY PROUDEST ROMAN—TRUE CHARM, BY COHOES

kay, before I start chatting, take a good look at me. Gorgeous, aren't I? Thanks. Don't mind if I agree. Now don't think I've got a swelled head, just because I know I'm handsome. I'm not conceited — I'm just proud.

From the day I was born, January 31, 1975, people have "oooed" and "ahhhed" over me. Some say it's because of my "markings," which means the amount of white on me. Not many other horses have so much white on their face, and the white on my hind legs makes me look special when I strut. And my coat is redder and brighter than most other horses, too.

But it's more than that. You see, I've gotta be proud, with a dad named Proudest Roman and a mom called True Charm. I'm not sure why Mom's other kids had such odd names, like Blackie Daw and Sweetest Nut (I'm not touching that one!). I heard they both won stakes races — which I know are the races for which you get extra carrots. But they had nothing on me…

I've heard humans talk from time to time about my name. They say my breeder, Colonel W. Randolph Tayloe, named me after a Roman man. I guess Horatius Cocles was a hero, and legend is he helped an army in some battle I've never heard of. I guess with a dad named Proudest Roman, my name makes sense. But I've sure tried to make people think of *me* when the name "Horatius" comes up, instead of some person from way long ago.

I used to be a racehorse, and I tried really hard. It was tough, and I hated getting dirty. But I was good, darn it, and I won some of those "stakes races" myself. Actually, if I recall, I won seven of them. Don't get me wrong, I won eighteen races, but seven were the type where the groom was extra nice, and the people in the barn could read my story in the newspaper the next morning.

I don't remember all their names — I know the Riggs Handicap was a good one, and that Red Bank Handicap, wow! It was fun winning that. I didn't always win, but, man, I tried. I even equaled a track record once, in front of a lot of nice people at a pretty track called Monmouth.

The race was a mile — I loved that distance! — and I remember people discussing the time. It was 1:35. I don't know exactly what it means, except that I was a little extra tired that night.

But those days are so far behind me that it's ancient history (just like that other Horatius' story). I've got a wonderful life now and a good buddy who takes great care of me. His name is Ricky Price, and I can't remember a time he didn't take care of me here at Thornmar. I'd have to guess, but I'd say it's been more than twenty cold seasons since we were lucky enough to become friends.

He messes around with me sometimes, but I can't blame him. If I had fingers, I'd always run my hands through my long mane and tail, and I'd spend lots of time brushing my beautiful coat. I mean, it pays to be slick — the ladies love it! I know they do, because sometimes when Ricky brushes me extra nice, they visit.

The past few years have gotten tougher for me, but that's just between you and me. I dated only fourteen girls last year, which might sound like a lot to you, but it sure left me clamoring over the fence a lot. I mean, sometimes I can see five or six gals hanging out across the way, looking like they'd like to visit. When I start making noise, you can bet most of them look, and sometimes I bow my neck. That really gets 'em.

This year, 2001, I met with only four ladies. Can you stand it? I know I can't, and I'm hoping Ricky might sneak me a few more when the owners aren't paying attention. Someone even said the other day that I'd never have any more dates. What jokers! They were just kidding, weren't they? It makes me a little bit nervous…

So far Ricky hasn't snuck any ladies in here though, and he's been extra good to me. He talks about "arthritis" sometimes, whatever that is. People sometimes say he spoils me, but even if he does, what's wrong with that?

I'm never mean, I love people and love attention, and did I mention I love the ladies? Ah yes, but I digress… Anyone who meets me says how great I am, and how much they wish they could take me home or buy one of my babies. They talk about my great body or my mind (I've always been smart) or my "attitude." I guess that means the way I behave, but why wouldn't I behave? I'd hate to embarrass myself, or my mom or dad.

Or heck, the kids might even hear about it. I'm proud of my kids, too. Safely Kept, now *she* was a runner…and Ricky once told me that my boy Oliver's Twist ran second in the Preakness, the biggest race in the whole state of Maryland.

Maryland, that's where I live, by the way. I'm proud of that, too, because I'm one of the best stallions Maryland has. People call my children "hard-trying" and "consistent" and "tough." Heck, my kids even take to the jumps, and I'm often on that list of top steeplechase sires. I mean, I don't read lists or anything, but Ricky

and other people tell me these things. Charles and Cynthia McGinnes are awfully good to me — guess it's their property I gallop around on. Tell them thanks for me — I'm not always this chatty around people.

Look over there, across that road and down in that ravine, way across those paddocks. Is that what I think it is?

Yeah it is, and, wow, she's pretty. I'm gonna just stand here in the corner and do my "suave" routine. Ouch, that leg hurts a bit…let me shift my weight. She didn't notice that, did she? No? Good. Now let me flick my long tail and toss my forelock around a bit to get it *just* right…

Excuse me, I've got matters to attend to. You can watch me all day if you'd like. If I had a mirror, I might, too. But I've just got to send a little whinny thataway…

HORATIUS AND RICKY PRICE

Island Whirl

B. H. 1978, BY PAGO PAGO—ALITWIRL,
BY YOUR ALIBHAI

I'm afraid he'll drop dead on me when he breeds, he gets so excited," said farm manager Will Johnson, laughing. "He still enjoys it so much." I visited Island Whirl at Sez Who Thoroughbreds in Ocala, Florida, in March 2001. The other stallion I photographed that day, Blue Ensign, was a near-white powder keg. You could almost see the flights of fancy rushing through his handsome head.

Island Whirl was quite different. He came out professionally, stood wherever asked, and seemed content in our company. His rich bay coat was slick, and his graceful body was toned with muscles. Island Whirl is a gentleman.

His groom calls him Paco Paco, a reference to Island Whirl's most unusual sire. Pago Pago, Australia's champion two-year-old in 1962-63, was imported to America in 1963. Sixteen years later, the grand old boy was shipped back to the land down under. Pago Pago sired fifty-five stakes winners, 219 winners, and earners of nearly nine million dollars.

In 1978, the year before the Australian champion's departure from American soil, Island Whirl was born. He was his sire's best American runner.

Island Whirl's accomplishments have been all but forgotten. The freewheeling speedster racked up six stakes wins, including the Hollywood Gold Cup, Woodward Stakes, and Whitney Handicap, all grade I races. He coasted home first in the Super Derby, the grade II Malibu Stakes, and Del Mar's El Cajon Stakes; hit the board in seven other added-money events; and earned more than a million dollars.

Island Whirl outgamed challenger after challenger in the 1983 Whitney. From the get-go, horses chased Island Whirl's broad hindquarters. Kentucky Derby winner Sunny's Halo went after him; then, Linkage. Fit to Fight moved next, and as they stormed down the famous Saratoga stretch, Bold Style challenged. Island Whirl held

them all off, using what trainer Laz Barrera called "quality speed." What did Barrera consider quality speed? Speed that carried over a distance.

Island Whirl retired to Florida's Happy Valley Farm in late 1983 and was syndicated for forty shares at $75,000 each (three million dollars). His initial fee was $15,000.

Two decades later, Island Whirl is still a Sunshine State resident. He's been a very useful sire, his runners averaging $44,625 in earnings. His only grade I winner, Mi Preferido, earned $696,750. Among his other graded stakes winners are Vivano, Forever Whirl, Jess C's Whirl, Fan the Flame, and R.D. Wild Whirl. His son Fighting K, earner of nearly $550,000, won the Island Whirl Handicap in honor of Dad.

The business has changed, and with fewer people breeding to race, Island Whirl is no longer in fashion. New stallions are the rage as the old guard quietly gives way.

"He's probably the best bargain in Florida for his one-thousand-dollar stud fee," said Johnson, the farm manager. "He'll throw you a good, solid racehorse. I love the horse. He's such a pleasure to be around.

"He's twenty-three (in 2001), he looks great, and he still has a great libido. He doesn't know he's old."

John Henry

B. G. 1975, BY OLE BOB BOWERS—ONCE DOUBLE,
BY DOUBLE JAY

An old gelding stood patiently in the entrance of the covered pavilion while the crowd that had come to see him filled the circular bleachers. As they caught sight of him, the crowd grew quiet. A television set above the horse's head clicked on, causing the gelding's long ears to pin. The crowd became lost in the flickering images on the screen.

They watched in wonder as a gallant horse strained toward the wire. Seemingly beaten, the horse surged, and at the wire he stuck his nose in front of a competitor named The Bart. The crowd buzzed, some lost in memories of John Henry's incredible 1981 Arlington Million triumph, some watching it for the first time.

A woman with a microphone began recounting stories of John Henry's career, and the gelding was led into the ring. He moved slowly, his plain head down and his manner relaxed or, more likely, bored. John Henry was an old pro at this game. The Kentucky Horse Park holds the Hall of Champions show twice a day most of the year, and John Henry makes appearances six days a week.

The feats and numbers spilling from the speakers were remarkable: thirty-nine wins in eighty-three starts, more than $6.5 million in earnings, 1980 champion turf male, 1981 handicap horse, turf male and Horse of the Year, 1983 champion turf male, 1984 champion turf male and Horse of the Year, winner of the Santa Anita Handicap twice, the Arlington Million twice...But words are somehow inadequate.

John Henry wasn't expected to be good. His life is a fairy tale come true. He was born at Golden Chance Farm in Kentucky in 1975, and those who worked with him remember a small, ugly colt with bad knees and an equally bad disposition. His sire had neither accomplished much at the track nor sired much of note, and John Henry's dam had not been much of a producer either.

The Ole Bob Bowers colt was sold at the 1976 Keeneland January mixed sale, and he did accomplish something of note, but it wasn't his price. Before the sale he banged his head against his stall, entering the ring with a noticeably bloody head. The unpleasant, plainly bred, bloody colt brought $1,100.

His disposition became the source of his name, as he had a habit of knocking his metal feed tubs down and crushing them flat. John Henry, a fictional character nick-named the "steel-drivin' man," seemed the perfect fit.

In January 1977 he was sold again for $2,200 and geld-ed. Gelding softened his attitude somewhat as he had become something of a danger. Sold yet again, this time privately, John Henry went to trainer Phil Marino, who ran the untested two-year-old gelding at Louisiana's Jefferson Downs, long since defunct. Jefferson Downs' regulars were the first to see a great horse in the making. The ornery John Henry broke his maiden in his first start.

It was the first of thirty-nine wins, many of which were memorable. John Henry's owners moved him from track to track and trainer to trainer, but when he first raced on turf at Belmont Park on June 1, 1978, he found his call-ing. Although he could win on dirt, he was remarkable on the grass, and when he was sent to trainer Ron McAnally in late 1979, he quickly became a superstar.

John Henry loved to run, and fans loved his head-strong ways and plain look. It was a great combination, and John Henry reeled off six consecutive stakes wins in early 1980. His most successful season was in 1981, when he won eight of ten starts, including the Santa Anita Handicap, Jockey Club Gold Cup, and Arlington Million. The Arlington Million featured a stretch drive for the ages, as John Henry closed gamely to nip The Bart on the wire. John Henry was named 1981 Horse of the Year, the first of two such honors.

At nine, an age when most horses have long since retired, the cantankerous old gelding regained his top form. He won six of nine starts, including his final four. That year in his second Arlington Million win, the old

horse, who was beginning to sprout gray hairs, prevailed easily by nearly two lengths.

John Henry had done enough, and owner Sam Rubin retired him. John Henry was sent to the Kentucky Horse Park's Hall of Champions. A racing comeback was attempted when John Henry was ten, but he aggravated a recurring leg injury and was retired for good. John Henry returned to his second career, an unlikely role for such a sourpuss: goodwill ambassador for racing.

More than fifteen years have passed since John stepped off the van at the Kentucky Horse Park, and his retirement has been interesting. He initially was ridden around the park on occasion, and he still poses with tourists, stands patiently as the announcer regales the crowd with his racing tales, and affords fans the opportunity to see a living legend.

Forego, another great gelding who resided there, died in 1997. About then, the popular Cigar moved into the Hall of Champions. The crowds come to see Cigar more often than John Henry, and the staff is certain that John Henry is jealous. But he has no need to be. He is a true racing hero, and countless fans are thrilled to run their fingers along his stall nameplate.

A large sign near his paddock chronicles his races and statistics, but all the numbers and all the words don't come close to explaining what made John Henry great. That tape of the 1981 Arlington Million does. It was his heart.

King's Swan

B. G. 1980, BY KING'S BISHOP—ROYAL CYGNET, BY SEA-BIRD

C ab Calloway, the old Hi-De-Ho performer with the broad-toothed smile and a penchant for the track, was a King's Swan fan. His wife collected porcelain swans, and he collected tickets at Aqueduct, so it was only natural that he should fall for King's Swan. He was not alone. "The King of Aqueduct" had countless fans.

King's Swan was easy to love. The durable gelding raced 107 times, first visiting the winner's circle in January 1983 and winning for the last time on November 12, 1990.

In King's Swan's final win, a colt named Joker's Farce passed the ten-year-old gelding. But in the final yards, pressed against the rail by the four-year-old competitor, King's Swan fought back to retake the lead. Tom Durkin, overwhelmed by the heart of the gallant gelding, screamed as if it were a Breeders' Cup event. "…Here he comes again! King's Swan! He's ten years old, and he's better than ever! King's Swan!"

Remarkably, King's Swan had three siblings out of Royal Cygnet who each raced more than a hundred times. His half brother Prince Siegfried raced 101 times over eight years, winning thirteen and hitting the board

an additional forty-one. Ornithologist raced 154 times in eight years and won or placed in sixty. Swan Prince raced nine seasons, winning twenty-three of 137 starts and placing in forty-three more.

It was only natural for King's Swan to be durable. What wasn't predictable was the heights he would attain.

On December 15, 1985, trainer Dick Dutrow claimed the then five-year-old King's Swan for a threesome from Maryland: Al Akman, Herb Kushner, and Dutrow himself. King's Swan had won eleven races, but he had finished off the board in his two stakes attempts. The son of King's Bishop ran third that December day for an $80,000 tag, but under Dick Dutrow's care the unmarked bay blossomed.

Al Akman recalled that when they got King's Swan, "he was a bit of a bleeder. After Dickie got him, he never bled

again. Dickie had a specialty for bleeders. Everyone knew it, but he would never tell anyone how he did it."

King's Swan quickly made Dutrow look smart, winning an Aqueduct allowance by more than three lengths. He followed with three scores in four races. Dutrow moved him up again, and for the first time, he hit the board in a graded stakes in May 1986, finishing third in the grade II Carter Handicap.

Dutrow sent King's Swan out in the first set each morning, and exercise rider Jeannie Uhl let the gelding take his time. As Akman remembered, "Dickie learned to give him his way. You couldn't take him directly to the track in the morning. You'd take him to the entrance of the track, stop, and let him stand there."

"He would survey the situation," Dutrow said. "After he looked around for a while, he would decide it was time, and then he would step onto the track."

King's Swan took his time walking to the paddock in the afternoons as well, but it was worth the wait. From 1986 through 1990, King's Swan won twelve stakes races and finished on the board in twenty-one more. His biggest win came in Aqueduct's grade I Vosburgh Handicap, but the list of Aqueduct stakes he won included the grade II Bold Ruler and six grade III races: the Stymie, Assault (twice), Aqueduct, Boojum, and Westchester. He set a track record at Aqueduct in 1987, running eight and a half furlongs in 1:41 4/5, and he won the Grey Lag Handicap carrying 130 pounds.

He won stakes races at Belmont and Laurel as well, but he moved up considerably at the Big "A." It was during these years that he attained his nickname "The King of Aqueduct." Bettors grew to love his determination and consistency, and the understated gelding attained hero status.

But time finally took its toll on King's Swan, and in his 1990 season he began tailing off. He ran third in two stakes,

then second in another to the speedy Once Wild. Dutrow put King's Swan in a high-quality allowance, and King ran sixth behind the young Pleasant Tap. His next allowance test yielded similar results, as King came home a tired fifth behind Out of Place.

Next came his final triumph, on a most appropriate stage. On that November day, when seemingly beaten by Joker's Farce, the ten-year-old warrior determinedly stuck his nose in front on the Aqueduct wire.

He raced once more, finishing fourth. Then his incredible racing career, which spanned nine seasons and 107 races, in which King's Swan carried sixteen different jockeys and earned $1,924,845, was over.

"I wanna retire him when he is a main event, and that's what he is now. I don't want to retire him when he's, you know, one of those preliminary fighters," Dutrow explained.

The New York Racing Association gave King's Swan a retirement ceremony, and the dependable gelding made one more trip from his Aqueduct barn to the paddock. As always, he stopped numerous times along the way to survey his track. King's Swan was adorned with his familiar white bridle and a purple blanket that read "KING'S SWAN—DECEMBER 22, 1990—THE KING OF AQUEDUCT." But this time on his way to the frontside, King had more than Dutrow's barn help meandering alongside. Television crews followed his every step, and famed television host Ray Gandolf interviewed fans, several of them jockeys, waiting for King in the paddock.

"He's like the Shoemaker of horses," jockey Chris Antley said, leaning forward for emphasis. "He kept doing it consistently. He's so old, and every year he made a comeback."

Cordero came next. "The other day when I rode him the last time, when he won, he looked like he was a beaten horse, and he was all out. I just kept pointing to the other horse and kept talking to him, and he just looked at that horse, and I know he was doing something extra. He fights; he's a fighter."

Richard Migliore intently considered what made King's Swan special. "You knew he was going to give you his best. Whatever it was that day, you were gonna get it, and you were going to get all of it. He never quits…never say die."

King circled the paddock, then stood for photos with seemingly countless people, including jockeys who had ridden him. Fans wore King's Swan buttons passed out with admission and cheered for the old-timer. He stepped back onto the Aqueduct surface, and his groom led him from the track one final time.

* * *

December 2001

"There was no way I could work at the track and take care of King, so I decided when King retires, I'm done," Jeannie Uhl said, laughing lightly as she pulled the saddle from King's Swan. The gelding shifted in the crossties. He now

lives at an idyllic farm, nestled in the quiet beauty of New York's Catskill Mountains.

King seemed to enjoy her voice. She continued, "The last year King was on the track I groomed him and exercised him. I rode him at 5:30 for Dickie at Aqueduct, then went over to Belmont to ride for Angel Penna Jr."

On Aqueduct mornings when King was finished training, he stood in an ice bucket while Jeannie applied a poultice to his legs. Friends visited, and groups of women congregated in King's Swan's stall. "Dickie would go by, he'd stick his head under the webbing when we were talking, and he'd say, 'I thought I heard a lot of cackling in there,' " Jeannie remembered fondly.

When I asked what King was like on the track, she thought for a moment. "He was my baby sitter. I always knew I was safe with him. He went out there to train and was a perfect gentleman coming back."

It was only natural that King's owners gave him to Jeannie. She was part of Ray Gandolf's television piece eleven years earlier, proudly wearing a "King's Swan" jacket as she moved around the horse's stall. When King retired, Jeannie followed soon thereafter.

King and Jeannie have been together ever since, living a life straight out of a child's tale. Jeannie saddles King for a ride almost daily. But when her schedule doesn't permit it, he is turned out with his friend Sam. A chestnut Quarter Horse with lots of white and a kind face, Sam suffers from navicular disease. The two buddies spend their days in a large paddock at the beautiful farm. The backdrop is so lovely it could be Yosemite.

Jeannie and King have many venues in which to ride, including an expansive indoor arena and a beautiful outdoor ring. The day I visited, she and King strode to the "sublime field."

"We call it that because, well, it is sublime," Jeannie said

and smiled from high on King's back. The field is rolled and checked regularly for holes; it's a safe place for a horse to stretch its legs.

On "cider and doughnut" days, others who board horses there gather for trail rides. King's Swan, almost always relaxed, becomes competitive when groups of eight or ten head to the trails. He canters in place, frets, and asks Jeannie to let him go.

King's Swan is a bona fide member of the Uhl family. "My mom says he's her grandkid. She fears he's going to be the only one," Jeannie laughed. "She tells everyone, 'my grandson has four legs and a tail.' "

In 1995 when King was fifteen, Jeannie called Dick Dutrow at Saratoga and said she'd like to bring King's Swan to the track. "You know Dickie. He said, 'We'll find a stall for him, just bring him up.' " Dutrow even climbed aboard the dependable gelding that August when King vacationed for a week at the Spa City. "He said he hadn't ridden a horse since Secretariat was a baby," Jeannie said.

King's Swan was quite lively when I photographed him. Maybe he remembered the sound of the camera from the countless times he'd been photographed. Or perhaps, as Jeannie supposed, he felt her excitement and "vibes" about the new visitor.

As they jogged around the "sublime field," King's Swan bowed his neck and fought for more rein. Jeannie finally conceded, and he broke into a strong canter. King pulled even harder, stretching his well-traveled legs. He was magnificent; his coat glowing brilliantly; his black mane and tail flowing behind him. Jeannie held the reins firmly but lovingly, a smile splashed broadly across her youthful face.

If you listened closely, you could almost hear Tom Durkin. "Here he comes again! King's Swan! He's twenty-one years old, and he's better than ever! King's Swan!"

Kris S.

DK. B/BR. H. 1977-2002, BY ROBERTO—SHARP QUEEN, BY PRINCEQUILLO

*L*arry Whaley gently pulled on the lead shank. The proud horse didn't want to move, but he had always been an agreeable animal. So the long, elegant black stallion slowly followed his friend outside, his legs tired but his action graceful.

Kris S. is showing signs of age, and Larry worries about his companion. He has worked with Kris S. since the stallion arrived at Lexington's Prestonwood Farm in late 1993. By then, Kris S. was already the sire of three Breeders' Cup winners.

Larry stayed with the classic horse through the farm's change of ownership to WinStar Farm, and he has watched another Kris S. offspring win a Breeders' Cup race. He has led the gentle horse to his paddock at night and brought him back up in the morning, taking extra time with his aging friend.

When several Kris S. auction yearlings sold for eye-catching sums in September 2001, an English fan wrote to an online racing forum: "Why is there so much interest in Kris S.? Is it because of Soaring Softly?"

Soaring Softly is indeed part of the answer, as she provided the stallion a then-record fourth individual winner in Breeders' Cup races. And the winners were each in different events: the Distaff, the Juvenile, the Turf, and the Filly & Mare Turf.

But it is much more than that. Kris S. has a classic combination of beautiful blood, solid conformation, and successful offspring. He offers a change from popular sprinter-type sires, and his durable progeny excel over longer distances, on either dirt or turf. This 16.3-hand sire hearkens to an earlier era, and magic names like Roberto, Nearco, Turn-to, Nashua, Bull Lea, Bull Dog, and Blue Larkspur dot his pedigree.

Kris S. had an abbreviated racing career, winning three of just five starts, including the Bradbury Stakes. He retired first to Meadowbrook Farms in Florida, and his stud fee in 1984 — when his first crop were just yearlings — was five thousand dollars.

But his foals have spoken for him, and his top runners

are known to most racing fans: champion Hollywood Wildcat, champion Soaring Softly, Breeders' Cup winner Prized, Breeders' Cup winner Brocco, grade I winners Dr Fong, Cheval Volant, Stocks Up, You and I, Kissin Kris, plus stakes winners Adonis, Class Kris, Evening Kris, and Arch. The list goes on, a total of sixty-three stakes winners as of May 2002.

In 2001, Kris S.'s stud fee was listed at $150,000, and interest in the old stallion had not waned. At the 2001 Keeneland September yearling sale, three of the top twenty-five high-priced horses were by Kris S., each selling for a million dollars or more.

Stallions cannot breed forever, and the time will come when Larry no longer leads Kris S. down that long pathway to his paddock. But there will never come a time when a classier horse graces that beautiful land. In that respect, Kris S. will never be topped.

* * *

In February 2002, after covering ten mares, Kris S. suffered a neck injury. The twenty-five-year-old stallion was sent to Lexington's Hagyard-Davidson-McGee veterinary clinic for treat-ment. Yet he continued to be uncomfortable, and on March 25, 2002, WinStar Farm announced Kris S.' pensioning.

In May, a much sadder press release followed. WinStar president Doug Cauthen said: "Kris S. has been a real warrior since his injury and recovered enough to graze comfortably for the last month. However, he had a setback this weekend and it was time to let him go out with dignity." Kris S. was euthanized May 7, 2002, and the beautiful stallion was buried on the farm in a handcrafted pine casket, painted WinStar green with the WinStar logo.

Six of the ten mares bred to Kris S. in 2002 are in foal.

KRIS S. WITH LARRY WHALEY

Life's Magic

B. M. 1981, BY COX'S RIDGE—FIRE WATER, BY TOM ROLFE

*L*ife's Magic stood quietly swishing her short, coarse tail, the intensity of summer keeping her movements to a minimum. Flies busied themselves on the large bay mare's thick, handsome head and around her kind eyes. Her lower lip hung heavy, but much heavier still was her belly, swollen with age and with life within. The mare was only four months along, but the heat made the load seem larger.

She lowered her head to nuzzle a pile of golden hay, and flies scattered. The grass had lost its spring flavor and was now holding steadfast despite high temperatures and little rain. She lifted her head again, and the flies settled back onto her face. It was summertime in Kentucky.

The groom's love for Life's Magic was readily apparent. She rubbed the mare's forehead gently and related stories of the mare's lack of luck. If something bad happened, it happened to Life's Magic, from episodes of colic to getting stuck in fences. And yet a gentler mare is seldom found.

Life's Magic dropped her head and relaxed, happy with the attention. She looks very much like her sire, Cox's Ridge, and she certainly performed admirably on the race-track. But her twelve foals of racing age had not yet approached her ability. In her belly, magic had begun anew, and a Thunder Gulch foal awaited its chance.

Fortunes have been spent and lost on this old gal, but she remains kind and humble. When she sold in 1986, the final bid was $5.4 million. When the gavel fell the next time, in 1987, the price was $4.4 million. Ten years passed before Life's Magic had another hip number applied, and in foal to Unbridled, she brought only $310,000.

In November of 2001, four months after my visit, Life's Magic sold again, in foal to Thunder Gulch. This time, the top bid was $75,000.

Life's Magic was one of the finest race mares of the 1980s, racing for red-hot trainer D. Wayne Lukas. Sporting the traditional Lukas white bridle, the big filly broke her maiden at first asking and ran successfully for three memorable seasons. Competition was sparkling those years, and names such as Miss Oceana and Princess Rooney sometimes gave her more than she could handle.

She handed Miss Oceana defeats as well, and Lukas had no fear of entering her against the boys. In the 1985 Brooklyn Handicap, Life's Magic lost to Bounding Basque by a half-length, and in the Norfolk for two-year-olds, she missed catching Fali Time by a nose.

Life's Magic's name was etched into trophies of many historic grade I races for distaffers, including the Oak Leaf, Mother Goose, Monmouth Oaks, Alabama, and Beldame. She earned Eclipse Awards for three-year-old filly in 1984 and top handicap mare in 1985. And what is remembered now as incredible, her dominant six and a quarter-length Breeders' Cup Distaff win over Lady's Secret, was no surprise at the time. In 1985 Life's Magic was that good.

She was retired after that Breeders' Cup and took her sensational credentials to the sales ring. She had won eight of thirty-two starts, earned $2,255,218, and finished off the board only nine times. Five of those were against the boys.

Sixteen years later Life's Magic was on the move again. Arthur Seelbinder is a member of the group that purchased Life's Magic in 2001. They looked at the $75,000 pedigree page and still saw the $5.4 million mare within.

He told the *Daily Racing Form*: "The opportunity to own such a fabulous horse, even at her age, is a great incentive to be involved in racing and breeding…Her foals haven't been that successful, but to get one or two foals would be very exciting, and you'd like to think that a foal out of Life's Magic could duplicate some of her ability."

After all, life is indeed magic.

***

Life's Magic foaled a chestnut Thunder Gulch colt on March 11, 2002, at Trackside Farm. The colt has strong bone, good size, and a forward attitude. And, of course, he has beautiful bloodlines.

Life's Magic was scheduled to be bred to Silver Deputy in 2002.

LIFE'S MAGIC WITH HER 2002 THUNDER GULCH COLT

Little Bold John

B. G. 1982, BY JOHN ALDEN—LITTLE BOLD SPHINX, BY BOLD AMBITION

ittle Bold John resides in the same barn in which he was born on January 19, 1982. It has been two decades since the big colt took his first clumsy steps at Hal "C.B." Clagett's Weston Farm in Upper Marlboro, Maryland.

Little Bold John's dam was the product of a breeding nick Clagett believed in, the cross of a Bold Ruler stallion (Bold Ambition) to a Restless Native mare (Restless Sphinx, the dam of Little Bold Sphinx). It proved very successful, for her son Little Bold John grew up to win thirty-eight races, nearly two million dollars, and countless fans' affections.

Little Bold John was not easy to break, tossing riders regularly and being a general nuisance. Once, the difficult colt jumped the fence, ran across the road, and tried to make an acquaintance with some fillies across the way. The decision was made to geld him.

The plain dark bay gelding took the slow route to fame.

Little Bold John actually won a stakes in his fourth start, Charles Town's Tri-State Futurity, but was placed fourth for a bumping incident. "For one minute we were the winners of a $60,000 purse," Clagett said. "Had that stood, I'd have paid my bills and kept him." Instead, Little Bold John was sold to businessman Jack Owens for $30,000.

Little Bold John's past performances, some three pages strong, record the busy gelding's rise and fall through the ranks. Beginning with maiden events in the autumn of 1984, Little Bold John moved quickly into allowances and stakes and then competed consistently in stakes after stakes after stakes.

He competed in seventy-three stakes races. Little Bold John won twenty-five and was second or third in eighteen more. His biggest win, the 1987 Donn Handicap, a grade II race at the time, rewarded his followers with a Donn-record win payoff of $113.80.

Over the years and many racing miles, Little Bold John's following grew. The courageous gelding with the fun name consistently went to battle with both attitude and perseverance for owner Jack Owens and trainer Jerry Robb. He competed primarily at Mid-Atlantic tracks, seemingly in every stakes for which he fit the conditions.

It's hard to imagine one horse winning them all, but for readers to understand how remarkable this old boy was, here's a list of his stakes victories: the Donn, the grade III John B. Campbell, Riggs (two runnings), Baltimore Budweiser Breeders' Cup, General George Stakes, and the Palisades, Edward L. Blake Memorial, Japan Racing Association, Native Dancer (two runnings), Chieftain (two runnings), Protagonist, Budweiser Maryland Classic, Jennings (three runnings), Resolution, Fort McHenry, Marylander, Polynesian, Congressional, Never Bend, and Thistledown Budweiser Breeders' Cup handicaps.

Robb bought Little Bold John in 1990 when the gelding was eight and tried to retire him. The horse wanted nothing to do with retired life, however, and before long Little Bold John returned to the racing wars.

He began the inevitable descent, and by the time Little Bold John raced his last, he was alternating between lower level allowance and claiming events. That last start came on Halloween 1992, and Little Bold John, at .80-1,

ALDEN'S IGLOO (LEFT) AND LITTLE BOLD JOHN

headed down the stretch as he had 104 times before. This time, near the quarter pole, he suddenly fell back.

"He pulled a suspensory ligament," Robb said. "Most horses, when they get hurt, pull up. But he came back to win the race, like he was three-legged. After that, I knew he'd end up killing himself if I kept running him."

This time Little Bold John's retirement lasted. Robb used the headstrong gelding as a pony for a while, but Little Bold John didn't take to that subservient job.

"He did okay until a horse tried to nip him, as they all do," Rob recalled. "Then he'd kick the hell out of them. He wasn't ready to give up the crown."

In 1996 Robb gave Little Bold John back to Clagett. Clagett had moved to Roedown Farm with his new wife. Weston Farm became the home of Clagett's son, Hal III. Little Bold John spent several years at Roedown with the senior Clagett, but now lives back at his nearby birthplace, Weston. The senior Clagett visits him regularly.

At Bowie in May 2001, a faded sign on Barn 12 still proudly announced, "JOHN J. ROBB RACING STABLE — HOME OF LITTLE BOLD JOHN."

At Weston the twenty-year-old Little Bold John, still flashing his strong attitude, spends his days like a teenager. The plain gelding has no use for primping or handling. He is happy running free with his buddies, two dark bays named Silent Alden (who's out of a half sister to Little Bold John) and Alden's Igloo.

The rambunctious trio, with just two small white socks among them, spend days wandering a large, sloping field, galloping in friendly races and grazing. One of their pleasures is a small pond at the field's lower edge, in which they splash, roll, and revel.

Days are full for the happy band of John Alden geldings. Among them, they ran 138 races, earned $1,978,512, and spent fourteen years on track. Little Bold John accounted for 105 of those starts, nine years' racing, and all but $22,106 of the winnings.

Alden's Igloo holds little regard for Little Bold John's racing exploits. When the two match up for long, sweeping runs, he holds an easy lead over the old stakes winner.

After spending nine years keeping ahead of the competition, Little Bold John looks quite content finally giving up the crown.

Little Current

CH. H. 1971, BY SEA-BIRD—LUIANA, BY MY BABU

L ittle Current is the oldest living American classic winner, and countless fans still remember his stirring wins in the 1974 Preakness and Belmont. But unlike champions such as Seattle Slew — Three Chimneys hosts between eight thousand and ten thousand visitors annually — Little Current receives perhaps ten out-of-state visitors a year. Little Current lives quietly far from the heart of Bluegrass Country, at a small veterinary clinic in Monroe, Washington.

The story of how he ended up in Washington state began like that of most older Thoroughbreds — a lack of success at stud. But, along the way, love intervened.

Little Current's owners are veterinarians Mark and Ann Hansen. Mark, a lifelong racing fan, became enamored of Little Current years ago while watching his races on television and reading articles about the horse's exploits in magazines. Although he never saw Little Current race in person, Mark visited the stallion at Doug Arnold's farm in Lexington, Kentucky, in 1990. "I had that feeling you get when you're around a great animal," he said. "He just had a presence about him."

By then, however, Little Current had already fallen from grace and the public's eye.

When Little Current was syndicated for four million dollars in late 1974, it was the eighth highest price ever paid for a stallion. His blood was impeccable, steeped in Darby Dan tradition. His female side alone included magic names like Luiana, Banquet Bell, Primonetta, Chateaugay, and Prayers'n Promises.

Queen Elizabeth II even visited Little Current at Darby Dan Farm in 1984, breeding some of her mares to the handsome son of Sea-Bird. But his bloodlines and race record proved not enough. In 1988 Little Current was moved to Arnold Farms.

Doug loved the stallion and tried his best to make him successful, but after four seasons Little Current was sold to a Louisiana breeder. By then the stud fee was listed at

$1,500, and the aging chestnut sired only thirty-three foals from 1993 to 1995.

After visiting Little Current in 1990, Mark Hansen kept an eye on the classic winner. In 1995, with the help of Doug Arnold, the Hansens purchased the twenty-four-year-old stallion and brought him to Washington state.

When Little Current stepped off the van, it was a dream come true for Mark. He and Ann bred Little Current to a few mares, and the horse had two named foals in 1997. But that was not Mark's reason for buying the famous racehorse. He simply loved him.

Even six years after their union, as I watched Mark brush Little Current for our photo session, his pride in the stallion was evident. His words and actions were almost childlike as he related stories of Little Current's playful antics and intelligence.

I hadn't seen Little Current since 1984, but there was no mistaking him. Little Current stood with his head high and his nose firmly planted against the stall rungs. His ears are finely tapered in Arabian style, his eyes extra large and wide-

set, his blaze slim and distinctive. The word "Little" is deceptive. With such a high head carriage, he appears even taller than his sixteen hands.

Little Current clearly enjoyed the attention and fussed

with Mark, reaching back occasionally to snatch at the rub rag. Mark spends much time with the old guy, and Little Current is a strong, content senior citizen.

The signs of age were apparent in the thirty-year-old stallion, the dip in the back and the rib cage slightly visible in the backlit stall. The decades of halter use have caused visible rubs behind his ears; his coat was thin; and his knees cracked when he lifted his legs.

But Little Current is fortunate to have veterinarians for owners. They give him special feed and vitamins, and worm him regularly. Little Current wears special horseshoes that have no nails and provide cushioning for his tired limbs.

On this day, however, Little Current's limbs didn't appear weary. Ann and Mark first let Little Current out in his pen to give him a chance to unwind. The pen in front of their clinic is perhaps fifteen feet by thirty feet, and while Mark intends to build a larger paddock some day, he worries about the old boy overextending himself.

Little Current took a few moments to get comfortable. But soon he bucked and galloped around the enclosure like a much younger stallion.

It was hard to envision him twenty-seven years earlier, storming down the stretch at Pimlico and Belmont Park. He had a very tough act to follow as Secretariat had won the Triple Crown the previous year. Little Current's time in the Preakness, 1:54 3/5, was just a fifth of a second slower than Secretariat's official time. And while Little Current's Belmont clocking didn't approach Secretariat's, his fractions for the final quarter and half-mile in The Test of the Champion were faster than those of Big Red's.

Little Current stopped showing off and dropped his head to graze. His legs shook slightly, and Mark pointed to them as evidence of his concern. With Little Current now relaxed, Mark put the shank back on and led the champion to new territory — a field across the street.

We picked the spot as it offered a more attractive backdrop than the clinic parking lot, and Mark gamely led his buddy there. Little Current definitely liked the change of venue, and the long-bodied chestnut circled Mark with renewed interest. But he had no desire to look our way, instead choosing to stare toward a large hill behind him. After all, he knew darned well all about his home in front of him. But that hill…ah, that hill…now, that was a place of mystery.

We tried for several minutes, but the old horse just wouldn't cooperate. Mark had an idea, and a moment later Ann brought a mare out of the clinic to give Little Current an incentive to enjoy the homeward view. It worked.

Little Current obviously didn't mind that the mare was one of his own daughters, and he displayed impressively like an active stallion. His nostrils flared and his breath blew heavily as he danced around Mark, thrilled with the assumption that his human friend was going to let him breed for the first time in five years.

He reared high above Mark's head with power and agility. His narrow face aimed down toward the man below, as Mark held on with a loving hand.

Little Current, his Sea-Bird blood flowing hot, was still breathtaking.

When Foolish Pleasure died, his remains were interred with no marker at his final home, a Wyoming haven of seemingly endless mountains, flowers, and blue skies. Sir Barton, who ended his days at a remount station, is buried in Washington Park, also in Wyoming, his remains forever guarded by a generic fiberglass horse. The park lacked the funds for a more formal marker.

When Little Current's time comes, the Hansens plan to ship him back to Doug Arnold's Kentucky farm for burial. If all goes to plan, Little Current will spend eternity beneath the hallowed bluegrass, a fitting resting-place for such a great and long-lived champion.

Lord Gaylord

DK. B/BR. H. 1970-1998, BY SIR GAYLORD—MISS GLAMOUR GAL,
BY AMBIORIX

After photographing the Pimlico workouts during Preakness week 1998, I decided to explore the area. I've always had an interest in equine cemeteries, and I'd been told about one at Worthington Farms in nearby Glyndon. A wonderful race mare named Lady Dean was buried there atop a hill with an overview of the Maryland Hunt Cup course.

I went to Worthington searching for the cemetery. Instead, I found Lord Gaylord.

He was standing in a back paddock, quite still amid the strong midday heat. Baltimore can be surprisingly hot in mid-May, and this day was tough. The old stallion watched with curiosity as I approached the fence, and he promptly and easily strode up. He pushed his long head forward trustingly, and I rubbed his forehead.

What a grand old horse he was!

His back was exceptionally long, and his belly had begun to fall. His coat was a rich mix of dark bay and black, and a small crescent star hung down on his forehead. He carried himself proudly despite his advanced age. His eyes were worldly, and his look, even at twenty-eight, was classic.

I took one last photograph of the old boy, standing regally as he watched me out of sight. He looked so stately and sad that an old Irish superstition came to mind. If someone watches a friend disappear from view, he will not see that friend again.

Lord Gaylord died four months later, and I sent a print to the farm to thank them for allowing my visit. Their gracious reply noted that the photograph, they believed, was the last taken of their old stallion.

"He was an extreme gentleman," farm manager Kevin Kellar said of Lord Gaylord. "He was the kind of horse who knew that he was special, and he always carried himself that way. He was very much a pleasure to work with."

Kellar worked with Lord Gaylord for two decades, arriving at Worthington Farms in 1979. Lord Gaylord was a young stallion then, and his first foals were three-year-olds. But it was Lord Gaylord's third crop with which he truly established himself, siring Lord Avie and Lady Dean.

Lord Avie won the Young America, Florida Derby, and Champagne, all grade I events; earned $705,977; and was named 1980 champion two-year-old colt. Lady Dean won eight stakes races, including the grade II Long Look and grade III Barbara Fritchie, and she earned $361,328.

Lord Gaylord sired six other winners of more than $300,000, including the popular graded stakes winners I Rejoice ($502,476), Notches Trace ($360,562), and I Am the Game ($369,051). In 1989 Lord Gaylord was award-

ed the Tesio Award as Maryland's best stallion.

By the time I saw Lord Gaylord in 1998, he'd been a pensioner for six years. He was still in good health, but time had caught up with him.

Lord Gaylord had always had allergies, and Worthington bedded the old stallion's stall with shavings, which don't create as much dust and mold as straw. But despite every effort to keep him comfortable, Lord Gaylord began to fail.

"He was just getting old," Kellar recalled. "We'd pensioned him years ago, and he was always a very robust stallion. But it was just getting to the point where he wasn't drinking water any more and he wasn't eating."

On August 26, 1998, in front of Worthington Farms' stud barn, Lord Gaylord was euthanized. The old boy had recently been excelling as a broodmare sire. The day he died, his talented granddaughter Tenski won a grade III race at Saratoga.

Lord Gaylord was buried near his daughter Lady Dean, high on a hill overlooking the famed Maryland Hunt Cup course. What a beautiful place to spend eternity.

What made Lord Gaylord such a good sire? His race record was unimpressive, with one win in six starts and earnings of $7,530. He was a half brother to two minor stakes winners. His dam, who won three of sixteen races, was a half sister to two minor stakes winners. Yet, nothing noticeable on the page would indicate that Lord Gaylord would sire runners that averaged $45,023, or that he would sire an Eclipse Award winner, or thirty-two stakes winners.

Looking at him, however, the answer was obvious. Lord Gaylord had class.

Mac Diarmida

DK. B/BR. H. 1975, BY MINNESOTA MAC—FLYING TAMMIE,
BY TIM TAM

*S*cotty Schulhofer still remembers his champion well. Recently reminiscing, he recalls leading the temperamental Mac Diarmida around a shed row one morning in 1978 and the horse rearing straight up. With that dark bay horse's legs and belly flashing before him, it was — and still is — the biggest any horse has ever looked to him.

When Mac Diarmida began racing, not many people noticed. His first three starts were on dirt, and the best he could do was one third-place finish. But when Scotty moved the big colt over to the turf, Mac responded emphatically with a five-length score under Jean Cruguet.

It was the beginning of grand things for Mac Diarmida, and Scotty chose his spots carefully. Mac won two allowance races, and then the Golden Grass Handicap. He next scored in a Monmouth Park allowance before easily winning the grade III Long Branch Stakes. Then, as people began to take notice, he swept through the Leonard Richards Stakes, the Lexington Handicap (beating John Henry), and the Secretariat and Lawrence Realization stakes, all graded events.

In his next start, however, the tenacious mare Waya ended Mac Diarmida's ten-race win skein in the grade I Man o' War Stakes. Mac Diarmida rebounded quickly, winning the Canadian International and the Washington, D.C., International, both grade Is. Among those in the beaten field of the International was Waya.

A maiden until February of his three-year-old season, Mac Diarmida had won twelve of thirteen starts after being moved to the turf, and he earned more than $500,000. Although only three, he was named 1978 champion grass horse over such stellar performers as Trillion, Waya, Noble Dancer, and Tiller, and he was quickly whisked off to stud in Florida.

Mac Diarmida probably would have fared better had he stayed on the racecourse. In thirteen years at stud, he sired 184 named foals, and very little of note. While breeders hoped their foals would inherit Mac's determination and attitude, they instead tended to inherit a trait not quite as useful: his large, gentle eyes. Mac Diarmida was pensioned early due to a decline in fertility just as his sire, Minnesota Mac, had been.

Mac Diarmida still lives comfortably in a paddock in front of the Cashel Stud office in Ocala, and they are very proud of their champion. There is a mare (his "girlfriend") kept in a nearby paddock to provide company, and he still receives occasional visitors or fan letters. The groom mentioned that Mac is a non-sweater and strongly dislikes standing in the sun. It is perhaps this physical problem that explains his favorite food, which he has loved since his racing days: potassium-rich bananas.

Mac Diarmida still has one very devoted fan named Chris Venis. Chris has loved Mac since those early racing years, and he visits the old champion every year, bringing his idol bananas and peppermints. He had a special halter made for Mac, which the horse wears daily. Its nameplate glows with the lovingly chosen words, MAC DIARMIDA, 1978 TURF CHAMPION.

Jessica Hartigan greeted me with a warm smile when I got to the Cashel office, and we walked to a nearby barn. Jessica's husband Kevin is Cashel Stud's owner/trainer, and Jessica primarily works with the broodmares.

A beautiful woman, Jessica stands only five-foot-two. Her small frame made it easy to picture her galloping horses in her younger days. Mac simply towered over her.

When Jessica brought Mac outside that sunny day in March 2000, Mac noticed his girlfriend watching and began to prance, arching his neck proudly.

The twenty-five-year-old stallion tried to rear, and Jessica easily held the shank as he went up slightly, perhaps a foot or so. She laughed. He would like to rear up higher, she said.

What a difference two decades makes…

Majesty's Prince

CH. H. 1979, BY HIS MAJESTY—PIED PRINCESS, BY TOM FOOL

I'm not doing a whole lot of advertising for him because he's twenty-two, and there are all those fancy things which keep coming off the production line," Hazel Marsh said in 2001 of Majesty's Prince. "We still keep up with his registration with The Jockey Club and the Breeders' Cup, but I'm not expecting a big flurry of calls."

Then she added, with regret: "Turf racing is only now becoming popular in this country. Unfortunately, it wasn't at the time when he was a young stallion."

If Majesty's Prince was born at the wrong time for breeding, it was the right time for racing. Bred by Hazel's late husband, John, Majesty's Prince was born in 1979 at their Gainesville, Virginia, farm. The Marshes held several shares in the Kentucky stallion His Majesty, and they sent their unraced Pied Princess to his court.

Pied Princess' dam, Melanie's Girl, was a wonderful broodmare. Of her fourteen foals, nine were winners and three won stakes. Pied Princess produced seven winners, but by far her best was Majesty's Prince. Majesty's Prince would have been nearly every mare's best foal.

The strong-willed chestnut raced four seasons, and his unusual blaze became his trademark. He was easy to identify on the track in the mornings, his blazed face bowed to his chest with draw reins.

And he was easy to identify in the afternoon, often heading to the winner's circle. The years, sadly, have dimmed the memory of his remarkable feats. Yet, of Majesty's Prince's twelve wins, five came in grade I stakes. Majesty's Prince won back-to-back runnings of the Man o' War and Sword Dancer, and he won the 1982 and 1984 Rothmans International (running third in 1983).

If he didn't win, he placed in nearly every major turf event: the Lexington; Hill Prince; Lamplighter; Hollywood Turf Cup; Washington, D.C., International; Lawrence Realization; Turf Classic; Bowling Green; and United Nations. When Majesty's Prince retired after his 1984 season, his record was twelve wins in forty-three starts with earnings just over two million dollars.

Mrs. Marsh rattled off the farms where Majesty's Prince had spent his stud career. He first went to Kentucky's North Ridge, then was moved to nearby Spendthrift. He spent years at McMahon of Saratoga Thoroughbreds in New York, then moved to Virginia's Rockburn Farm. It later became Rockburn and Meadowville Farms, but when manager Mark Hardin took ill in 2001, Majesty's Prince was vanned to Virginia's Legacy Farm.

It was at Legacy that I visited the old boy, still instantly recognizable by that handsome blazed face. A misty rain fell as the groom brought him out, and Majesty's Prince moved stiffly. His arthritic limp soon subsided, and he strode out fully, carrying himself with the classic pride of so many His Majesty foals. He was still fiery, keeping the groom on his toes throughout the visit.

Majesty's Prince did not stay at Legacy for long, however. "He was just there a short while, but he was not getting any business," Mrs. Marsh related. "So I brought him home.

"He has a wonderful personality, and he's a character, like all studs become. He's gotten used to all the love and attention he's given."

Majesty's Prince has sired some notable runners, including grade II winners Majesty's Turn and turf specialist Dr. Kiernan. "He's becoming a good broodmare sire," Mrs. Marsh said. "Several of his fillies were stakes winners in their own right, and quite a few are producing stakes winners."

Perhaps that will be Majesty's Prince's legacy at stud.

My Juliet

DK. B/BR. M. 1972-2000 (EST.), BY GALLANT ROMEO—
MY BUPERS, BY BUPERS

*J*ockey Tony Black remembers the day well. A quarter of a century ago, he entered Aqueduct's starting gate aboard My Juliet, a small filly who had most recently won Keystone Racetrack's Doylestown Handicap.

To his immediate left, Angel Cordero Jr. sat astride the Kentucky Derby and Belmont winner Bold Forbes. Bold Forbes had been freshened all summer, and he had recently returned in a devastatingly easy allowance score, with fractions of :22 1/5, :44 4/5, and 1:09 2/5.

"I was a kid, that's all, and I'd been riding for six or seven years," Tony recalled. "Well, Cordero had been saying that it would take a jet airplane to beat Bold Forbes. He was just being Angel…Angel was a great rider, and he was so charismatic.

"So Cordero turns to me in the gate and says something like 'Just don't bother me leaving the gate, kid.' I thought, 'Yeah, right…'

"I've got that attitude then that you get from success. I was having moderate success in Pennsylvania and Maryland. You're young, you're dumb, and you don't know you're overmatched."

Tony continued. "I left the gate with all the confidence in the world — she always gave you that — and she had Bold Forbes everywhere on that track where he didn't want to be. He went to go inside, she was inside; he went to go outside, and she was there. He finally got out, and I drifted him wide, and as we came down the stretch, we drew away.

"Angel came back and he claimed foul, and they took *him* down. Turns out, he'd bumped It's Freezing coming out of the gate.

"When he claimed, I knew I'd pulled out all the stops, and I took my best shots to beat him. But if she ended up being taken down because of it, she wasn't going to win anyway. I guess I just wasn't smart enough to be intimidated."

My Juliet won seventeen stakes races, but that 1976 Vosburgh with Tony Black would forever be her crowning moment. She was named the year's champion sprinter.

The filly's name was appropriate: she was by Gallant Romeo and out of My Bupers.

A $7,500 yearling purchase, My Juliet began her career in a four-furlong maiden race at Fonner Park in April 1974. She missed the win by a head. After several months off, she reeled off five easy scores, including Churchill Downs' Pocahontas Stakes.

The beautiful, dark bay filly with the high-stepping action and a unique white inkblot star and snip was on her way.

My Juliet won stakes across the country, including Pimlico's mile and one-sixteenth Black-Eyed Susan, Belmont's seven-furlong Vagrancy, Aqueduct's one-mile Next Move, Santa Anita's six-furlong Las Flores, and Detroit's Michigan Mile and an Eighth Handicap over males. She carried weight, winning under 128 pounds. She won on fast or sloppy tracks. And she was smart.

She had incredible speed, once running a quarter in :20 3/5 and a half in :43. Yet she could also run a distance. As Tony Black said, "Of course, when you have speed you can do a whole lot, but with her, she was so willing you could rate her; you could put her anywhere. If you can gauge a horse for intelligence, she sure was at the top."

However, the exquisite four-year-old filly suffered a major setback in the midst of her 1976 campaign. In winning the Vagrancy in May under 127 pounds, My Juliet fractured her left front cannon bone. She underwent surgery, and the bone was set with a plate and two pins.

She came back on October 1, and by the end of the month she'd won four straight, including the Vosburgh. My Juliet, racing with a foreleg set with hardware, earned the nickname "The Bionic Filly." The nickname was a natural, during a time when television's Steve Austin and Jaime Sommers — the Bionic Man and Bionic Woman, respectively — were household names.

My Juliet had earned her championship.

She was retired with twenty-four wins in thirty-six starts and earnings of $548,859.

She was one of those rare top race mares who also became a wonderful producer. Her first foal, Bold Julie (by Bold Forbes), was a minor stakes winner. Two of her offspring — Stella Madrid and Tis Juliet — won grade I events. Her last foal, whom she produced in 1998 at age twenty-six, is a winner named Valiant Victory.

Fellow photographer and horsewoman Tina Hines and I visited My Juliet at Pleasant Retreat Farm near Paris, Kentucky, in autumn 2000. Tina had worked with the sweet filly when My Juliet was an unraced two-year-old at Fonner Park. Tina had been instantly smitten, and her love for My Juliet has lasted for more than twenty-five years.

Accompanied by a Spanish-speaking groom, we wandered into the field where My Juliet kept company with both mares and beef cattle. Even from a distance, it was easy to tell she was the oldest horse there. The twenty-eight-year-old mare was dozing in the sun as we walked up.

She was pleased to wake to human company, and as cattle and horses milled about, she moved forward slowly to be rubbed. My Juliet's trusting face hung low, her hind end atrophied. Nearby mares kept a watchful eye on us, protecting her.

It seems that those who ever worked with My Juliet consider her to be the most intelligent, gentle horse they've ever been around. While My Juliet's body was etched with the passing years, her grace and dignity were impossible to miss.

Tina recounted stories of My Juliet's early days, and for perhaps a half-hour we stayed with the mare. Leaving was difficult, but Tina finally kissed her "Juliebug" on the nose, and we walked away. As we turned to take one last look, My Juliet was watching us through beautiful, tired eyes. I knew it would be the last time we would see her.

Several months later, during the winter, My Juliet passed away. She was buried where she died. Her death was not announced for almost a year, but when it was, the racing world mourned.

Tony Black, who teamed with her a quarter century earlier, felt a deep loss.

"I always meant to go see her, and visit with her," he said pensively. "But you know, you get busy, and I just never got down there. I meant to."

However, Keystone Racetrack, long since renamed Philadelphia Park, provides Tony with a wonderful reminder of the beautiful mare.

At one end of the grandstand, in the picnic grove, there's a nice little café. Several names were considered for the café before one was chosen.

"I go by in the morning when I'm galloping a horse or breezing one, and I pass it, and I can always see her name across it — the My Juliet Café. I feel so good that they named it after her. She deserved it.

"She was a real sweetheart."

Near East

GR. G. 1977, BY DAMASCUS—SHENANIGANS, BY NATIVE DANCER

He doesn't look a thing like his legendary half sibling. He is a thick, adorable old gelding with long, white eyelashes and a careful manner. His coat, which appears white from a distance, is a lovely mixture of white and gray, with a smattering of black. He carries his large head low, approaching visitors with the trusting interest of a child's pet. His name is Near East.

His famous half sister, well, she was different from anything we'd ever seen…

She appeared like a shooting star, blazing her way into our hearts through ten wins and eight records. Her body was oversized, but her look was racy and lean. Her near-black coat, high head carriage, and strong will were among her trademarks — all frozen forever in three-year-old form. And, like a shooting star, she departed quickly and completely, leaving us wondering if we'd ever really seen her. Her name was Ruffian.

Owned by Stuart Janney's Locust Hill Farm, their mother, Shenanigans, was a lovely gray mare with kind eyes and white eyelashes. Shenanigans' dam, Bold Irish, was a gift from Janney's mother-in-law, Mrs. Henry Phipps. The mare was a nice gift.

Shenanigans produced only six foals, but each was extraordinary. Each was a winner, and three won stakes. Icecapade came first, in 1969. The gray horse won seven stakes and thirteen of thirty-two starts. He also became a tremendously successful sire.

A lovely Bold Ruler filly followed. Named Laughter, she won four of twelve starts, but her greater destiny was as a broodmare. She produced five stakes winners and a filly named Laughing Look. Laughing Look's three stakes-winning offspring include Coronado's Quest and his half brother, Warning Glance.

Shenanigans' 1971 foal, On to Glory, became a successful Florida sire. The star-crossed Ruffian arrived in 1972. Buckfinder, who followed two years later, was another near-black stakes winner for Locust Hill Farm. Then came the gray colt named Near East.

"Frank Whiteley always said he was one of the most

NEAR EAST (LEFT) AND WARNING GLANCE

rider, the elder Janney occasionally saddled up the old gray horse. "My father rode him, so when Dad died, (Near East) was over there (at Locust Hill). I brought him over to my place," said Stuart.

The farms were close, and the trip a short one. Near East has been at Stuart's for more than a decade now, and the gray gelding spends his time turning white and enjoying his pasture companions. He is the final living foal who spent youthful days kicking up heels and circling the grand old mare Shenanigans.

Near East shares his large field with two South Carolina gaited horses, a New Zealand Thoroughbred named Lincoln, and a family relation, Warning Glance.

talented horses he ever trained," Janney's son Stuart recalled. "But he and my father had a debate about whether to geld him."

Near East was a ridgling, and Whiteley believed the horse's discomfort impeded his racing career. He eventually persuaded Janney to have the horse gelded, but Near East was by then an older racehorse.

"Frank would say that there's no end to what he could have done," Stuart said. As it was, Near East raced for seven years, won fourteen of fifty-four starts, and earned more than $200,000.

Near East was retired to Locust Hill Farm. An expert

Near East is good friends with his great-nephew, Warning Glance, a lovely chestnut gelding. With Near East as a role model, Warning Glance, fourteen years his junior, has calmed down considerably since his racing days. Known for his high spirits, Warning Glance won seven stakes for Stuart and earned $647,863.

Stuart and his family can watch Near East and Warning Glance from their front window. Stuart speaks of them with a combination of sentimentality and common sense. "If they do that much and give you that much fun, that's where they need to be."

They should all be that lucky.

Northern Baby

B. H. 1976, BY NORTHERN DANCER—TWO RINGS,
BY ROUND TABLE

*I*t's easy to overlook Northern Baby, Stone Farm's handsome old stallion whose racing exploits were overseas and whose best runners often jumped fences. After all, Stone Farm's imperious Halo demanded fans' attentions, and Gato Del Sol's heart-warming story inspired countless fans and horsemen.

Yet the twenty-six-year-old Northern Baby grazes in quiet comfort, pensioned after two decades of service. Forgotten by some, and unknown by others, are what a powerful racehorse he was and what a fine stallion he has been. Northern Baby is the all-time leading steeplechase sire.

Northern Baby was a $120,000 yearling from the 1977 Keeneland summer sales. A son of Northern Dancer, he looked like his sire in both size (15.3 as a stallion) and build. He was purchased by the bloodstock agency Horse France and shipped to Europe, where François Boutin trained him for owner Mme. A.M. d'Estainville. Northern Baby was competitive in many of Europe's top races.

His biggest win came in England's group I Champion Stakes, but he also annexed France's group II Prix Dollar and group III Prix de la Cote Normande. Northern Baby placed in races such as the Epsom Derby, Coral-Eclipse Stakes, and Prix Ganay, all group I races. He won or placed in twelve of his seventeen starts, nine of them stakes, and entered stud in Ireland in 1981.

When Northern Baby was returned to America for the 1982 season, his fee at Arthur Hancock III's Stone Farm was $75,000.

Some of Northern Baby's best foals were among his first. Ireland's champion older male Coolcullen was from his first crop, foals of 1982. Thrill Show, champion miler in France, was born in 1983.

That year also brought Northern Baby's first outstanding American runners. Rampage won the grade I Arkansas Derby and earned $374,086. Summer Colony earned more than $400,000, and Moonstruck earned $234,517. The last two excelled in steeplechasing, and an appreciative new audience emerged.

More champions followed for Northern Baby, including Eclipse Award-winning turf female Possibly Perfect ($1,377,634). Northern Baby's offspring impressed on different surfaces at different distances, against both sexes, and around the world. And he continued to sire top steeplechase horses, including Eclipse Award winners Highland Bud and the flashy chestnut Warm Spell.

Fashionable new stallions came to the forefront, however, and Northern Baby's stud fee dwindled. He sired seven grade I winners and a like number of champions. His statistics remained strong, and one crowd in particular noticed — the jump crowd.

Northern Baby was pensioned in 2000, but breeders called Arthur Hancock, inquiring about the aging sire. Arthur reopened Northern Baby's book for 2001 with a stud fee of $5,000, giving breeders one more chance. Four of the mares bred took and three carried their pregnancies, and at the time of this writing Northern Baby has two 2002 arrivals with one more to come.

Now the beautiful old boy, again pensioned, resides proudly in the first stall on the right in Stone Farm's stallion barn. His stall nameplate gleams with the awe-inspiring names of his parents: Northern Dancer— Two Rings. They are older names of quality and timelessness.

Inside the stall is a gentle old stallion whose exploits thrilled European audiences more than two decades ago, and whose offspring wowed countless crowds around the world. Northern Baby is a name of quality and timelessness as well.

Northern Sunset (Ire)

CH. M. 1977, BY NORTHFIELDS—MOSS GREINE, BY BALLYMOSS

*S*he hasn't had a foal since 1999, a Carr de Naskra," groom Robert Warner said, stroking the chestnut mare's thick neck. "What she'll do when she does have a foal, she takes it out over the hill, away from the other mares and foals, and she'll exercise it.

"They get as far away from everybody as they can, and she just circles that baby, just really, really exercises it. I mean, it just stands out like a sore thumb, watching them. She is really remarkable."

Robert has worked with horses for more than fifteen years now, since starting with his stepfather at old Crimson King Farm. He's been with Payson Stud in Lexington for eight years, and his pride in Northern Sunset shines through.

Northern Sunset is easy to be proud of. By the time she was named Kentucky's Broodmare of the Year at age eighteen in 1995, she was the producer of four outstanding racehorses.

In 1982 Virginia Kraft Payson, owner of Payson Stud, paid $105,000 at the Keeneland January horses of all ages sale for a five-year-old Northern Sunset, who was carrying her first foal. The resulting bay colt, named Salem Drive, was also his dam's first top-notch stakes performer.

Salem Drive won thirteen of forty-six starts for Payson, including four graded stakes. He placed seventeen times, earned $1,046,065, and stands at Payson Stud.

Lac Ouimet came next. A strong Pleasant Colony colt, he won six graded stakes, including the Jim Dandy, and earned $817,863. He too stands at Payson, where he consistently sires quality runners. Through April 2002, his average earnings per starter was a very respectable $61,038.

Northern Sunset's best performer was another son of Pleasant Colony, St. Jovite. In 1992 he was named champion three-year-old colt in France and Ireland and Horse of the Year for Europe.

Among his wins were the King George VI and Queen Elizabeth Diamond Stakes and the Irish Derby. In the latter, he shattered the course record by three seconds and won by twelve lengths, the largest winning margin in a European classic race in the twentieth century. He was the highest-weighted horse in the world in 1992, seven pounds higher than U.S. Horse of the Year A.P. Indy.

St. Jovite also entertains the ladies at Payson Stud.

L'Carriere is the most recent top runner Northern Sunset pushed around as a foal. Born in 1991, the New York-bred gelding earned $1,726,469, winning eight races including two Saratoga Cups.

L'Carriere was the crowning touch on Northern Sunset's career as a broodmare. She was awarded her profession's top honor: Broodmare of the Year.

She looks the part. When Robert brought her out in June 2001, the muscles of twenty-four-year-old mare rippled. While not overly tall, she has an exceptionally broad chest, full quarters, and solid legs. Her coat is an enchanting combination of red and golden hues, with white hairs scattered throughout. She is an unusually handsome, sturdy mare.

Robert proudly held the shank. "Anything out of the ordinary she pays attention to. She's just very particular about who fools with her, and if she doesn't like you, you can't catch her.

"A lot of times if she's there and you're talking with someone, chit-chatting and not paying attention, she just takes off like *that*. She leaves. She doesn't care for chit-chat.

"Shy Princess is her best buddy now. She had another mare, Made Glorious, but she died last year," said Robert. "She would have a baby early or Made Glorious would have hers early, but they would always pair up. They were best friends. No matter how far apart they were at the beginning, they were always together by the end.

"Made Glorious is buried here on the farm. She was Mrs. Payson's first stakes winner."

Northern Sunset was bred in 2001 but did not take. Her life now consists of days spent with Shy Princess in Mrs. Payson's "pool paddock," where Mrs. Payson can watch them from poolside.

Robert put Northern Sunset back into her stall, and the chestnut mare turned to watch us leave. The groom said simply, "She's been of great service. She's been a blue hen mare, really.

"She's a class act."

Our Mims

B. M. 1974, BY HERBAGER—SWEET TOOTH, BY ON-AND-ON

heir love story had an unlikely beginning. "She was out in a field with some other mares," Jeanne Mirabito remembered. "We went out into the field, and a co-worker grabbed Whiskey Jade to bring her in. Another horse came up, and I ducked as she tried to kick my head off."

The identity of the mare startled her: Our Mims.

It had been more than two decades since Jeanne, as a seventeen-year-old, had seen news clips of Our Mims. The name of the strapping bay Calumet filly had long since been shuffled from the forefront, but Jeanne still remembered Our Mims' three-year-old championship season.

Sweet Tooth, one of Calumet's most important mares, produced Our Mims in 1974. The next year, Sweet Tooth dropped a chestnut colt named Alydar. Mornings at Saratoga in 1977 were memorable when Our Mims and Alydar stood together before jogging off for their morning exercise.

Our Mims came into her own at three in 1977, winning the Fantasy Stakes, Coaching Club American Oaks, Alabama Stakes, and Delaware Handicap, earning $368,034. She won or placed in thirteen of eighteen starts for Calumet Farm and trainer John Veitch.

Our Mims retired to Calumet in early 1978, and she pro-duced several Calumet foals. None approached their mother in quality on the track, but two carried on the line with bravado. Our Mims' 1983 filly Mimbet produced Breeders' Cup Sprint winner Elmhurst, and her 1988 colt Slewvescent has become a successful sire. Among his offspring are Tout Charmant and Lazy Slusan.

When Calumet Farm dispersed its stock in 1991, Our Mims was sold for $190,000, and she eventually made her way to a quiet Paris, Kentucky, farm.

Jeanne worked at the farm where she first saw Our Mims' flying hooves in 1998. She sometimes took extra jobs to support her own horses, and she met two very special ladies while working in Paris: Our Mims and My Juliet.

Champion sprinter My Juliet was a sweetheart, easy to adore. She was still a producer, and her 1998 arrival was named Valiant Victory.

Our Mims, well, she was a bit more difficult. She was an intelligent mare with a strong will, and she had not produced a foal for years. As with many pensioned and inactive mares, the then twenty-four-year-old spent much time outside. Her days of constant attention were but a memory.

"She wasn't being worshipped," said Jeanne, who immediately began paying homage.

Our Mims shared a paddock with some cows, and Jeanne visited the bay mare daily at lunchtime. Jeanne would eat her own lunch as Our Mims ate the grain Jeanne brought along. Our Mims would then flatten her ears and shuffle away.

Days passed, and soon Jeanne wasn't the only one looking forward to the visits. "I would watch her all during lunch," Jeanne said. "And then, one day, she started watching me, too."

Jeanne brought a tack box into the paddock and began grooming the old champion.

Our Mims relaxed under her touch, although Jeanne was in no hurry to try her luck with the mare's feet. Our Mims' hind end, which she had shown to many top fillies in the seventies, was still very quick. "I'd already been shown the power of her kick," Jeanne said.

As Jeanne picked up the tack box to leave one afternoon, however, Our Mims lifted a hoof. Jeanne took the hint, and picked out the old mare's feet. Those hooves had stood in famed winner's circles, supported foals, and taken Our Mims on countless trips.

Like in numerous children's tales, the kindness paid off. The forgotten champion soon began meeting Jeanne at the gate to receive her adulation.

Jeanne eventually left the job, but kept tabs on both mares. She later approached the owner about buying that sweetheart My Juliet, but as My Juliet was still producing, the offer was turned down. Instead, he offered Our Mims.

Jeanne jumped at the chance. She knew she lacked the resources to give Our Mims a proper "sprucing up." Jeanne contacted Shon Wylie at ReRun, a Thoroughbred placement organization, the motto of which is "recycling racehorses." Shon and Jerry Wylie took Our Mims into their Carlisle, Kentucky, barn in September 1999. They set to work, calling an equine dentist and a vet and providing Our Mims substantial feed. ReRun and another Thoroughbred assistance organization, T.U.R.F., footed the bills.

When Our Mims' story became known, several farms offered to take in the gallant old mare. Calumet Farm offered a home.

SUE ROSENBACH

OUR MIMS (LEFT) AND PLUSH DISH

Three Chimneys' farm manager Dan Rosenburg, who had worked in Calumet's broodmare division, offered as well. But there was no real choice: Our Mims had already chosen.

On February 9, 2000, Our Mims took one more van ride — to Jeanne Mirabito's nearby farm. Friendly posters with brightly painted sunflowers and "Welcome Home, Our Mims!" awaited her.

Outside her stall, the wood is painted with red scalloped edges and blue writing in respect to Calumet. The stall door also bears the colors — and her name. Photos of Our Mims' racing days line the barn walls, and her stall is decorated with the names of races in which she was first or second. The stall sign reads "1977 Filly Champion." Jeanne takes photos of Our Mims' visitors and hangs the prints on a wall.

The old mare has quite a few visitors, and Jeanne keeps in touch with many longtime fans by e-mail. Others have come to know Our Mims through ReRun articles and fund raisers. There are Our Mims greeting cards, and a lovely statue, and a "Bucket Baby" stuffed horse.

Our Mims does her best to repay ReRun. When she was twenty-seven, she appeared in the "war horse in hand mare class" at the 2001 Turfway Park All Thoroughbred Charity Horse Show. Jeanne mentioned with a smile: "She tied for first...Increased her winnings by $125."

Our Mims also appeared in the show's costume class, appropriately decked out in a queen's robe and crown, in Calumet colors of course. Jeanne led her around, humbly dressed in a black and white servant's apron.

Our Mims made an appearance at Keeneland's Breakfast With the Works on October 13, 2001, where she nuzzled up to Calumet's longtime secretary, Margaret Glass. Mrs. Glass' seat, a wheelchair, didn't slow Our Mims down for a minute.

Jeanne's writing background shines in her e-mails. After the Keeneland appearance, she proudly related: "You should have seen her! She absolutely loved it. The old girl was prancing and showing off like she was three again.

"In fact, on the way from the barn to the paddock some-one…said, 'She looks like a winner. What race is she in today?'

"All in all, she made a grand impression. She didn't want to leave. Just like at Turfway, Mims wanted to walk around and check out what was going on…"

Other e-mails tell more stories about the old Calumet champion. "She is sometimes, er, often, is stiff with arthritis but then again there are times when she absolutely flies across the pasture. I have had to limit her time with the young horses because if there is opportunity to run, she generally considers it a race and WILL win, no matter what it costs her old body. I am amazed that she refuses to slow down.

"But if I keep her with slower horses she still gets the benefit of the race at less of a price. I can only pray that she never figures out what I have done."

One note mentions Our Mims' amusing run-in with hornets, and another tells of a poignant tale from early 2001. Our Mims' best friend is Plush Dish, a Thoroughbred mare whom Jeanne refers to as Mims' bodyguard. Our Mims usually wants to be left alone, and Plush Dish protects her.

Our Mims switched roles soon before Plush Dish's 2001 foal was born, watching Plush carefully. When the maiden mare was in labor, each of her contractions was met by a reassuring nicker from Our Mims. When the red-bag birth foal arrived extremely small, Mims was stricken with worry. She watched and listened from her adjacent stall as the fifty-pound filly struggled, unable to rise.

Our Mims wouldn't eat and couldn't be comforted as she waited. The foal, smaller than the Mirabitos' dog, fought hard. She was down on all pasterns, and they put a tiny sweatshirt on her to warm her that read "Girls Are Tough."

The foal got sicker, and Our Mims listened intently to the nearby bottle feedings. The only time Our Mims ate was when the foal drank, and then it was only small bites. The night that things looked bleakest, a miracle happened. Jeanne arrived for the 4 a.m. bottle-feeding, and the filly, standing, greeted her. Jeanne moved forward, and the spirited filly kicked her. Our Mims went back on her feed. The filly was named Stormy Miracle.

* * *

Nearly three decades have passed since Sweet Tooth foaled Our Mims at Calumet Farm. Sweet Tooth was interred in the Calumet cemetery long ago. Sweet Tooth's dam, Plum Cake, is buried there as well. So are Real Delight and Blue Delight, Our Mims' third and fourth dams. Jeanne hopes, when the time comes, Calumet will consider Our Mims' interment. But if not, she will begin her own equine cemetery and name it "Champion Hill."

I asked John Veitch about Our Mims one sunny Saratoga morning in 2001. He mentioned her determination, intelligence, and work ethic. She was fine to work with, very professional. But as I walked away and John got to his car, he stopped. He turned and yelled back, with a slight smile, "But she wasn't a pet!"

At age twenty-eight, Our Mims lives in a barn surrounded with love and reminders of a bygone time. Perhaps she wasn't a pet on the racetrack. But she is now, albeit a strong-willed, aloof one. Our Mims is content.

As Jeanne's thirteen-year-old daughter Cassidy tells her mother: "I groom all the other horses in the barn and they say 'Thank you.' I groom Our Mims, and she says 'You're welcome.' "

Our Native

B. H. 1970-2001, BY EXCLUSIVE NATIVE—OUR JACKIE,
BY CRAFTY ADMIRAL

he old bay stallion struggled to rise in his stall, but his tired legs had finally betrayed him. His groom, Pancho, stayed with him that day and night, as veterinarians assessed the situation. As sunlight filtered into the barn the following morning, Pancho was still with his friend, and still the old horse could not rise.

Around noon Sunday, August 26, 2001, the thirty-one-year-old stallion was euthanized. He was laid to rest in an unmarked grave.

* * *

Twenty-eight years earlier Our Native stood in the Kentucky Derby starting gate, three stalls from a chestnut colt with the blue-and-white Meadow Stable bridle and blinkers. Twice a Prince, a Derby longshot, reared in the gate, and while struggling, struck Our Native. But Our Native still ran courageously that day, finishing third to the Meadow Stable colt named Secretariat. They met again in the Preakness, but the results were the same.

Secretariat has been interred in the Claiborne cemetery for more than a decade now, and countless visitors still regularly leave flowers. In contrast, Our Native lived a very quiet life at Lexington's High Point Farm with his owner, veterinarian Edwin Thomas.

Thomas began his career in Lexington more than a half-century ago, and while it took years of hard work, he certainly made his mark. Among his many accomplishments was the first successful major surgery in the state, and possibly the country, to treat twisted intestines. It was such news-making surgery that a *Blood-Horse* article chronicled Thomas' notes.

Nowadays, Thomas has a hitch in his stride. He moves with a cane and supervises farm activities from his car. He was the owner of Our Native, but he and Our Native were more than just owner and horse. Thomas' pride in his bay stallion shines through in his words. "I have bred and raised an Eclipse Award winner (Rockhill Native) with a partner, but I consider Our Native to be the best horse that I have ever bred and raised due to his courage,

demeanor, soundness, and his entire life performances."

When seeking a stallion in 1969 for his best broodmare, the Crafty Admiral mare Our Jackie, Thomas chose freshman sire Exclusive Native due to his low stud fee and his sire line. Thomas was a devoted Polynesian fan, and unable to afford breeding to Native Dancer, he searched for others from that same line. Polynesian was a sound horse who raced fifty-eight times. He had good bone and a tendency to produce strong offspring. As a veterinarian, Thomas had seen their durability firsthand. When Exclusive Native entered stud for a very reasonable $1,500, Thomas had his chance.

The match was a tremendous success. When the year-ling Our Native went through Keeneland's ring in September 1971, he topped the sales.

Thomas was not the only person to appreciate the strength of Exclusive Native when combined with Crafty Admiral. Four months after Our Native was a sales-topper, Louis Wolfson bought a Crafty Admiral mare at the 1972 Keeneland January sale for $18,000.

In 1974, the year after Our Native's successful three-year-old season, Wolfson bred his mare to Exclusive Native. The mare's name was Won't Tell You, and her 1975 colt was named Affirmed.

As the 1973 spring classics approached, Thomas bought back into Our Native because, as he said, "Of course, I've got great dreams." His biggest dream, that of winning the Kentucky Derby, did not materialize. But Our Native won two grade I races, the Flamingo Stakes and Monmouth Invitational, and earned $426,969.

In 1977, when Our Native was still a young stallion, Thomas and his wife, Mary Elizabeth, bought High Point Farm with a partner. Rockhill Native was born that year, and he was destined to become, arguably, Our Native's most famous runner. In 1979, he was champion two-year-old, earning $267,112.

Mary Elizabeth passed away in 1985. She missed the years when Our Native was a successful broodmare sire, as well as the years of his pensioning. But Thomas continued, and Our Native's groom took special care of the stallion.

Pancho Camache has worked with Thomas for almost a quarter century now, taking care of Our Native with pride and respect. Our Native trusted Pancho, and Pancho trusted Our Native. Our Native would tell Pancho what he wanted, and if Pancho could accommodate him, he certainly would.

When I last visited in May 2001, Our Native looked excellent at age thirty-one. He grazed in a paddock in front of the stallion barn, and an old teaser in an adjacent paddock kept him company. Our Native's mane was long and his face still handsome. His body looked full, and his back had barely any sway. Only a few white hairs were visible along his temples. Other than his front legs, he appeared a much younger stallion.

In the past year and a half, however, Our Native's right front foot had rotated, and it

aimed noticeably inward. Not only had it lost its flexibility, but it also put the stallion at risk if he moved quickly. Like his owner, Our Native moved with a hitch in his stride, but Our Native's was more pronounced.

Still, Our Native was content, and he found me interesting, as long as Pancho stood nearby. He looked from me to Pancho and then back to me, seeking assurance that I was an acceptable intruder. After all, he received only a dozen or so visitors a year. Pancho moved to the old

OUR NATIVE AT AGE TWENTY-EIGHT

bay and rubbed him a minute, and Our Native relaxed.

Three months after my visit, those old legs that were causing him so much trouble finally gave out. Pancho could not help him, nor could Thomas or the additional veterinarian who was summoned. It was time to let Our Native go. In the stud barn named the Our Native Barn, the old horse breathed his last.

Not far away, the Our Jackie Barn houses broodmares, and on a nearby hill, Our Jackie is buried. Her daughter Salud lies in another plot near her. Neither plot is marked.

Our Native's grave is unmarked as well, and that is how Thomas wants it. Our Native was buried "right around the midst of the activity," so he could still be a part of the farm he helped to create. For a few years the mound will be visible, Thomas said, but in time it will blend in. "I'm a self-effacing individual. I'm truly made that way." He does not need a marker to remember Our Native.

Thomas' days are less full now, with one less paddock to visit. But he takes comfort in knowing that his friend of three decades did not suffer long. "He was like me, getting around.

"He didn't walk exactly straight, but he sure seemed to enjoy life."

OUR NATIVE WITH PANCHO CAMACHE

Pam the Ruler

B. M. 1973-2001, BY STEVWARD—JIM N' PAM, BY FAIR RULER

She never did become a household name, although the dreams of her breeders were probably no different from the dreams of others. But Pam the Ruler did buck the odds to become a winner, on the tough New York circuit at that. She was one of those names in the program that you always looked at a second time. In forty-two starts over four years, Pam the Ruler returned to the winner's circle on six occasions.

As a racehorse she was difficult to work with, a headstrong mare who warranted the backstretch stories told about her. She couldn't be taken to the track or led to the post by ponies, as she would inevitably try to savage them. She had to have things her own way or she was very unhappy; and when she was unhappy, everyone around her was unhappy. But when she raced she was tough, winning both at Belmont Park and Aqueduct.

Pam the Ruler was retired and produced several foals for her owner, including a Triocala colt, later named Tri State Ruler. Not long after Tri State Ruler's arrival, Pam got a new owner named Sandy Zaconick. She became Sandy's property and companion, and spent the rest of her days in Sandy's care.

Pam subsequently had two more foals — a colt by Conte Grande and a dark bay Blues Alley filly, named Pam's Blue Sky.

The colt was so large and difficult that he was gelded, but he still didn't reach the races. Named Rip Finch, he trained at Belmont and proudly took the place of his mama by providing backstretch personnel with plenty of stories. Eventually, due to Rip Finch's chronic leg problems, Sandy brought the seventeen-hand gelding back to her farm in upstate New York.

Pam's Blue Sky, a small, sweet filly, finally reached the races at Finger Lakes in western New York at the age of four. She made one start — the only start in which Sandy Zaconick's silks ever appeared — and ran last, technically

a DNF, or "did not finish." Sandy, ever proud of the filly with a chronically sore shoulder, brought her home.

Pam spent the rest of her days in the company of her two last foals, and she had a good life. She was a happy mare, full of fire and personality right to the end. When the trio was taken trail riding, Pam was always the leader. When it came time for Sandy to brush them, Pam provided the most pinned ears, tail swishes, and nips. She watched her gelding and reprimanded him when he acted too foolish, and she protected her filly when the gelding threatened.

But Pam's failing eyesight and health problems finally became insurmountable, and Sandy was forced to make the choice that all loving owners dread. In the late afternoon of April 27, 2001, Pam stood in her stall. She had just finished her evening feed. Several human friends, including me, were providing her with molasses-coated alfalfa squares and orange slices,

which she happily accepted. Sandy chose a final resting spot where Pam would have an eternal view of the pond she loved, the barn in which her children resided, and the kitchen window from which Sandy could always keep an eye on her.

Pam's final moments were happy ones. The first shoots of spring grass were rich under her tired feet as she was led outside. Her friends Rip and Sky called to her from their stalls, wishing to join her in the beauty of the afternoon. The taste of a fresh golden delicious apple was sweet on her tongue, and loving hands stroked her neck as she watched the afternoon sun glow through clouded eyes and freshly budding trees. It was a day of daffodils and warm breezes, and of spring's cyclical symphony of life renewing itself.

At 5:30 p.m., Pam the Ruler, good friend and hater of ponies, quietly left this life.

Pleasant Colony

DK. B/BR. H. 1978, BY HIS MAJESTY—SUN COLONY,
BY SUNRISE FLIGHT

*P*leasant Colony ambles from the open stall into the paddock yard, his large ears propped forward atop his long, distinctive face. A homely old man, he moves with purpose and grace toward his destination, a large goat snuffing the grass. When he reaches him, Pleasant Colony drops his head for a better look.

Satisfied that the goat is pretty much as he left it, Pleasant Colony lifts his head and hones in on a stallion across the road. Slavic is grazing where he left him, too, and Pleasant Colony relaxes.

The paddock is large and comfortable, five acres of sloping hills with old split-rail fences and large trees everywhere. It is spring, and dogwoods burst with pinks and whites. The grass is deep, richly green but not manicured, and only the sound of birds breaks the stillness. It is the heart of Virginia horse country at one of the oldest Thoroughbred farms in the state, and Pleasant Colony feels at home.

He should. It's only twenty-eight miles from where the Kentucky Derby winner was born, twenty-four years ago.

Kentucky Derby winners often do not live up to their expectations at stud, but Pleasant Colony was an emphat-ic exception. Champion three-year-old in 1981 after winning the Kentucky Derby and Preakness, Pleasant Colony entered stud at his owner's Buckland Farm, on Lexington's Paris Pike.

It was there in 1984 that I first formally met the big horse. The groom, Nils LaCour, was very careful with his charge. Pleasant Colony wasn't exactly social. In fact, he was rather shy around people. He didn't dislike them, and he certainly wasn't tough, but he'd rather be left alone in his quiet routine. Nils was a soft-spoken boy with a gentle hand and a world of respect for the 16.3-hand dark bay.

When he set Pleasant Colony loose in the paddock, the horse wheeled and galloped off heavily, the sound of his hooves memorable on the damp earth. After much coaxing, Pleasant Colony returned for a moment and stuck his

head over the fence. He decided we had nothing to offer him and wandered off to graze in a far corner.

In 1984 Pleasant Colony's first foals were yearlings, and there was no way to know whether he'd be a successful stallion. His first crop consisted of twenty-seven foals, and while only five won at age two, six eventually won stakes. His leading first-crop earner was multiple stakes winner Lac Ouimet, who earned $817,863. Pleasant Colony was on his way.

Pleasant Colony was not known as a sire of two-year-olds, but his durable offspring won at all ages on either track surface. Pleasant Stage won the Breeders' Cup Juvenile Fillies and was champion two-year-old filly, while Pleasant Tap earned more than $2.7 million and was named champion older horse at the age of five. St. Jovite was champion two-year-old in Ireland, champion three-year-old colt in both Ireland and France, and was named European Horse of the Year.

Sir Beaufort, Shared Interest, Pleasant Variety, Colonial Waters, Behrens, Roanoke, and Cherokee Colony won grade I races for Pleasant Colony, and most of them shared something else with their sire as well. Almost all were oversized, not overly handsome horses, with strong action and stamina.

Colonial Affair was perhaps Pleasant Colony's most famous runner. When the big colt splashed under the wire in the rainy 1993 Belmont Stakes, jockey Julie Krone became the first female rider to win a Triple Crown race. They assumed their place in the history books.

After retiring in late 1981, Pleasant Colony lived contentedly at Buckland Farm. His son Pleasant Tap joined him upon his retirement. But in 1997 Buckland's owner Thomas Mellon Evans passed away, and both Pleasant Colony and Pleasant Tap were moved to beautiful Lane's End Farm in nearby Versailles.

In January 2000, a press release from Lane's End indicated that Pleasant Colony was suffering the effects of age and his breeding future was in question. Lane's End was forced to make a difficult decision. The lead story of *The Blood-Horse*'s Stud News on April 15, 2000, read: "Pleasant Colony Pensioned."

Three weeks later, *The Blood-Horse* featured another headline: "Pleasant Colony Makes New Home at the Horse Park." On April 27 the big stallion arrived at the Kentucky Horse Park, presumably to live out his days.

The problem that had recently plagued Pleasant Colony, an inability to retract his penis, continued. He was noticeably underweight, and the near-constant activity at the park upset the shy stallion. Pleasant Colony paced his fence line when horses passed, and the horse-drawn carriages that circled the park every fifteen minutes kept him on edge.

Pleasant Colony was moved again, this time to Blue Ridge Farm near Upperville, Virginia. On May 25, 2000, he arrived at the farm, which was recommended by one of Thomas Evans' sons. It neighbors the famed Rokeby Stables, and both farms are beautiful reflections of an old-fashioned lifestyle and grace.

The area is like a scene from an old hunting print in which stone fences are enveloped by undergrowth and dreams were realized and lost long ago. Blue Ridge Farm is an old F.B. Voss painting, a Munnings, a Vaughn Flannery — subtle pastels and occasionally brilliant tones wrapped in timeless beauty, with ageless brush strokes.

There, on that canvas, a moving scene is played out. A large hill-crested paddock is rich with the dark greens of spring, and shadows dance seemingly everywhere. A goat stands quietly to the side, and an old open-stalled barn beckons. In the distance, paddocks and stallions with lowered heads provide the backdrop.

There, surrounded by budding dogwoods and quiet friends, an elegant, shy stallion stands proud. His plain head is raised high, his large ears forward, his lean body strong. A dash of white is streaked behind his temples, and his dark coat shines with indistinguishable reflections and accomplishments.

There, he is beautiful.

Proud Birdie

B. H. 1973, BY PROUD CLARION—BERNIE BIRD, BY BOLERO

I went to Marablue Farm twice before I was satisfied with my portrait of Proud Birdie. I felt I owed it to the farm to "get it right" and to represent Proud Birdie as the noble, strong stallion he is.

Few farms mention pensioned stallions in their annual stallion brochures and promotions. Marablue, however, is a proud exception. Pages of photographs and text, as well as a web page, are devoted to its favorite stallion, whom owner Doug Henderson refers to as "The Grand Old Man."

The web site entry begins: "Marablue Farm will forever be linked with Proud Birdie. Although the stallion…is officially retired from the breeding shed, he is still an integral part of the farm where he began his stallion career two decades ago."

Doug Henderson purchased Proud Birdie at the 1975 Ocala Breeders' Sales Company two-year-olds in training sale, and he was richly rewarded. Proud Birdie won the grade II Everglades Stakes and the Bahamas Stakes and Cabrillo and Christmas Day handicaps. He ran second in the Fountain of Youth and third in the Florida Derby, but his most impressive win was over a mud-splattered field in the grade I Marlboro Cup in 1977.

Retired to stud at Marablue Farm near Ocala, Florida, Proud Birdie started well and quickly became a popular sire. He sired grade I winner Birdonthewire, grade II winner Score a Birdie, and grade III winners Hidden Tomahawk, Birdie's Legend, Georgia Bird Dog, and Star's Proud Penny. His Huizcazda was a multiple group I winner and champion older male in Mexico, and Algodonal won a group I race in Venezuela.

When I visited Proud Birdie in March of 2000, he was living the life of a sassy old pensioner. He was in no mood to cooperate. The groom tried his best, but Proud Birdie simply refused to find us interesting. His look was one of intelligent disinterest, the "I've seen it before" attitude often prevalent in horses of class. I took several photos, but knew that they were merely "for the record." For the moment, Proud Birdie had defeated me.

When I visited a year later, Proud Birdie was brought

out again. He again looked grand, the groom obviously having spent time cleaning the stallion. His white points shone brightly against his black legs, and his coat was a shiny, brilliant blood bay. His legs were no longer straight, as time had begun playing with his knees, but he looked remarkable for twenty-eight.

Again, the self-proclaimed King of Marablue scoffed at me, and I wondered how in the world the brochure photos showed a stallion with ears tilted forward.

Just as I was losing hope, Proud Birdie decided to indulge me. He stood quietly for several seconds, viewing me with a lofty air, obviously humored by my simple attempts at intriguing him. He was polite enough, just once, to aim his large ears forward toward my lens.

Raise a Man

CH. H. 1977, BY RAISE A NATIVE—DELTA SAL,
BY DELTA JUDGE

Milfer Farm near Unadilla, New York, is not where a person might envision top Thoroughbred stallions. The state's Taconic Valley and Saratoga region are known for their Thoroughbred horse farms. But Milfer Farm, in a less populated part of the state, consists of six hundred acres of rolling hills, brisk breezes, and brilliant displays of fall foliage. There is no other farm in the area, and possibly the state, with a stronger stallion roster.

When Spectacular Bid moved to Milfer in 1991, it was a tremendous coup for the state, not simply for his breeding potential but also his sheer star status. In the decade since, Jon and Deb Davis have brought several other major stallions from the Bluegrass State to the Empire State, including Cure the Blues, Take Me Out, and, in 2001, Phone Trick.

Farm manager Joel Reach estimated that two hundred fans visit annually to see Spectacular Bid, and many stop to peek at Phone Trick or Take Me Out. Far fewer notice an angular, high-headed chestnut in the back stall, and those who do often don't remember what a topnotch racehorse he was. But Raise a Man was a strong force in West Coast racing two decades ago, even gracing a cover of *The Blood-Horse* in 1980 when he defeated The Carpenter in the grade II San Felipe.

The accompanying article began, "This is the time of the year when the good 3-year-olds begin to put in an appearance, and one of the best—make that, the very best—that has shown so far in California is Northwest Farm's Raise a Man.

"It is a name to remember, because Raise a Man is a stylish-looking colt, a colt of obvious quality that almost certainly will be heard from in the spring classics."

While Raise a Man didn't quite live up to those words, he won three other major stakes races in his two-year campaign: the grade II Malibu, the grade III San Vicente Stakes, and the Phoenix Gold Cup.

Upon his retirement, Raise a Man began his stud career at Gainesway Farm in Kentucky. He had solid bloodlines, a son of Raise a Native and the stakes-winning mare Delta Sal, a Man o' War descendant who raced fifty-four times.

In 1984, when Raise a Man's first foals were yearlings, his stud fee was $22,500. Yet as the years went by and Raise a Man did not reproduce himself, his opportunities waned and he was moved to New York. From Milfer, he was even shuttled to South Africa for the 1990 and 1991 seasons, where he was very popular with breeders.

Raise a Man has been a good sire, the type often referred to as "useful," although his name has not yet appeared in any marquee horses' pedigrees. His top runners include two-time South African champion older mare Splendid Ann, South African champion sprinter Whistling Dixie, grade II winner Raise a Stanza, South African grade II winner High Raiser, and grade III winner Highland Crystal.

Perhaps his most popular American runner was a rangy colt named Vinnie the Viper, who earned $516,821 in his New York-based career, winning the grade III Sport Page, Gravesend, Paumonok, and Sporting Plate handicaps.

Raise a Man is still an active stallion, although few people call for breeding contracts, and his name has quietly slipped from the stallion registers. Although he has sired twenty-four stakes winners, few people visit Milfer to view this classy stallion.

Yet every day, Raise a Man is led to his paddock before Spectacular Bid or Take Me Out. The kind-hearted stallion has shown his age in recent years, and his hocks are sometimes unsteady as he walks on his tired hind legs.

But he still strides out as proudly and professionally as any stallion. While his body may be tired, his aged eyes are brilliant and his head still high.

Raja Baba

B. H. 1968, BY BOLD RULER—MISSY BABA, BY MY BABU

*E*very day at Hermitage Farm, Raja Baba is quietly led from the stallion barn to his paddock. He has walked that familiar path for decades now, although his stride is no longer certain and he moves quite slowly. Stallions in adjacent paddocks — names from Barbizon to Party Manners — have come and gone; and yet Raja Baba remains, a living testament to his famous sire.

Raja Baba has been a pensioner for fifteen years, the same amount of time he spent as an active stallion. When young, the rich bay had several small white spots scattered along his coat. Now his spots are much more plentiful, the hollows above his eyes have deepened, and white splashes seem to have been painted haphazardly across his body. Where he once had a star, his face is streaked with white and the star is no longer distinguishable. And while he is still quite alert, his hearing does not seem to be what it once was.

Raja Baba is in remarkable shape for age thirty-four. A 1981 *Blood-Horse* magazine article mentions that while Raja Baba is "correct in front and back, he is slightly over at the knee." Nowadays, the word "slight" no longer applies. Harriet Jones, widow of former Hermitage Farm owner Warner L. Jones, visiting the pensioner in 2000, wrote that while his health is very good, Raja Baba suffers from "old legs."

Few people knew Raja Baba was still alive when, at thirty-two, he was featured on a *Blood-Horse* cover in December 2000. After all, he made his first appearance in a *Blood-Horse* advertisement after winning a minor two-year-old stakes in 1970. It is probable that he is the oldest living son of Bold Ruler, as few horses live well into their fourth decade.

Raja Baba didn't hit it big at the track, although he won the Francis Scott Key Stakes and Alligator and Delaware Valley handicaps for the Michael G. Phipps family; and even as a full-grown stallion he stood only 15.3 hands. But it was as a sire that the old adage "blood will tell" bore

Lassie Dear and three other stakes winners. Lassie Dear became a grand broodmare herself, producing Weekend Surprise, the dam of A.P. Indy; Honor Grades; and Summer Squall.

When Raja Baba retired to stud with a fair record of seven wins in forty-one starts, he was well received due to his female line and fashionable sire. And when his first crop included multiple graded stakes winner Royal Ski, Raja Baba was on his way to the top. While Raja Baba's initial stud fee was $2,500, by the height of his stud career a share was reportedly sold for $380,000.

Raja Baba was America's leading sire and leading juvenile sire in 1980, in a year when he had no major classic horse or champion. He did have one September weekend that year when three of his offspring — Raja's Delight, Well Decorated, and Sweet Revenge —- won major stakes in successive days, but they were just icing on the cake. Raja Baba already led both stallion lists at that point.

His offspring include two Breeders' Cup winners, Sacahuista and Is It True. In 1987, however, the year of

true for this son of Bold Ruler. His dam, Missy Baba, produced fourteen foals, including twelve winners and six stakes winners.

Among Missy Baba's offspring were successful racehorse and sire Sauce Boat, and Gay Missile, the dam of

Sacahuista's Distaff win and a year before Is It True's Juvenile, Raja Baba unfortunately had to be pensioned at age nineteen due to a fertility problem.

In 1980 Warner Jones, then-master of Hermitage Farm, described Raja Baba as "…one of the kindest horses I've ever been around. My grandchildren can go out and catch him in his paddock…" Raja Baba still enjoys company in his paddock and watches with wide, proud eyes when visitors approach.

Nowadays, he keeps company with the young stallion Pembroke. Pembroke's coat glow, and he occasionally breaks out into youthful displays of speed in his paddock.

In a paddock near his, a small bay stallion stands quietly with crooked legs and an aged face. On occasion he himself jogs a short distance, his flowing forelock streaked with white. But, more often, he just watches the daily routine being played out before him.

A visitor to the Hermitage Farm stallion barn cannot help but stop at his beautiful wooden stall door and look with great respect at the two words engraved on the attached metal plate: RAJA BABA.

It is a giant name for such a small, kind old horse.

Rockhill Native

CH. G. 1977, BY OUR NATIVE—BEANERY, BY CAVAN

*I*t's been more than two decades since he won an Eclipse Award, but Rockhill Native can still break into an impressive gallop on occasion. He resides quietly not far from Keeneland Racecourse, the site of one of his most impressive wins.

Retired trainer Herb Stevens still remembers Rockhill Native's temperamental attitude. "He loved people, but I'll tell you one thing, if you didn't watch him, he'd bite you. He was a nice horse — he did love people, but he would bite, and he kicked his groom a couple of times."

Memories come easily with a horse of quality, and Mr. Stevens continued. "His owners were Mr. and Mrs. (H.A.) Oak, and they'd visit the barn. Mrs. Oak had a pink cloth-coat that she wore, and she was there playing with him, and he bit her. From then on, every time she came by the barn, she wore that coat so he could bite on it. She took the buttons off it, though, so he wouldn't bite them."

Rockhill Native earned enough to keep Mrs. Oak in coats. The gelding launched his career at Churchill Downs, where he won three straight races, including the Jefferson Cup. He moved on to Monmouth, finishing second in the Tyro, then winning the Sapling by three lengths. The Hopeful at Saratoga was his easiest yet, as he won by six and a half lengths, but he was disqualified for interference and placed sixth.

He came back to win the Futurity and Cowdin at Belmont Park, then finished second in the Champagne to Joanie's Chief. With seven first-place finishes in nine starts, he was voted the Eclipse Award champion two-year-old colt or gelding.

Rockhill Native was a slim horse with fine features, a brilliant final kick, and a wonderful nickname: Rocky. Times such as :58 2/5 for five furlongs, 1:03 for five and a half, and 1:22 for seven were impressive in any company. In addition, the chestnut gelding was by the popular Our Native. Fans adored Rocky.

Returning at three, Rockhill Native won four of eight starts, including the Blue Grass Stakes, en route to the Triple Crown. In the Kentucky Derby he was favored at 2.10-1, made a strong showing early, but eventually weakened to finish fifth. It was his only actual off-the-board finish. He ran next in the Belmont Stakes but by then was 12.80-1. Rocky finished a respectable third to Temperence Hill and Genuine Risk, just three and a half lengths behind the winner.

It was Rockhill Native's final start. He bowed a tendon, and the popular gelding was retired to Herb Stevens' Kentucky farm with an official record of ten wins, two seconds, and three thirds in seventeen starts, and earnings of $465,122.

Rockhill Native lived in comfort with Stevens for about a decade. But when the farm was sold in 1991, Rockhill Native was moved. When the horse didn't seem happy at his new home, a friend offered to keep the Eclipse Award winner, and Stevens readily agreed.

Rocky moved one more time in the early 1990s, and a retired pony of trainer Elliott Walden's named Hubie joined him several years later. Hubie and Rockhill Native quickly became best buddies, and they spend their days wandering the expansive field together. On occasion Hubie wanders too far away as Rockhill Native grazes, and when the chestnut gelding notices, he whinnies and gallops to his companion. The two often pass the time with their curious heads propped over the fence boards watching cars come and go.

"I drive by every so often and holler at him," Stevens said fondly of his old champion. "Rocky's a little bossy with (Hubie) every so often, but that's all right. Rocky's got a nice home."

ROCKHILL NATIVE (LEFT) WITH HIS FRIEND HUBIE

Sans Supplement

GR. M. 1974, BY GREY DAWN II—TOUT COMPRIS, BY TANTIEME

*W*hen the groom entered the barn to bring out Sans Supplement, the twenty-seven-year-old mare was certain that we were the blacksmith, dentist, and vet combined. She tried her best to keep her large, gray hind end between the groom's shank and her halter. After several attempts, with Sans Supplement craftily moving slowly but certainly, another groom entered the stall. With only one hind end and two grooms, she was cornered. She submitted grudgingly.

Sans Supplement had reason to worry about us. She primarily lives outdoors, as many older pensioners do. Time spent in her stall, especially combined with fussing, cleaning, and primping, just wasn't natural to her.

Neither was standing politely for her portrait. We tried for perhaps fifteen minutes as she danced and fretted, and the groom decided being closer to her equine friends might help. He moved her near her paddock, but that was not the answer. She couldn't wait to join them, and a good friend named Approver stretched her long, bay neck over the fence. Sans Supplement nosed back, lamenting how miserable her day had recently turned.

I couldn't help but smile when a friend sent excerpts from a *Blood-Horse* article about Sans Supplement's biggest victory, the 1976 Alcibiades at Keeneland. Her breeder/trainer/owner Don McKellar told Ed Bowen: "Sans Supplement is by Grey Dawn II, and Grey Dawn II's horses tend to be hard to train. It took us three weeks before she would go into the starting gate, but Tony just took his time, kept talking to her, and she is no problem now."

Tony was exercise rider Tony Garcia, and the trainer credited both him and groom Louis Twyne for her success. Sans Supplement was such a fiery little lass that, on occasion, she needed to be tranquilized for the standard practice of applying hind shoes. With such a filly, the groom and exercise rider were invaluable.

McKellar wasn't happy with her progress early in her

three-year-old season. He sent her to his farm near Lake Forest, Illinois, where she promptly broke through her small paddock's plank-board fencing. She was uninjured, but McKellar placed two Black Angus calves in the paddock with her for company.

Sans Supplement won four of her twenty-two starts and earned $134,224, but two of her wins were major. In addition to the grade II Alcibiades, she won the Laurance Armour Handicap as a three-year-old.

McKellar didn't breed Tout Compris to Grey Dawn II because of the stallion's attitude. "The mare, Tout

Compris, is a small mare, and we went to a larger sire." It worked, as Sans Supplement is large with very strong bone and has a look warmblood breeders would envy. The names of mother and daughter are cleverly connected. On French menus *tout compris* means everything included; *sans supplement* means, generally, "at no charge."

Since retirement, Sans Supplement has created a strong produce page as well. Of her twelve foals, eleven became winners. One was Minamino Elegance, a graded stakes-placed Japanese runner. Another, a colt by Distinctive Pro named Big Stanley, won nine of twenty starts including the grade II Tropical Park Derby and earned nearly $400,000. Another was a champion.

Itsallgreektome, her seventh foal, became her best known. The popular gray gelding raced five years, winning two grade Is, eight of his twenty-nine starts, and earning $1,994,618. However, he is perhaps best remembered for close second-place finishes in the 1990 Breeders' Cup Mile and the 1991 Breeders' Cup Turf. Itsallgreektome was named champion turf horse in 1990. A name like his is tough to forget.

Sans Supplement produced her last foal in 1995 and has since been pensioned at Howard and Susan Kaskel's idyllic Sugar Maple Farm in New York. That final foal, a gray filly named Cryptocari, resides in a nearby paddock.

Sans Supplement has several melanomas as many older grays do, but she seems quite comfortable. She shares a paddock with three other mares, standing out due to her brilliant gray-flecked coat and strong build.

Thankfully, for her and those around her, she no longer wears hind shoes.

Seattle Slew

DK. B/BR. H. 1974-2002, BY BOLD REASONING—MY CHARMER,
BY POKER

There is only one living Triple Crown winner: Seattle Slew. Since Sir Barton swept through the Kentucky Derby, Preakness, and Belmont Stakes back in 1919, there has always been at least one. Gallant Fox came next, then Omaha, War Admiral, Whirlaway, Count Fleet, Assault, and Citation. In the 1970s, Secretariat, Seattle Slew, and Affirmed joined the heralded ranks.

For more than eighty years, a Triple Crown winner has grazed in a field somewhere, providing fans a chance to remember and to dream anew.

Once, there was a close call. In the twenty-five years between Citation's and Secretariat's Triple Crowns, previous Triple Crown champions died one by one. In 1970, when Citation died at age twenty-five, only Count Fleet remained.

When Secretariat finally won the coveted honor in 1973, Count Fleet was a swaybacked, thin old pensioner. Later that year, as if he had waited for the torch to be passed, Count Fleet died at the very advanced age of thirty-three.

There have been eleven Triple Crown winners, but Seattle Slew blazed through the 1977 Triple Crown in an unprecedented way: undefeated. After winning the Belmont Stakes, he had a perfect nine-for-nine record.

Seattle Slew's bloodlines, while good, were not extraordinary, but the competitive fire within him was. He won fourteen of seventeen starts, earning $1,208,726. He was favored in each of his starts except one, the 1978 Marlboro Cup, which featured the first-ever meeting of Triple Crown winners. Affirmed was favored, but the elder Seattle Slew easily prevailed, winning by three lengths. In *The Blood-Horse*'s ranking of the top one hundred horses of the twentieth century, Seattle Slew ranked number nine, the highest of any living Thoroughbred.

Though the Bold Reasoning yearling sold for $17,500 in 1975, one share in the famed stallion sold in 1984 for three million dollars.

Seattle Slew has been a remarkable sire, and the list of his important offspring is a long one. Among his more than one hundred stakes winners are champions Swale, Digression, Capote, Surfside, Slew o' Gold, and Landaluce, and Horse of the Year and leading sire A.P. Indy.

Interestingly, Slew is genetically unable to sire a chestnut horse, and a strong preponderance of his foals are either bay or dark bay.

His sons have already sired such horses as Golden Missile, Stephen Got Even, Thirty Six Red, and Gorgeous, and as a broodmare sire, he is already represented by many stakes winners, including Golden Attraction, Escena, and Cigar.

* * *

Nearly every racing fan knows the name Will Harbut, the groom of the mythic Man o' War. Will was quite a showman with "the mostest hoss that ever was," regaling audiences with stories of his grand red stallion for some sixteen years.

There is little showman in Tom Wade, although he has been showing Seattle Slew to tourists and breeders for twenty years now. His workday begins and ends with the venerable Seattle Slew. His life and that of his horse are forever linked.

Tom began working with Seattle Slew at Spendthrift Farm in 1982, not long before that farm's well-recorded fall from grace. When Seattle Slew was moved to Three

Chimneys Farm in 1985, Tom's boss at Spendthrift told him to put the horse onto the trailer. Tom did, but instead of leaving Seattle Slew he stayed with the horse, and the duo moved to Three Chimneys together.

In the main stallion barn, Seattle Slew reigned supreme among the stallions, including two of his own offspring, Capote and Slew o' Gold. As the years passed, the grand stallion became revered as his sons and daughters not only won but also began producing their own successful offspring. Three Chimneys averaged between eight thousand and ten thousand visitors a year, the vast majority asking to see Seattle Slew. Tom showed his famous stallion daily, quietly answering questions, fixing the stallion's sun-bleached forelock and allowing visitors to be photographed next to the icon.

Every evening, weather permitting, Tom led Seattle Slew to his paddock and every morning brought him back in. The near-black stallion was tacked up and, around 7 a.m., was the first to exercise. Almost every Three Chimneys stallion is ridden daily, an unusual practice for a major farm. When Slew was younger, he was galloped a mile or more, but as he reached the quarter-century mark, the routine varied. The rider would start him at a jog, and if he sensed Seattle Slew was feeling strong, he would allow the stallion to gallop.

But Seattle Slew's routine was forever changed in January 2000 when he suffered a sudden lack of coordination. The twenty-six-year-old walked with great difficulty, his hind end unstable and his body twisted. Tom was forced to make a difficult call to Mickey and Karen Taylor, Slew's majority owners, and they immediately flew to Kentucky. They were heartbroken at the sight of their grand stallion in such discomfort. Mickey Taylor noted later: "He

was bent over to the right and walking like a crab — almost sideways."

Bone scans determined that Seattle Slew was suffering from changes in his vertebrae due to arthritis, putting pressure on the spinal cord. At first, anti-inflammatory injections alleviated the pain and Seattle Slew bred seventeen mares. Seven of the first nine conceived, but the next eight came up empty. And Seattle Slew was still uncomfortable.

The stallion was shipped to Rood & Riddle, a nearby equine hospital, where two vertebrae were fused with a titanium device called the Bagby Basket. The surgery was a success, and Seattle Slew returned to Three Chimneys. In press releases, farm manager Dan Rosenberg stated that Slew's recovery and comfort were their only concern and that the champion's breeding future was uncertain.

Through it all, Tom Wade was there.

Seattle Slew moved into a smaller barn away from the

SEATTLE SLEW WITH TOM WADE

busy main stallion barn. Tom lived at Three Chimneys for a while, sleeping in a small apartment or tack room to make sure his friend's every need was met.

Seattle Slew recovered, and his progress was videotaped and monitored. Three times daily he was walked between a quarter- and half-mile with a groom on each side. Tom accompanied his charge many times, and sometimes Mickey Taylor himself lent a hand. Behind the barn, a thirty-foot small round paddock provided Slew a chance to relax and graze.

On February 12, 2001, Seattle Slew returned to another activity in which he reveled: He successfully bred his first mare since surgery. Remarkably, his fertility had returned, and Slew had another chance to improve on his already historical stallion statistics.

One summer morning in 2001, Tom grazed Slew as the sun glowed off the stallion's muscled coat. It was quiet, and when Tom spoke to the horse his words could not be discerned. Always soft-spoken, Tom swept his hand across the robust stallion's back.

Photos of the pair in 1984 show a thick stallion with a young man on the shank. The man has dark hair, a full beard, and a gentle, calm expression. Tom no longer has the beard, and his hair is now peppered gray, but Slew still looks much the same.

When he was young, the horse was considered an ugly duckling. He was so clumsy he was nicknamed Baby Huey. But the years have been kind to Seattle Slew. While the fictional ugly duckling evolved into a swan, Seattle Slew is no swan. He is more unique than that. His look is his own.

The horse lifted his handsome head to survey the land, and the sun glowed through his eye. That eye, that liquid brown eye, is so much a trademark of the famed stallion that it is sometimes called "a Slew eye." Countless Slew ads and promotions have featured it. His grade I-winning steeplechaser, Yaw, had it. Grade I winner Capote has it. His grade I-winning filly, Flute, proudly flashes those same startling eyes.

Tom Wade doesn't want to hear that Slew is showing signs of age, and the occasional tourist that mentions it will receive no response. His job isn't the defense of America's greatest living racehorse. His job, which he does admirably, is taking care of America's last living Triple Crown winner.

Other horses have recently come close to winning the Triple Crown, including Thunder Gulch, Real Quiet, and Charismatic. Two of the near misses, Silver Charm and Point Given, retired with fanfare to Three Chimneys and now reside in the main stallion barn. They are merely reminders of how difficult the Triple Crown really is.

Seattle Slew is the last living reminder that the Crown is attainable at all.

* * *

Soon after beginning the 2002 breeding season, Seattle Slew again began suffering from a lack of coordination. A second surgery was performed on the stallion March 2, 2002, and just four days later Slew was returned to Three Chimneys for recovery.

On March 31 came a most surprising press release: "Seattle Slew Moves to Hill 'n' Dale Farm." Mickey Taylor noted: "I believe that it is in Slew's best interest to be in a setting which allows him to be more isolated from mares coming to the breeding shed."

After spending more than half his life at Three Chimneys, twenty-eight-year-old Seattle Slew was moved to Hill 'n' Dale Farm on April 1 and placed in a stall removed from other stallions or distractions. Tom Wade, as he had been for twenty years, was by his side.

The great Seattle Slew breathed his last on the morning of May 7, 2002, twenty-five years to the day after his incredible Kentucky Derby win. He was buried at Hill 'n' Dale. As he had during the stallion's life, Tom Wade made certain to place blankets carefully over his friend's body for his final journey.

And then there were none…

Shelter Half

DK. B/BR. H. 1975, BY TENTAM—GAY MATELDA,
BY SIR GAYLORD

When he used to go to the post, he kept his head down like he was half asleep," part-owner George Huguely reminisced, still amused twenty years later. "He acted like he couldn't care less."

Recalling the races Shelter Half won, it's hard to picture him that way. He was a very fast horse. In Monmouth's Select Handicap, Shelter Half equaled the six-furlong stakes record of 1:08 2/5. In the Phoenix Handicap at Keeneland, he ran the same distance in 1:09 1/5, defeating the brilliant Cabrini Green. Although he hit that proverbial "brick wall" at a mile, he won six sprint stakes at five different tracks for Fourbros Stables.

Fourbros Stables consisted of two sets of Maryland-based brothers: Geoff and George Huguely and Tommy and Bobby Manfuso. They bought Shelter Half as a yearling for $14,500 and were lucky with him from the start. Unbeknownst to them, their trainer entered Shelter Half in a $30,000 claimer for his debut, and fortunately no one else saw the Virginia-bred colt's potential. During his four-year racing career, Shelter Half won fourteen of thirty-one starts and earned $236,337. A bet-

tor's dream, the crack sprinter failed to finish in the top three only four times.

Shelter Half's retirement was announced in 1980, and he took up stud duty the next year at Maryland's Glade Valley Farms. His sire was the tremendously popular Tentam, who stood at Windfields Farm. His female line was as strong, as his dam, Gay Matelda, was winner of such races as the Alabama and Gardenia stakes. The Sir Gaylord mare produced eight foals to race, all winners, including Shelter Half and grade II winner Reine Mathilde.

For two decades now, Shelter Half has quietly been a wonderful regional sire. Throughout his stud career he has consistently sired quality runners, and his average earnings per starter is a stellar $47,309. Shelter Half is known for his fillies and for passing on his speed. His top earners include stakes winners In the Curl ($749,891), Born to Shop ($538,373), and Jeweler's Choice

($458,543). To date, the compact dark bay has sired twenty-two stakes winners and the earners of more than $13.5 million.

As often happens with older sires, however, Shelter Half's popularity waned despite his impressive statistics.

Since 1994, his largest foal crop numbered ten in 1997, and in 1996 he had only three foals.

When I visited Shelter Half in March 2001, the twenty-six-year-old stallion stood tied to the wall as the groom rubbed him. The intelligent stallion nipped playfully whenever the groom moved near his head, but otherwise stood professionally. A chilly mixture of rain and snow fell outdoors.

Outside, Shelter Half was an indifferent model who, just like twenty years ago, kept his head low, as if he were half asleep. He couldn't have cared less about my feeble attempts to rouse his curiosity. He was a thick horse when running, but he now had a bullish appearance and a wise, aloof bearing.

For a moment on a far off hillside, a horse moved and Shelter Half's thick ears bounced forward. Then the moment was gone, and the brilliant old sprinter went back into his indifferent mode.

Shelter Half was never as nationally known as were several other members of his foal crop, such as Alydar, Affirmed, and Believe It. But the brilliant sprinter has made his mark on the Mid-Atlantic region, both as a racehorse and sire.

Silver Buck

GR. H. 1978, BY BUCKPASSER—SILVER TRUE, BY HAIL TO REASON

Florida is a state of fast-changing weather, and Ocala often receives seemingly spontaneous downpours — rains that wash away layers of earth. The land on which Bridlewood Farm sits was once Indian territory, and after such rains arrowheads and other Indian artifacts are sometimes unearthed. Silver Buck welcomes the company in his paddock when farm personnel search the ground for freshly unveiled treasures. He lowers his head and follows them quietly with keen curiosity, very much enjoying a break in his routine.

Blood does not come much bluer than Silver Buck's. He is a C.V. Whitney homebred by Buckpasser, out of the Hail to Reason mare Silver True. Silver True was out of a Mahmoud mare and in addition to winning the Spinaway Stakes, Silver True produced two stakes winners.

But Silver True was simply a continuance of a long distaff line of timeless, magic-laced names. For generations, her relatives appeared proudly in the Whitney Stud books, beginning with Silver Buck's seventh dam, Elusive. And through three generations of Whitneys — W.C. Whitney, H.P. Whitney, and C.V. "Sonny" Whitney — the mares produced stakes winners sporting the family's famed Eton blue-and-brown Whitney silks.

Silver Buck was a combination of this strong female line with the great Buckpasser added on top.

With every reason to be a good racehorse, Silver Buck did not disappoint. In a two-year campaign the dark gray won seven of sixteen starts, including grade I wins in the Suburban and Whitney handicaps. A beautiful animal, his fine features belied the fact that he stood a sizeable 16.2 hands high as a stallion.

Silver Buck spent his entire stud career in Florida, standing his first season for $20,000. As he aged, his fee dwindled, and he moved from farm to farm. But unlike many stallions, his best was yet to come. At age sixteen while standing at Silverleaf Farms, his most successful runner was born: Silver Charm.

In 1997 Silver Charm won the Kentucky Derby and Preakness, failing by a half-length to capture the Triple Crown. Silver Charm was a crowd favorite, and Silver Buck — already sire of major stakes winners Forever Silver, Silver of Silver, and Silver Survivor — reached the pinnacle of his popularity.

Unfortunately, however, Silver Buck's time in the breeding shed was limited, not because of lack of interest by breeders, but because of his own fertility.

When Silverleaf Farms went on the market in 1999, Bridlewood Farm took in the twenty-one-year-old stallion. He stood at Bridlewood for a season, but his fertility declined quickly and he was pensioned.

Statistics tell the sad tale. While Silver Buck consistently sired about forty horses annually, the number swelled to a high of fifty-two in 1998, the year after Silver Charm's Derby win. In 1999, only twenty-seven foals were born, and by 2000, fourteen. Even more sadly, the number for 2001 stands at one.

Saddest of all is that there will be no more offspring. Silver Buck is a reminder of another time, a time when a man known as "Sonny" Whitney attended races with a freshly pressed suit and an engaging smile to watch the horses descended from those that his family bred for generations.

Six Crowns

CH. M. 1976-2002, BY SECRETARIAT—CHRIS EVERT,
BY SWOON'S SON

 he's a real sweetheart," the groom said, fixing the twenty-five-year-old mare's foretop. "A real sweetheart." Six Crowns has been one of racing's sweethearts since her birth in 1976. A member of Secretariat's second crop, she was the first foal of the popular race mare Chris Evert. As Dad was a Triple Crown winner and Mom won the Filly Triple Crown, the foal's name was a natural.

A sweet photograph of the young lady and her mother graced trade magazines, showing the long-faced Chris Evert drinking near her adorable, fuzzy filly. Racing fans fell instantly in love.

Six Crowns was not as talented a race mare as her famous dam, but she was successful. In her two-year campaign, the chestnut carried owner Carl Rosen's silks to five wins in fifteen starts. Sporting a long tail and a large star and snip, Six Crowns won the Meadow Queen Stakes, ran third in the grade I Ladies Handicap, and placed in five other stakes.

She retired with $136,274 in earnings and began her second career, that of broodmare. Six Crowns' second foal, born in 1982, was a handsome bay colt with a large star. Named Chief's Crown, he was one of the best racehorses in America in the 1980s. His biggest wins were the inaugural Breeders' Cup Juvenile, the Norfolk, Hopeful, Cowdin, Blue Grass, Marlboro Cup, Flamingo, and Travers. He ran second in the Preakness, third in the Kentucky Derby and Belmont, and earned more than two million dollars. He retired to Three Chimneys near Midway, Kentucky, where he was a popular and beloved sire.

Sadly, owner Carl Rosen did not see Six Crowns' foal succeed. He died in 1983, a year before Chief's Crown made history by winning the first-ever Breeders' Cup race.

Six Crowns' 1985 foal was a near-black Mr. Prospector filly with an unusual star and a strong will to win. Named Classic Crown, the D. Wayne Lukas-trainee won grade I races at both two and three, and retired with four wins in fourteen starts.

Each of Six Crowns' seven foals that raced won, and Six Crowns deserved her well-earned retirement from her second career. After her 2001 El Prado filly was born, Six Crowns was pensioned.

When I drove down the driveway to the broodmare barn in May 2001, Six Crowns was waiting. She had been brought in from her paddock, her hooves were painted, and her coat was brushed clean. She waited on the driveway, a groom loosely holding the shank.

At twenty-five, Six Crowns' body was very slim and her countenance tired. The groom fixed her foretop and scratched her chest, and Six Crowns' head dipped gently toward him.

She enjoyed the attention on this warm morning and nuzzled us as we took turns being photographed with her. Her equine friends suddenly jogged over the crest of a nearby paddock and moved toward us eagerly. Six Crowns raised her head high to watch them. Her face was so beautiful.

The Rosen family called Chris Evert their foundation mare and retained each of Chris Evert's five fillies for breeding. When Chris Evert died at age thirty, she was buried at Three Chimneys.

Six Crowns, the last remaining Chris Evert, will be buried there as well.

* * *

No amount of care could compensate for the passing of time. On Valentine's Day 2002, at the age of twenty-six, Six Crowns was euthanized, as time had taken its toll. She was laid to rest in Three Chimneys' broodmare cemetery, next to her dam.

Smarten

DK. B/BR. H. 1976, BY CYANE—SMARTAIRE, BY QUIBU

t age twenty-six, he doesn't look like a Derby winner. Not "the Derby" winner, but the winner of nearly every other Derby…

Smarten claimed four: the Illinois Derby, Ohio Derby, American Derby, and Pennsylvania Derby. He didn't compete in the 1979 Run for the Roses, but his connections were wise to avoid the gray dynamo named Spectacular Bid.

Smarten avoided Spectacular Bid in many nice races, winning eight stakes and placing in ten others. When he did face the Bid, in the 1979 Meadowlands Cup, he finished three lengths behind the magnificent gray. By the time Smarten retired at the end of 1979, the near-black son of Cyane had earned $716,426.

Smarten, born in Maryland on April 17, 1976, returned to his native state to stand at Windfields Farm. Spectacular Bid, a Kentucky-bred foaled February 17, 1976, continued running in 1980, shattered records, and entered stud at Claiborne Farm.

Smarten, perhaps, turned out to be the better sire. While many racing fans were surprised, true studiers of pedigree weren't.

Smarten's female line was unusually strong. His dam, Smartaire, was a remarkable producer of three other stakes winners: champion Smart Angle, Quadratic, and Smart Heiress. Quadratic became a successful sire, and Smart Heiress and Smart Angle both produced major stakes winners.

When Windfields was sold in 1987, Smarten stayed on the property, now Northview Stallion Station. In his nineteen-year stud career, Smarten sired 506 runners. Among them were a champion, four grade I winners, and nine additional graded stakes winners. Twelve of his offspring earned more than $300,000.

Very impressive statistics indeed, for a stallion who stood his entire career in Maryland. Smarten led the Mid-Atlantic sire list only one time, in 1989. But two years after being pensioned in 1996, he led Maryland's all-time leading sire list with progeny earnings ($23,162,100) and all-time leading two-year-old sire list ($3,662,780).

Northview stallion manager Harlan Appleby enjoys the quiet senior stallion. "He's just an old horse, old and calm…He'll walk around like an old mare; then all of a sudden he'll act like he's going to bite you, just to let you know he can still do it."

Smarten eats senior feed but still has trouble keeping weight on. From 6:30 a.m. to 2:00 p.m., he goes outside with the other stallions. Smarten moves slowly around his paddock, as younger stallions Crowd Pleaser and Partner's Hero frolic youthfully nearby. Smarten wanders over to visitors, slowly stretching his noble head over the fence for attention.

The Aberdeen Proving Ground is not far away, and muffled explosions are occasionally heard as weapons testing is conducted. Neither the farm help nor Smarten seems to notice. On occasion Smarten stands a bit unsteadily, his knees long since tired of straightening completely. But he is still a strong, proud old man, a wonderful good-will representative for Northview.

"A lot of people are amazed that Northview hasn't sent him somewhere else or even put him down," Harlan said. "As good as this horse has been to this farm…"

There was no need to finish the sentence.

Son of Briartic

CH. H. 1979, BY BRIARTIC—TABOLA, BY ROUND TABLE

*J*ulie McMurry, whose husband Packy owns and manages Royal Match Stud near Enumclaw, Washington, regrets that Son of Briartic didn't have more opportunity to make a national mark. However, Son of Briartic has become Washington's perennial leading sire, his sons and daughters winning primarily regional and Canadian stakes.

Born on April 29, 1979, Son of Briartic has a double dose of Round Table. He is out of a Round Table mare and by Briartic, himself out of a Round Table mare. The flashy chestnut colt with the thick blaze and white legs was one of the most successful Canadian runners of the early 1980s.

Son of Briartic won six stakes, including the Toronto Cup, Sir Barton Stakes, and Kingarvie Stakes. But his most impressive score was the 1982 Queen's Plate. Peter Gzowski chronicled his race preparation and the race itself in the 1983 book *An Unbroken Line*.

Son of Briartic raced again at four but didn't equal his three-year-old form. He raced five times in 1983, finished third once, and earned $3,391. He retired with a $380,470 bankroll and eight wins in thirty starts.

The budding stallion began his second career at owner David Kapchinsky's Paddockhurst Farm in Alberta, Canada, but when Kapchinsky eventually offered the horse to the McMurrys, they proudly accepted. "He basically had bred every mare in Alberta twice, and he (Kapchinsky) felt the horse was running out of the market there," Julie recalled. "He came here at the worst possible time, right after the old track was closed. They announced the sale (of Longacres) a month before we completed the sale."

Son of Briartic relocated to Washington in October of 1990. He had already been the leading freshman sire in Canada, so he was immediately popular. For more than a decade now, he has lived in comfort near majestic Mt. Rainier.

Royal Match Stud's web site lists the stallion's particulars: "15 3-1/2 hands, very compact stallion. Exceptionally short cannon bones, excellent feet, good substance for his size. Crosses well with most physical types, except very small fine boned mares. Closely Inbred to Round Table, Son of Briartic consistently delivers sound durable campaigners that provide their owners with years of excitement."

He has done that for countless owners, and he quickly ascended to the top of the Washington stallion list. By the time I visited in July 2001, he had led the way for a remarkable seven years.

Son of Briartic is a strong, handsome horse and a real gentleman. His class was evident as he ambled across his field, his liver chestnut coat glowing. His muscles rippled as he moved through thick grasses, and when brought in for grooming, he stood like a champion. The groom told me stories of the stallion's gentleness, including her personal favorite. Son of Briartic had been caught sleeping in his stall with a cat curled up between his front legs.

Although still interested, Son of Briartic was pensioned after the 2001 season. "He just was no longer a consistent breeding horse," Julie said. The costs of keeping a mare at Royal Match Stud long enough to guarantee a successful breeding were prohibitive.

Royal Match Stud changed its emphasis to broodmares around the same time, and their stallions were moved to other homes. But not Son of Briartic.

When asked whether he'd live at Royal Match Stud for the rest of his life, Julie answered quickly: "Oh yes, definitely." Then she added, pensively: "The saddest part of it is that Son of Briartic was a far better horse than the numbers show. His legacy will be significantly curtailed because he just couldn't get the opportunity with the best mares. He's accomplished marvelous achievements in light of his opportunity."

Spectacular Bid

GR. H. 1976, BY BOLD BIDDER—SPECTACULAR, BY PROMISED LAND

On February 16, 2001, I baked a birthday cake. While cooking does not come naturally to me, I poured my heart into its preparation. I chose bran cake with white sugar frosting, using twice the recommended ingredients. Leaving some items out, like vanilla extract and egg yolks, I added extra sugar and molasses. Then I peeled carrots and tucked them into a container. Finally, I wrote a birthday greeting across the front, pushed a small circle of peppermints into the icing, and covered the cake for the night.

The next morning, my friend Annie and I drove two hours to visit the birthday boy. The day was windy and bitterly cold, and wind chills dipped the temperature under ten below. We got to his place about one o'clock.

After shoving the carrots into place, we went to the barn, where the man of honor was waiting. It was February 17, 2001, Spectacular Bid's twenty-fifth birthday.

Farm manager Joel Reach and his son Justin had Bid prepared beautifully. They led the fuzzy stallion outside his stall, and Justin offered him the cake. Bid took a look, sniffed at it curiously, and quickly swept two "candles"

into his mouth. Other carrots scattered, and the first part of the photo session was over.

Justin brought Spectacular Bid out into the bitter cold. Milfer Farm is high atop a hillside, and the snow-traced wind cut deep as Bid cut a cold path through the fresh powder. I wished my coat were as thick as Bid's and wondered if even that would have been enough.

Spectacular Bid looked fabulous for twenty-five, his body still strong and his manner proud. He held his head high, and although the sub-zero winds swirled up under his tail, he didn't act up. He was used to being shown, and understood his role.

He also understood when he had fulfilled his obligation. After standing for an updated conformation photograph, Spectacular Bid pinned his ears and began to dance. Still lively, Bid knew how to bite, and he was signaling that he'd like to stop fussing around. We obliged, and the stallion's modest birthday party was over.

By three o'clock Spectacular Bid was covering a mare, and we were on our way back home.

* * *

Countless words have been written about Spectacular Bid's racing exploits and misadventures with safety pins. It has oft been recorded what Buddy Delp said of his greatest runner, and contemporary stories usually mention Bid's less-than-grand stud career.

Nevertheless, what Spectacular Bid did on the track is nothing less than remarkable. He earned his way onto *The Blood-Horse*'s list of the greatest racehorses of the twentieth century, ranking tenth.

Spectacular Bid won twenty-six of thirty starts, earned $2,781,608, was a champion for three consecutive years, and earned four Eclipse Awards. He won thirteen grade I stakes events, equaled or broke eight track records, set a world record of a mile and a quarter in 1:57 4/5, and won five times carrying 130 pounds or more. His races and records were so extraordinary, in fact, that in his final start not a single horse faced him.

Spectacular Bid galloped around Belmont Park's large oval alone in the 1980 Woodward Stakes, but even that he did in style. The stout dark gray galloped strongly under Bill Shoemaker, stopping the clock in an impressive 2:02 2/5 for the mile and a quarter.

Great things were expected when Bid, syndicated for twenty-two million dollars, retired to Claiborne Farm. Spectacular Bid and Secretariat gamboled in adjacent paddocks, and the gray and the chestnut both attracted thousands of visitors annually. More came to see Secretariat, of course, but Spectacular Bid was more interesting to watch as he aged. Each year, the famed gray lightened noticeably, until it was difficult to see the dark racehorse in the dappled stallion.

Secretariat died in 1989. Two years later Spectacular Bid was on the move. While Bid was one of the greatest racehorses of modern times, he was having surprisingly little success at stud.

"He's gotten a lot of criticism that he hasn't cloned himself," Dr. Jon Davis said. "But as the Meyerhoffs say, 'How can you clone Superman?'"

Davis had faith in this particular Superman when he contacted Claiborne Farm. Davis owns New York's Milfer Farm, and in the decade since has brought several proven stallions to the state.

Spectacular Bid was a big one. While not setting any records at stud, he had proven capable of producing a grade I winner (Spectacular Love) and many graded stakes performers. He was perhaps not Kentucky material, but such a famed and durable horse was a boon to New York.

When Spectacular Bid arrived in late 1991, local newspapers carried stories of the popular gray horse. Cars drove by the property, their occupants straining to catch a glimpse of the great horse. People drove up, and seeing gray mares in broodmare bands, jumped out to take pictures. Joel jokingly considered spray-painting all the gray mares' sides with "Not The Bid."

In the ensuing decade, peace returned to the farm, even though Spectacular Bid still lures several hundred visitors annually. The old stallion has stayed remarkably handsome and healthy, defying his years. But in 2001, at age twenty-five, Bid has finally begun showing his age.

He has countless black and gray spots. He is what is commonly called a flea-bitten gray, and he will never be close to white. His thick winter coat becomes tinged in yellow, and he has lost weight in the past year.

In November 1995 Spectacular Bid suffered an episode of colic. While suffering from abdominal discomfort, he injured his right front fetlock. Infection set in, and he was shipped to Cornell University for surgery. In July 1996 the stallion was returned to Cornell for a second ankle surgery. The attending physician, Dr. Alan Nixon, used a technique at the forefront of equine medicine to save the great horse.

Nixon implanted special ceramic beads, impregnated with time-released antibiotics, into the ankle. The antibiotics, released over several months, did the trick. Spectacular Bid, despite losing the mobility in his ankle, returned to the farm. He was stall-bound, then hand-walked during his recovery. But Bid has long since returned to his old schedule, and the fused ankle, while noticeable, seems to cause him no discomfort.

In his twilight years, Spectacular Bid has also taken on an unusual new role.

"I had my blinders on as far as breeding was concerned," Davis said, "thinking in terms of flat racing only. But then I embraced the idea that an athlete is an athlete, no matter what venue it's in. At least one of (Bid's) sons has been successful as a sport-horse sire, a Denmark stallion named Mytens. And some of Bid's Thoroughbred progeny have excelled at dressage and eventing.

"I went out on a limb a little. I asked the syndicate members about letting Bid be a sport-horse sire, and they agreed. The stud fee is the same, and the semen is transported. I've advertised Bid as a sport-horse sire."

Spectacular Bid now sires both racing Thoroughbreds and sport horses. Davis hoped to get twenty-five to thirty-five Thoroughbred mares to Bid in 2002. Semen will be shipped for another ten or so sport mares.

* * *

While Spectacular Bid has not been a tremendously successful sire, he has excelled as a broodmare sire. That strength has not gone unnoticed by breeders. "The joke that people say when they book to Bid is, 'Can I get a filly?'" Davis said. "I hope Bid will stand the test of time as a broodmare sire."

Either way, the gray stallion who spends days gracefully wandering Milfer's lands has stood the test of time as one of the greatest racehorses America has ever known.

Star de Naskra

DK. B/BR. H. 1975-2000, BY NASKRA—CANDLE STAR, BY CLANDESTINE

Star de Naskra was a champion, and a gentleman. I was fortunate enough to photograph Star de Naskra winning the 1979 Whitney Handicap in a stirring performance over Cox's Ridge and The Liberal Member. Less than two lengths separated the top three finishers, as front-running Star de Naskra refused to concede. That was the year he won his championship, and although the Whitney was run at a mile and one-eighth, Star de Naskra was voted champion sprinter.

Carlyle Lancaster bred and raced the Maryland-bred colt, who began his career with an easy maiden win by three and a half lengths at Bowie. It was onward and upward, as the compact bay colt got used to traveling, racing at twelve tracks as a two- and three-year-old. While victorious on occasion, the colt didn't win a graded stakes in his first two seasons.

The four-year-old Star de Naskra was a stronger animal with solid hindquarters and boundless determination. He won the six-furlong Bold Ruler Stakes by five lengths in 1:09 1/5, the grade II Carter Handicap at seven furlongs in 1:21 4/5, a mile allowance by more than six lengths in 1:34 3/5, and Belmont's seven-furlong Celanese Cup in 1:22.

Disqualified from his Celanese Cup win, he came right back to score in the grade II Cornhusker Handicap, an eight and a half-length jaunt in 1:48 2/5. Then came his Whitney win on a sunny Saratoga afternoon.

Star de Naskra faltered in his final two 1979 starts, but with seven wins in ten races he was named champion sprinter and retired to Pillar Stud near Lexington, Kentucky.

Several years later, he was moved to Spendthrift Farm. Some of the stalls had back windows, and Star de Naskra's distinctive face was usually poking through watching the scenery and the ever-present tourists. His finely pricked ears always seemed to be forward, and those who moved close enough to offer grass or a treat were greeted eagerly.

Star de Naskra moved again in 1992 to his final home, the beautiful Darby Dan Farm. He occupied a front paddock, content to watch cars come and go and happy to say hello to visitors. He quickly became a Darby Dan staff favorite.

When I visited in July 1999, Kentucky was deeply entrenched in a heat spell, and temperatures hovered in the nineties. Stallion manager Ron Kahles shook my hand and went into Star de Naskra's stall, replacing the stallion's halter with a beautiful show bridle. Star de Naskra walked out pleasantly.

I looked around for someone to assist us, but Ron thought it wouldn't be necessary. We moved to an open area where Star de Naskra immediately stood beautifully. The stallion was in display mode, and he held his refined head high.

Ron spoke glowingly of the old horse. Star de Naskra had a thyroid condition that made these hot days particularly difficult, and Ron pointed to the stallion's legs. Even on this mid-summer day, extra hair grew on his chest and legs. But Star de Naskra never complained. He always moved with a champion's grace.

He bred professionally and stood still for vets, blacksmiths, and fans. Yet one thing, just one thing, really could irritate the old boy. "He hates Meadowlake," Ron said, shaking his head with a smile. "He sees him coming, and he gets mad." There was no love lost by Meadowlake, either. Who started the feud was unknown and irrelevant. The two stallions just didn't like each other's company.

Star de Naskra took ill in 1999. He rallied, but due to reproductive problems was pensioned in March 2000.

The infirmities of his condition finally became too much for Star de Naskra, and the gentle stallion breathed his last on October 1, 2000. Farm employees wept for the loss of their friend, and he was buried in their stallion cemetery.

Star de Naskra rests forever beside some of the greatest horses to have grazed those historic lands: Ribot, His Majesty, Graustark, Roberto, Black Toney...But none was more of a gentleman than he.

Stay Out Front

CH. M. 1966-2001, BY CURROCK—BELLE'S GAL,
BY HELLCAT

*I*n Margery Williams' classic 1922 children's book, *The Velveteen Rabbit*, the main characters are toys in a young boy's nursery. Many of them are new, shiny, and quite brilliant. But in a corner cupboard, an old model-horse stands nobly.

"The Skin Horse had lived longer in the nursery than any of the others. He was so old that his brown coat was bald in patches and showed the seams underneath, and most of the hairs in his tail had been pulled out to string bead necklaces."

One lazy day in the nursery, the Velveteen Rabbit asks the old horse what it means to be "Real." He answers thoughtfully.

"It doesn't happen all at once," says the Skin Horse. "You become. It takes a long time. That's why it doesn't happen often to people who break easily, or have sharp edges, or who have to be carefully kept. Generally, by the time you are Real, most of your hair has been loved off...and you get loose in your joints and very shabby. But these things don't matter at all, because once you are Real you can't be ugly, except to people who don't understand."

* * *

In early 2001, a photograph of a thirty-five-year-old mare appeared in a Florida racing paper. Her name was Stay Out Front, and she lived at Sorted Oaks Farm.

When I set foot on Sorted Oaks a month and a half later, awaiting me in a worn paddock was a remarkable sight: a real-life, breathing — beautiful — Skin Horse.

She stood resting on three legs, her fourth cocked comfortably beneath her. Her body was slim. Her mane hung thick on the near side, and much of her hair was worn off along her shoulder, face, and back. What appeared to be a saddle was merely tanned skin.

This incredible mare was among the first horses ever bred by Sorted Oaks, and her story and that of the farm are forever linked. I had never heard of either the mare or the farm. But the instant I saw Stay Out Front at Sorted Oaks, I knew I would forget neither.

Sorted Oaks Farm sprang from humble beginnings in Indiana for Edward DeVries Sr. and his wife, Dorothy.

"We always had riding horses, and we were boarding a

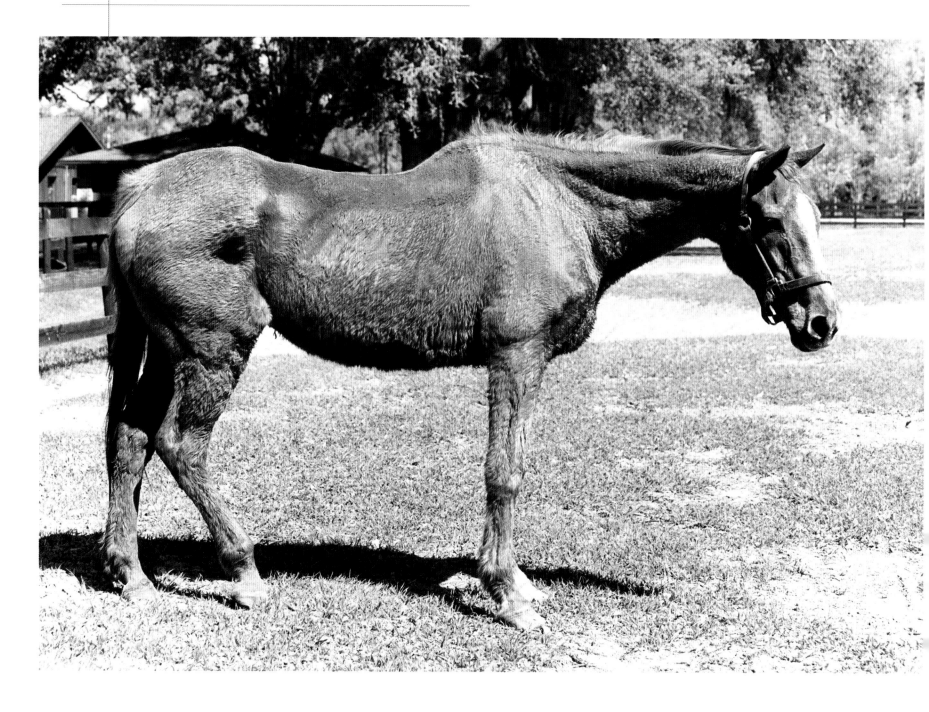

Thoroughbred for a friend of ours," Edward DeVries Jr. recalled. "He decided he didn't want it any more, and he gave it to us. His name was Dusty Velvet. He ran at old Cahokia Downs (in Illinois) in 1959."

Edward continued. "In 1959, or maybe it was 1960, we bought four horses from a fellow in Ohio. There was Belle's Gal, and Who Dudette, Hesagohi, and Buckeye Breeze. We bought a few more the next year."

Edward remembered the horses' names easily, although in 1960 he was just a child. More amazingly, he remembered the names of four decades of Sorted Oaks' homebreds. His parents began a tradition of giving their horses three-word names, beginning with S, O, and F (Sorted Oaks Farm). Keeping them sorted out is no easy matter.

STAY OUT FRONT WON THE 1972 SUWANEE RIVER HANDICAP AT GULFSTREAM PARK.

In 1963 the DeVrieses bought property in Ocala, Florida, and as the new Sorted Oaks Farm took shape, they moved their humble operation south. They purchased their first stallion, a Curragh King stakes winner named Currock. He would be the sire of one of Sorted Oaks' best.

Belle's Gal, their first mare, wasn't much of a racehorse. She raced three times but never placed. She had a breathing problem and became a broodmare.

Belle's Gal was being boarded at nearby Ocala Stud when she produced a chestnut filly in 1966. The daughter of Currock was lovely, and a blaze slid down her pretty face between her nostrils. They named her Stay Out Front. The name was prophetic.

"All of Belle's (descendants) are basically real laid back, quiet mares," Edward said. "They kind of gave you the impression of being lazy, until they got to the track."

At the track, however, racing in Dorothy's name, the chestnut filly with the blaze face sparkled. "She beat some of the best horses in the country, and going six furlongs to a mile she really was something," Edward recalled. "At one and one-sixteenth or one and one-eighth miles, though, that kind of stretched her out a little bit."

Stay Out Front showed her stuff early, winning the Miss Florida Handicap as a two-year-old. In doing so, Stay Out Front became the first stakes winner bred by Edward Sr., and the first for Dorothy as an owner.

She placed in the Twilight Tear and Yo Tambien handicaps at four, won the Columbiana Handicap at five, and the Suwanee River Handicap the following year. The Columbiana Handicap chart reflects how sparkling she could be: "STAY OUT FRONT was sent to a clear lead at once, raced along the inner hedge while being patiently rated, rallied gamely when challenged in the stretch to prove best despite being bumped by TOP ROUND in midstretch."

All told, the durable Florida-based filly won fourteen of eighty-eight races, finished second eighteen times, and third in nine more. During her six-year campaign, she earned $130,290.

The new Sorted Oaks Farm, 120 acres strong, was completed in 1967 when Stay Out Front was a yearling. When she retired, Stay Out Front came home as a broodmare.

She only produced three colts and three fillies over fifteen years, but keeping their names straight is a test for even the most fertile mind.

First came Shape of Fame. Born in 1974, he raced 153 times, won or placed in forty-eight, and set a mile track record of 1:36 1/5 at Ellis Park.

Next came She's Out Front. Also a winner, she was best known for her son, Skip Out Front. Skip Out Front won the grade I American Handicap and placed in nine other graded stakes, earning $871,996.

Stay Out Front's 1982 filly, Safe Out Front, was her only foal not to race. When Stay Out Front and her filly were being shipped for breeding, the mare inadvertently stepped on the filly's ankle, breaking it. Safe Out Front stayed home,

where she produced four-time stakes winner and grade I-placed Slide Out Front.

Slide Out Front, purchased by John Franks, became an impressive producer herself. Her first foal, multiple graded stakes winner Silent Eskimo, earned more than one million dollars.

Stay Out Front produced three other foals, and each was a winner. In a break from family policy, R. and R. Markey was named for family friends. But State of Funshine and Son of Front kept the tradition alive.

Son of Front was Stay Out Front's last foal. He was born in 1989, when Stay Out Front was twenty-three.

In 1998 Edward Sr.'s wife, Dorothy, passed away. The duo had built Sorted Oaks into a thriving, successful farm, and memories resided thick and tangible at the property. Edward wanted a change. The farm was sold, and Sorted Oaks relocated on a lovely forty-acre site in Ocala. The family's first stakes winner, Stay Out Front, had a new home at age thirty-two.

Edward Sr. still lives at Sorted Oaks, although he no longer runs the farm. Edward Jr. takes care of the business. They have four horses in training scattered at three Florida tracks, and thirty-two horses on Sorted Oaks.

* * *

The published photograph of the thirty-five-year-old mare was fresh in my mind when I drove up Sorted Oaks' driveway in March 2001. Tall, thick trees laden with Spanish moss offered welcome shade. The buildings seemed timeless, the feel of countless humid Florida seasons on each surface. The sun beat down, challenging anything that moved.

The farm manager, Joe Everman, emerged from the barn and shook my hand. He said to follow him to the front paddock, where Stay Out Front spent her days.

I couldn't wait to meet her, but when I saw her standing

asleep, I was a bit taken aback. I'd seen old horses, but I had never seen anything quite like Stay Out Front.

When Joe walked up to her slowly and quietly, the dozing mare awoke. At first I felt sorry for her and thought about asking for a brush. But I wasn't sure what brushing would do to her remaining hair, and I decided to leave her as she was. She truly wore the patina of age.

I thought about the tired old girl, thirty-three years earlier, winning the Miss Florida Stakes. I could envision the win photo: a pretty, young filly with a slim blaze standing proudly, jockey up, victorious smiles all around. Her life was in front of her.

Joe's love for the thirty-five-year-old mare was evident. He rubbed her shoulder gently, reassuring her both with hands and voice when other mares approached. Stay Out Front moved forward a few feet, then was pushed back by equine friends. Reassuring her again, Joe spoke so softly the words were nearly unintelligible. "It's all right, girl."

Stay Out Front still had her hearing, and his words immediately relaxed her. When she did move, she moved surprisingly well. I reached out to her face, wondering what she felt like. She leaned into my hand endearingly, and I gently rubbed her temple. She felt soft, and warm, and her tired eyes closed contentedly.

I stayed there for moments, gently rubbing her forehead and down her weathered neck. The longer I stayed, the more beautiful she became.

On the way out, Joe stopped at two paddocks. Behind the barn a large chestnut gelding, Stay Out Front's final foal, was intent on grazing. His tail swished gently with the heat of the day. Son of Front looked quite content.

In another paddock a lovely chestnut mare, Safe Out Front, stood quietly, happy to see visitors. She hobbled forward trustingly, moving quite well on an ankle broken so many years earlier, when she was just a foal.

Two of Safe Out Front's offspring, Secret of Front and Spirit of Front, also live at the farm. Secret of Front's foals live there as well, an unnamed yearling colt and a filly named Stays Out Front.

In 2001, that was four generations…

Back in the barn office, Joe gave me a beautiful eight-by-ten-inch photograph of Stay Out Front. Copies had been made with her name and age superimposed. Everyone at the farm was so proud of their old girl. They knew they were lucky to have her as long as they did.

* * *

Early in 2002 Edward Jr. recounted the sad news.

"She was doing well, but she was having trouble in the back end some. We were giving her shots, and then she'd be all right. She'd fall down on me, then in a half-hour or so she'd get back up. I think she was having mini-strokes.

"On December 15th she went down again. We gave her most of the day to get back up. We even tried to help her get up, but she just couldn't. This time, she just couldn't."

On December 15, 2001, just weeks shy of her thirty-sixth birthday, Stay Out Front was euthanized. She was laid to rest on the farm, and a headstone was to be placed upon her grave.

* * *

Stay Out Front's reaching thirty-five was a milestone, but she was more than a number to the DeVries family and those at the farm. They continue to care for Stay Out Front's three generations.

The Jockey Club does not require death certificates, and many horses' deaths go unrecorded. There is no way of knowing how many mares have made it to the remarkable age of thirty-five, or even older.

Stay Out Front is the oldest mare I've ever found or read about. But on that sunny March day she became much more than a number to me, too.

She became "Real."

Stop the Music

B. H. 1970, BY HAIL TO REASON—BEBOPPER, BY TOM FOOL

e beat Secretariat," the groom smiled in June 1998, as he led Stop the Music to his paddock. He reached over and petted the twenty-eight-year-old stallion.

"Of course, it was by DQ," another groom laughed lightly, leading another stallion.

When released, Stop the Music snorted, turned on his heels, and ran. He stopped perhaps a hundred yards away, watching us as we watched him. He bowed his neck, snorted again, and trotted up, his knees high and his tail like a flag behind him. He came to the fence, pushed his handsome head over, and said hello.

Stop the Music is perhaps better known for that one win via disqualification than for the ten times he actually finished first or for his contributions as a sire and broodmare sire.

On October 14, 1972, Stop the Music finished two lengths behind a rising star named Secretariat in the Champagne Stakes. Unfortunately for Secretariat fans, the chestnut colt had bullied his way past Stop the Music.

Stop the Music had lost to Secretariat before and finished second by eight lengths in their next meeting, the Laurel Futurity. But on that chilly October day, Stop the Music received the laurels.

Stop the Music also won the Dwyer and Saratoga Special and placed in thirteen stakes before heading back home to Greentree Farm in Kentucky for stud duty. His dam, Bebopper, was a lovely Tom Fool mare who dropped grade I-winning Hatchet Man the year after she foaled Stop the Music. Stop the Music's sire was the durable Hail to Reason, and Stop the Music was a handsome, well-conformed stallion.

Stop the Music's paddock was near the famed Greentree cemetery where his dam was laid to rest in 1988. When the Greentree stallions were relocated, however, Stop the Music was moved to neighboring Gainesway Farm where he continued his stud career. On November 30, 1999, his pensioning was announced due to declining fertility. Said Gainesway's Michael Hernon of the twenty-nine-year-old stallion: "Stop the Music's influence on the breed will be felt for many years to come."

Stop the Music sired forty-five stakes winners

through March 2002, including five grade I winners. Temperence Hill, 1980 champion three-year-old colt, won nine stakes, including the Belmont, Super Derby, Jockey Club Gold Cup, Travers, and Suburban. Music

Merci won twelve of thirty-five starts, including the Del Mar Futurity. Dontstop Themusic won fifteen races, including the Vanity and Spinster. Missy's Mirage won nine stakes, including the Hempstead and Shuvee. And

the lovely Cure the Blues won the Laurel Futurity.

Stop the Music's line continues most strongly through Cure the Blues, whose death at twenty-one in 1999 was a significant blow to racing. Cure the Blues became a tremendously successful stallion, siring champions such as Le Glorieux, Saoirse, Prudent Manner, Lucratif, and Honky Tonk Tune. Among his other top runners were Gaily Gaily, Stop Traffic, Rock and Roll, Take Me Out, and American Chance.

Now Cure the Blues' sons, including American Chance and Take Me Out, carry on the line.

And through it all, Stop the Music marches on.

Stop the Music was thirty-one when I visited in July 2001. He no longer lived near the hectic stallion barns but in a quiet area on the property. When I walked up, he ambled slowly to the fence and poked his now white-templed face over to say hello.

Gainesway pensioners often live very long lives, and Stop the Music's nearby companion was thirty-two-year-old Lyphard. Not bad company — two old friends aging gracefully.

Thirty Flags and Nasrahni Native

A t Allaire du Pont's Woodstock Farm in Maryland, seven horses that served the farm well relax and frolic in a "pension field." Chief among them are two older mares, one familiar to race fans, the other a one-time starter at Charles Town.

Thirty Flags, twenty-two, is a beautiful Woodstock homebred, by Hoist the Flag out of stakes winner Thirty Years. Under trainer Allen Jerkens' attentive eye, Thirty Flags won two stakes, placed in six graded stakes, and earned $275,243.

Her second dam, Battle of Roses, was a stakes-placed half sister to Jaipur, Rare Treat, and Rare Exchange. Her third dam, stakes winner Rare Perfume, was half sister to two stakes winners, Scent and Ambergris. Her fourth dam, Fragrance, was also half sister to three stakes winners, including the prominent filly Rosetown.

Thirty Flags has produced three stakes winners for Woodstock: Manlove (now a successful stallion), Byars, and multiple graded stakes-winning Dixie Flag.

The obscure pensioner is Nasrahni Native, twenty-one, by Windsor's Rebel out of Dancer's Rhythm. She raced once, ran fifth, and earned eighty-one dollars. The man listed as her trainer is certain he did not train her, and her breeder and first owners have apparently disappeared from the racing scene.

Nasrahni Native's mother won two of thirteen starts and earned slightly less than five thousand dollars. Nasrahni Native's three half siblings did not even race.

Her second dam, Just for Helen, was unplaced in her only start, although Nasrahni Native's third dam finished third in a minor stakes. It is back to the fourth generation before a recognizable name appears, as Nasrahni Native's fourth dam was Cassiope. While not a prominent producer, she was a Hyperion mare who won two stakes races.

According to Bloodstock Research statistics, Nasrahni Native has no offspring, yet everyone at Woodstock knows better. She gave birth to thirteen foals and raised a dozen other mares' foals. Nasrahni Native was a nurse mare.

* * *

Dolly Pouska has been in the nurse-mare business for more than forty years. Dolly was raising foals in Maryland to sell as hunters when someone asked whether she had any surrogate mothers. Dolly had never heard of such a thing, but her friend replied that they had nurse mares in Kentucky.

Dolly had one such mare at the time, and she put her to work. For Dolly, this odd business quickly became a full-time job. She now keeps between forty-five and fifty mares at the ready at her North East, Maryland, farm.

She provides a necessary service. When mares die or suffer injuries while foaling, left behind is a needy, whinnying baby demanding attention. Some mares reject or even turn on their foal. With the money involved in Thoroughbred racing, a mother to guide an abandoned foal through its early days is a must.

Woodstock Farm is unusual, however, in that many of its foals are raised on nurse mares as a matter of course. When a mare is shipped to Kentucky for breeding, her foal is kept home and paired with a nurse mare. Farm manager Richard Bennett said that Woodstock's philoso-

NASRAHNI NATIVE
DK. B/BR. M. 1981, BY WINDSOR'S REBEL— DANCER'S RHYTHM, BY SENSE OF RHYTHM

"THE MARRIED COUPLE": NASRAHNI NATIVE (RIGHT) AND OLE ATOCHA

phy is that traveling stresses the foal and puts it at risk of injury. Woodstock is a large farm with a full staff and comparatively few horses. It welcomes the nurse mares.

Beginning in 1986, it welcomed Nasrahni Native. On February 1 that year, Woodstock mare Ring o' Bells dropped a filly. In came Nasrahni Native. That began a cycle in which Nasrahni Native gave birth to a foal at

Dolly's (a foal raised on bucket feeding), ventured to Woodstock early in the year to adopt a newborn, was bred to a non-Thoroughbred, and then returned pregnant to Dolly's in the fall.

Nasrahni Native took several years to get used to her role. But from 1986 to 1998, this stout mare gave birth to thirteen foals. She also raised a dozen foals at Woodstock Farm.

Nasrahni Native's actual foals, Dolly Pouska proudly related, brought good money as show horses. The willing mare was both a good birth mother and good surrogate mother — not a bad return on Dolly's original investment. (When Nasrahni Native went through Timonium's sales ring in 1985, Dolly brought her home for four hundred dollars.)

Nasrahni Native's years of faithful service to Woodstock Farm did not go unnoticed.

"Woodstock took several of my nurse mares over the years," Dolly said. "Mrs. du Pont tells me, 'Don't you dare take

THIRTY FLAGS
B. M. 1980, BY HOIST THE FLAG—
THIRTY YEARS, BY BOLD HOUR

them to the sales. I've used those horses, and they can have a home here. We'll put them here in the pension field.' "

* * *

When Richard Bennett led me into Woodstock's pension field in December 2001, he asked whether I'd heard of the Greentree Gashouse Gang. I knew of Greentree's famed band of pensioned geldings, but it was a rare farm manager to mention it. I liked Richard right away.

He had been at Woodstock for eighteen years, which he quickly said was not long compared to other employees. He was the one who recommended Thirty Flags and Nasrahni Native for my photo session, and he seemed equally proud of each. He may have been even more proud of Nasrahni Native, because she had produced foals for thirteen consecutive years — a remarkable feat.

The seven horses grazing in the pension field included one laid-up two-year-old, and they were a peaceful bunch indeed. Thirty Flags grazed with the grace of a true grand dame, her bay body long and beautiful. She grazed alone but stayed close, and she found us mildly interesting.

Nasrahni Native stayed close to a sweet bay gelding, Ole Atocha, whose biggest racing moment was a second in the Donn Handicap. They went everywhere together, never wandering apart, and the staff affectionately calls them "the married couple."

It was a wonderful field of old friends, on a beautiful old property of hope and tradition. Behind the office, a quiet equine cemetery memorializes the remains of the great Kelso and displays markers for other beloved runners such as Politely.

The famed gray-and-yellow silks of Allaire du Pont have been a proud symbol of success for generations, and Mrs. du Pont knows from whence the success came.

That's why Nasrahni Native, the Windsor's Rebel mare who raced just once and never had a recorded foal, will live out her life next to Thirty Flags.

Timeless Moment

CH. H. 1970-1998, BY DAMASCUS—HOUR OF PARTING, BY NATIVE DANCER

*D*earborn stallion advertisements from the mid-1970s show him as a compact, golden chestnut with a thick foretop and bright eyes. The beauty of the stallion was matched by the elegance of his name: Timeless Moment.

Ben Walden Sr. was wise to buy the handsome racehorse to stand at his blossoming Dearborn in Midway, Kentucky. The chestnut stallion spent nearly two decades repaying him and his family.

* * *

Bred by Paul Mellon, Timeless Moment impressed Walden immediately. "I first saw him in the paddock one day at Saratoga, the day he made his first start," Walden told *The Blood-Horse*. "I was impressed with him physically, and although he didn't run too well that day, I followed him throughout his career."

Timeless Moment got better with age and, by the time he retired at four in 1974, he was a multiple graded stakes winner. His biggest score was the 1974 Nassau County Handicap, a grade III race at Aqueduct over the mighty Forego. The year before he had won the grade III Princeton Stakes and the Sport Page Handicap.

When Timeless Moment entered the sales ring at Belmont's paddock sale in 1975, Walden, in partnership with Harry Mangurian Jr., bought the flashy young stallion for $400,000. Timeless Moment was whisked down to Dearborn.

In addition to his race record, Timeless Moment carried handsome bloodlines to Midway. He was by the great Damascus and out of the Native Dancer mare Hour of Parting. Hour of Parting was sadly destined to have only four foals, but two, Timeless Moment and Farewell Party, were major stakes winners.

Timeless Moment rewarded Dearborn by consistently producing strong, sound, marketable offspring. Years passed, and Ben Walden Jr. took over the farm. It was renamed Vinery, and by the 1990s it had become one of the top farms in the nation.

Timeless Moment's runners were always competitive, but in 1991 and 1992 his first champions graced the racing world. Culture Vulture, an angular chestnut, was the

1991 highweighted two-year-old filly in France. In 1993 she was the highweighted older mare in both England and Italy for seven to nine and a half furlongs.

Americans took greater notice of his other champion. Gilded Time, a golden chestnut, won three stakes, including the Breeders' Cup Juvenile, and was named champion two-year-old colt.

However, the timing wasn't perfect for Timeless Moment. Alistair Roden, stallion manager at Vinery for more than a decade, recalled: "In 1991 Timeless Moment was still active, but his fertility was going downhill. Then he had two champions, and in 1993 he got a lot of mares."

But the timing was right for Timeless Moment's finest son. "When we got Gilded Time, it was a good time to go ahead and retire Timeless Moment," said Alistair. Gilded Time started standing at Vinery in 1994, and Timeless Moment was pensioned before that breeding season.

"We retired Timeless Moment (from breeding) and thought we'd put him in the back of the farm," Alistair said. "Back there, there were a lot of trees and a really nice little barn, all beautiful and peaceful. He lasted back there for two days," Alistair laughed, his voice thick with smiling memories. "We had to bring him right back up front and back into his old routine."

Alistair described Timeless Moment as "a kind and gentle horse, always easy to work with. He was always a bit frisky, was always a 'good-feeling' horse. He was the neatest breeding stallion. When he'd come into the barn he was very aggressive, but then he'd just glide up onto the mare. He was so gentle with them."

Timeless Moment was healthy until the final six months of his life, when he began losing coordination in his hind end. He continued in his daily routine, and the loving staff, who called him the "Elder Statesman," gave him a thick New Zealand blanket for comfort and warmth.

* * *

I photographed Timeless Moment twice in 1997, the final time when he had just months to live. The farm was bustling with activity, overflowing with young stallions with worlds of promise. Timeless Moment, then twenty-seven, stood quietly in his paddock. He moved slowly toward me, watched me for several minutes as I photographed him, then audibly sighed and slowly shuffled past.

The old chestnut stallion was slim and unsteady, his mane unkempt and his eyes overflowing with decades of life. His legs clicked with the sound of arthritis, and the blanket shifted slightly, offering its own soft sounds.

Timeless Moment no longer noticed that I was there, but instead became intrigued by a young stallion in the adjacent paddock. Timeless Moment watched pensively, his eyes fixed, his tiredness complete.

The young stallion was full of life, jogging around the paddock. He was the nation's leading freshman sire, with a world of promise. He was a compact golden chestnut, with bright eyes and a thick foretop. The beauty of the young stallion was matched by the elegance of his name: Gilded Time.

Valid Appeal

B. H. 1972-2002, BY IN REALITY—DESERT TRIAL, BY MOSLEM CHIEF

Mrs. Muriel Vanderbilt Adams was a Thoroughbred owner for nearly three decades. While she made a great impact on Florida's racing and breeding industry, sadly she did not live long enough to know it.

Mrs. Adams came upon her love for racing naturally. Her grandfather, William K. Vanderbilt, owned the beautiful Haras du Quesnay Stud in France. Her mother, Mrs. Graham Fair Vanderbilt, was a noted sportswoman whose best-known racehorse was the Hall of Famer Sarazen.

Mrs. Adams' colors first appeared just before World War II, and two decades later she raced Desert Trial. Desert Trial, a lovely filly and fierce competitor, won seven stakes including the Del Mar Oaks, Milady Handicap, and back-to-back runnings of the Ramona Handicap. She earned $106,385.

Upon the mare's retirement, Adams bred her to the Florida stallion In Reality. A bay filly resulted in 1970. The following year, Adams sent Desert Trial back to In Reality.

Before the second In Reality foal's birth, Mrs. Adams died of a heart attack on February 3, 1972. Her Thoroughbreds were dispersed at a Hialeah auction, and a newcomer to racing made several wise purchases.

Harry Mangurian Jr., whose new Mockingbird Farm was being built in Ocala, Florida, bought both the in-foal Desert Trial and her In Reality two-year-old. The In Reality filly cost $40,000, and Desert Trial, heavy with foal, brought $92,000. As added incentive, the mare came with a pre-paid season to Dr. Fager.

Desert Trial's 1970 filly was named Desert Vixen. The foal Desert Trial carried at auction, born May 12, 1972, was Valid Appeal.

Desert Vixen, a lovely bay filly with a long, slim face and bright star, had a remarkable three-year-old season. From mid-June through September, she blazed through eight straight wins against the best fillies and mares in the country. She was named champion three-year-old filly, and she came back at four to earn older filly or mare honors. The Florida-bred earned $421,538.

Valid Appeal was a rich bay colt with a thick jaw and

1975: "He's more of a docile type, inclined to be a little lazy, whereas she was more willing to exert herself upon request. But both are nice to handle and a pleasure to a trainer."

Valid Appeal entered stud at Mockingbird, and from his first crop came the brilliant Proud Appeal. Proud Appeal won seven stakes, including the grade I Blue Grass, grade II Gotham, Great American, Youthful, Bay Shore, and Swift stakes.

Valid Appeal was on the rise. Unlike many Florida stallions that are quickly whisked to bluer grass when success finds them, Mangurian kept Valid Appeal close. Mockingbird Farm, and the entire Florida breeding industry, were rewarded.

sprinter's physique. He was foaled at the famed Tartan Farms. Mangurian boarded his horses at the adjacent Tartan, but when his own farm was ready, Valid Appeal and Desert Trial were led next door. They were the first two horses to set foot on Mockingbird Farm.

Valid Appeal won only one stakes in three seasons, the grade II Dwyer over Wajima. But he placed in four other graded stakes, won eight races, and earned more than $200,000. Trainer Tommy Root Jr., who conditioned Valid Appeal and his champion sister, compared them in

Tom Drier came to Mockingbird Farm in January 1982, working his way from groom to farm manager in 1986. He helped tend to Valid Appeal and remembers Desert Trial well.

He remembers what a sweetheart the old mare was. He remembers her other two stakes winners, each by In Reality, named Court Trial and Classic Trial. He recalls her final foaling, and the burst uterine artery, and the difficult decision that had to be made. He remembers when she was laid to rest in the peaceful Mockingbird/Tartan Farm cemetery.

Desert Trial and Valid Appeal meant the world to Mangurian and his Mockingbird Farm. "She got Mr. Mangurian hooked on the game," Drier said, "and he got him through all of his years in the game."

Valid Appeal was small, a mere 15.1 hands (although listed at 15.2). But Drier had a world of respect for the diminutive stallion.

"He was such a smart horse in the breeding shed, he really worked his mares. Most stallions go in there already up on their hind legs. But being small, he had to think of ways to make the mares smaller. He would work on their stifles or hocks, and he'd get them to crouch a bit. He was such a smart horse, and his get were smart, too. That was part of his success.

"He was a little guy that really loved his job."

Valid Appeal's way with the ladies paid off. In twenty-one crops, the compact bay stallion with the short nose and distinctive look sired eighty-six stakes winners, five grade I winners, and runners that averaged a very impressive $69,899 in earnings. His total progeny earnings, nearly $46 million through April 2002, make him Florida's all-time leading sire.

Valid Appeal had only one bad habit; he bolted whenever he was let out in his paddock. His handlers tried every trick they could think of to curtail the irritating and dangerous game, but the little stallion just loved to be set free.

Once settled in his paddock Valid Appeal enjoyed human company, and he loved to be scratched. Anyone willing to scrub on the top of his hind end was a very welcome visitor, indeed.

Valid Appeal was pensioned from stud duty in late 1997, and in late 2001 the twenty-nine-year-old stallion became part of the sale of Mockingbird Farm. Harry Mangurian Jr., dispersing his stock and property holdings, sold the farm to Eugene Melnyk. As part of the deal, Melnyk would provide Valid Appeal a lifetime home in his familiar paddock and stall.

Sadly, the deal never had to be fulfilled. "He wanted to be a horse, and he wanted to be outside," Drier said. Valid Appeal had always preferred his paddock to a stall's confinement, and it was in his paddock that Valid Appeal reached his end.

Drier had taken a new job at nearby Sez Who Thoroughbreds, but happily agreed to continue tending to Valid Appeal as the farm sale moved forward. Until the week before his death, the old stallion, who had just turned thirty, had been in unusually good health. Then, he took a sudden turn.

"He got really, really weak," Drier said. "He couldn't hold his head on the level for more than thirty or forty-five seconds, then it would go back down. He was uncomfortable. Maybe he was lonely. He was the last horse on the property.

"You could see his body was closing down," Drier continued. "Right up to the last days he'd come up and try to nip you. But the last day, I put my leather coat out for him and he wouldn't even try."

Mangurian was contacted, options were discussed, and the sad decision was made. Drier could not bring himself to be present the morning of January 5, 2002, when the grand little stallion breathed his last. But the devoted horseman helped transport his old friend to the timeless Mockingbird/Tartan Farm horseshoe-shaped cemetery.

"He's buried right next to his mother, Desert Trial. He's also up there near Intentionally, his grandsire," Drier said. "He has family ties all up there around that ring."

Mockingbird Farm issued a press release for their fallen star, which noted the ironic timing. Valid Appeal and Desert Trial were the first horses ever to step foot on Mockingbird Farm. Three decades later, Valid Appeal was also the last to depart.

The Vanderbilt Mares

*D*ecember 6, 1999. Gray gloom lay thick over Aqueduct, and intermittent rains had turned the track to slop. Light fog enveloped the afternoon scene, the backstretch barely visible from the front side. It was a dark day, when racing was not conducted, and yet a horse and rider emerged from the shrouded backstretch. They were barely visible, first walking and then jogging slowly down the backside. The horse moved deliberately, its neck bowed, the rider holding it back.

As they rounded the far turn into the long, muddy homestretch, their features emerged through the colorless murk. The horse was galloping now, a chestnut filly with a long tail and blazed face. The rider, nearly inert, wore the familiar cerise-and-white silks of the great sportsman Alfred Vanderbilt.

Tears flowed freely as countless horsemen and friends, old and young alike, watched from Aqueduct's fourth-floor clubhouse. They watched in silence, unable to hear the lonely sounds of the solo horse's breathing and hoofbeats through the glass. The horse swept beneath the wire, the famed silks glowing through the grayness, made its way around the clubhouse turn, and disappeared back into the afternoon fog.

The infield toteboard glowed: ALFRED GWYNNE VANDERBILT, 1912-1999.

A solo set of deep hoofprints remained.

It was the last set of hoofprints ever left under Vanderbilt silks.

* * *

Alfred Vanderbilt, in describing why he bred his mare Geisha to Discovery, once said: "Well, I gave the mating of Geisha to Discovery a great deal of study, and the somewhat nebulous value of my twenty years' experience, and lo and behold, here came Native Dancer. Quite naturally, I'm not going to tell you that I have given a great deal of study and the background of my twenty years' experience to the mating of all my other horses, many of whom cannot get out of their own way. One can feel much more of an expert if one does not mention these others."

Mr. Vanderbilt didn't sing his own praises, but while Native Dancer shone above them all, many other

LOW CUT
GR. M. 1978, BY THE AXE II—SHOW OFF,
BY OLYMPIA

SHIVER MY TIMBERS
B. M. 1974, BY NORTHERN DANCER—IVORY TOWER,
BY HILL PRINCE

Vanderbilt colorbearers spoke for him. Low Cut and Shiver My Timbers, descendants of the famed Gray Ghost of Sagamore, were among them. The two mares, both fourth-generation Vanderbilt-breds, are among the few remaining mares bred by Mr. Vanderbilt.

Shiver My Timbers, a slim bay mare, is by Northern Dancer and out of a Hill Prince mare. Northern Dancer's broodmare sire was Native Dancer. Low Cut, a strong gray mare, is by The Axe II out of the multiple stakes-winning Olympia mare Show Off. Show Off was out of a Native Dancer mare named Look Ma.

Shiver My Timbers was born in 1974, and Low Cut followed four years later. Both fillies grew up at Sagamore Farm in Glyndon, Maryland, and each raced without much success. Mary Eppler, who eventually trained horses for Mr. Vanderbilt, started at Sagamore in 1979. "Low Cut was the first horse I broke for Mr. Vanderbilt," she said. "Later, (her foal) Up in Front was the first horse I trained."

While Low Cut and Shiver My Timbers didn't inspire much applause from race-going crowds, their offspring did. Both mares retired to Sagamore, where Barbara Twilley tended to the broodmares and Mary Eppler broke the offspring.

"From Up in Front on, I trained all of Low Cut's babies," Mary said. "They were the best to break, unlike Shiver's, who were the toughest to break. Local Problem — he was a real problem. I put the tack on him, and he fought for five hours before I could even get back into the stall to take the tack off. They were very, very tough.

"All of Low Cut's were just wonderful," Mary continued. "You could have used them as the lead ponies for Shiver's babies."

The mares' babies, both the tough and the polite, showed their true cerise-and-white colors at the track.

Shiver My Timbers produced two stakes winners. Local Problem, by Sagamore stallion Restless Native, earned $281,633 and won eleven of his fifty-four starts, including the Gen. Douglas MacArthur Handicap. Over the Brink, by Overskate, won twelve of forty-six starts, including the Bertram F. Bongard and Damon Runyon stakes, and earned $275,470.

Known for the witty naming of his foals, a tradition that undoubtedly caused Jockey Club employees angst, Mr. Vanderbilt had fun with Low Cut. Among Low Cut's foals were Ogle (by Oh Say), Up in Front (Mr. Leader), Down in Back (D'Accord), Half Staff (Personal Flag), Gash (Distinctive Pro), Way Out Front (Opening Verse), Nice Slice (Distinctive Pro), and Opening Address (Opening Verse). Some names, such as Opening Address, are delightfully subtle.

Two were stakes winners. Ogle earned $276,455 in an eight-season career, winning or placing in twenty-eight of eighty-six starts. He won the Breeders' Cup Handicapper Championship Stakes at Penn National and placed in four stakes. An over-sized gray, Gash raced twelve times, won four, and earned $127,301. He won the New York Stallion Times Square Stakes and finished third in the grade II Peter Pan.

Alfred Vanderbilt's son Nicholas, his only child interested in racing, was tragically lost in a British Columbian climbing expedition in 1984. With no children interested in continuing his Sagamore dreams, Mr. Vanderbilt sold the property three years later.

Broodmare manager Barbara Twilley accepted a job on Long Island, and Shiver My Timbers and Low Cut went with her. Two years later, when Barbara returned to the rolling hills of Maryland, Alfred Vanderbilt's two mares were again in tow.

Barbara and the mares lived at Halcyon Farm, just miles from their old Sagamore home. A decade passed as Sagamore's beautiful old barns ached for fresh care and paint, but the two mares grazed contentedly in Halcyon's expansive fields.

What Mr. Vanderbilt meant to the sport defies description. He was a last reminder of a better time, when racing was a sport of honor and pageantry. He always had a polite word for passersby, and he spent his lifetime improving the sport he loved. He didn't dwell in the past but relished the opportunity to share time with others. He had a soft spot for the ladies and always seemed to have freshly baked chocolate chip cookies tucked in a coat pocket. He had a willing smile and a magic heart.

Even that, however, doesn't come close to describing how unique "Mr. V" was.

While nearly blind toward the end of his life, Mr. Vanderbilt visited the track every morning to listen to the sounds and talk with friends, including the morning of November 12, 1999. That day, he returned to his Long Island home and died suddenly of a stroke. He was eighty-seven.

OPENING ADDRESS, A DAUGHTER OF LOW CUT, REPRESENTED HER REVERED OWNER ONE FINAL TIME.

As the Vanderbilt children had no interest in carrying on their father's racing interests, Mr. Vanderbilt's will directed his horses be sold at auction. Many of his trophies were sold as well.

Trophies engraved with names like "Find," "Loser Weeper," "North Sea," and "Discovery" found their way onto internet sites and were scattered around the world to web-savvy buyers. The horses were sent to Fasig-Tipton Timonium in February 2000.

The lovely gray Low Cut, in foal to Vanderbilt's last stakes winner, Traitor, sold for $20,000. The twenty-two-year-old mare had never before worn a hip number, but it would not be long before she would wear one again.

Shiver My Timbers was spared the auctioneer's gavel. Her final foal came in 1994, a Personal Flag colt. The birth was difficult, and the twenty-year-old Shiver My Timbers burst a uterine artery. The attending veterinarian, Dr. Win Stevens, used a blood-slowing medicine before transporting the stricken mare to his clinic. Surgery was performed, and she was saved.

She would not have another foal, however. Shiver My Timbers, an unmarketable twenty-six-year-old pensioner, found solace at Halcyon Farm.

Almost two years later, on December 2, 2001, Low Cut again entered the Timonium sales ring. In a poignant gesture, Halcyon Farm's Stiles T. Colwill bought the twenty-three-year-old gray mare for $1,200, and Low Cut headed back to Halcyon.

"She was shaking when she got in the ring," Barbara Twilley recalled. "And she was shaking when she got on the van."

Low Cut returned on a Monday and was moved into a stall across from Shiver My Timbers. The two old mares hollered at each other all week. That Friday, as Barbara led Shiver My Timbers to her paddock and another groom led Low Cut to hers, Shiver pulled Barbara toward Low Cut.

They released the mares into the same field, and the reunited duo galloped off, up a gently rolling hill.

Every morning at eight, the pensioned pair gallop up their hill together. The thick gray mare is stunning, her tail high and her ears forward in happy freedom. The bay mare gallops more tenuously, her ears flicking uncertainly.

The two stop on the hilltop and view their surroundings. Has anything changed overnight? The gray mare drops her head to graze. Low Cut, twenty-four, is nearly white now, with a strong look that harks back to Native Dancer.

The bay mare takes her place behind Low Cut. A worrier, Shiver My Timbers' head disappears behind her gray friend when she grazes, but pops up frequently. Her eyes are large and poignantly expressive. A white star that might have once been small has spread up her delicate face. She bears little, if any, resemblance to the Gray Ghost.

"She's twenty-eight, going on two," Barbara said of Shiver My Timbers. "She's very high-strung, flighty." Shiver My Timbers is losing her sight, but Barbara added with a slight smile, "She's just like Mr. Vanderbilt was. She sees what she wants to see."

Low Cut's dam is buried at Halcyon; one day Low Cut and Shiver My Timbers will be as well. They are the oldest living mares bred by Alfred Vanderbilt and, sadly, two of the last.

They have a combined commercial value of $1,200. But the two old friends are truly priceless.

* * *

Opening Address won one of nineteen starts and earned $57,520. Unbeknownst to Mr. Vanderbilt, however, Opening Address was to represent him perhaps most proudly of all.

On that dreary dark day at Aqueduct, the four-year-old daughter of Low Cut held her head high and galloped in lonely flight down the homestretch, rekindling warm memories and breaking horsemen's hearts with what would never be again.

Viva Sec and Water Lily

I n my lifetime no stallion's offspring were followed as closely as Secretariat's. *Time* magazine mentioned his first foal (an Appaloosa named First Secretary), and we waited eagerly for his first runner (a filly named Sexetary, who finished fourth in her debut at Keeneland). I remember the first Secretariat to run at Saratoga, a big, thick gray colt named Brilliant Protege. He didn't win, but I photographed him dutifully, looking eagerly for similarities between him and his famous sire.

Viva Sec was one of Secretariat's more popular runners, due in part to her interesting name and her long race record. Almost two decades after her retirement I photographed Viva Sec, eager to find similarities between her and her legendary sire as well.

Two smiling women met me at a small farm on the outskirts of Lexington, Kentucky, happy to show their beautiful mare. They asked if I'd like to photograph other mares they tended to as well, including Water Lily. I hadn't known Water Lily was there, but the pensioned mare was the dam of one of my all-time favorites, Talinum.

Christine Hansen brought out Viva Sec first, and the mare circled anxiously several times. She didn't care for her situation on this unusual day. Her body is quite long and lean, and at twenty-three she still looks remarkably like a racehorse — a high-strung, eager racehorse. While she didn't remind me of Secretariat, she was a very attractive older mare.

Viva Sec depends upon Water Lily for comfort. The two are best friends, so rather than make Viva Sec tolerate the photo session alone, we decided to put them together. How often are two such quality mares together, let alone best buddies?

Next Meghann McKnight brought out Water Lily, who moved slowly with heavy, long strides. A big-boned mare with a strong look, she is full-bodied and quite sensible. She is a classic broodmare, combining grace, class, and quality.

With her companion nearby Viva Sec relaxed, and the damp sheen developing on her shoulders subsided. The farm was pastoral and choosing a location for photos was easy. The two women resembled teenage girls with their prized show ponies, and easy laughter broke the stillness.

WATER LILY
DK. B/BR. M. 1976,
BY RIVERMAN—FIRST BLOOM,
BY PRIMERA

VIVA SEC
DK. B/BR. M. 1978,
BY SECRETARIAT—VIVA LA VIVI,
BY ROYAL NOTE

Viva Sec and Water Lily are both content, and the years' passage has been kind to them. With patience and loving care provided in abundance, the two mares have an idyllic home in which to spend their twilight years.

* * *

Water Lily began her racing career in France in 1978, and in two years of racing, she won one of eleven starts. She won the Prix Yacowlef and placed in two group III events, before Nelson Bunker Hunt purchased her and shipped her to America at the end of her three-year-old season.

At four, Water Lily won her first three starts for trainer Lefty Nickerson, including the grade III Next Move Handicap. After failing in three subsequent attempts, however, she was retired. Lefty said of Water Lily: "She's a very classy filly to handle. She's an extremely intelligent filly."

Turf writer William Rudy was smitten as well, reporting after the Next Move: "Water Lily is a glistening dark bay or brown, almost black except for distinctive brown patches on her head, and an attractive feminine look."

Grade I winner Talinum has been Water Lily's leading winner to date, earning $737,818. Another of her foals is grade I placed, and she has seven winners in her fourteen foals of racing age.

She is now living the life of a pampered pensioner.

* * *

A member of Secretariat's fourth crop, Viva Sec is out of Viva La Vivi, described by William Rudy as "the lovely stakes-winning filly which used to have a cup of morning coffee (decaffeinated, it is presumed) with her trainer, Harold Hodosh."

Viva Sec campaigned for four seasons, winning ten of her thirty-five starts, and earned $307,022. She won the ungraded Dark Mirage and Grey Flight stakes, and placed in several graded races.

Viva Sec has yet to reproduce herself, but she has been quite successful. She has produced five stakes-placed runners, and of her nine runners thus far, seven are winners. Her second foal, stakes-placed Escrow Agent, is the dam of the handsome stallion Vicar.

* * *

Viva Sec produced a lovely dark bay filly by Grand Slam on March 18, 2002. She will be bred back to Grand Slam.

WATER LILY (LEFT) AND VIVA SEC

Wajima

B. H. 1972-2001, BY BOLD RULER—ISKRA, BY LE HAAR

From the beginning, he was no ordinary horse. A member of the cherished final crop of Bold Ruler, Wajima as a yearling was a thick, correct individual with unusual eyes and a finely tapered nose. At Keeneland, his look and pedigree prompted a group of four men, including top Japanese horseman Zenya Yoshida, to pay the highest price ever, at that time, for a sales yearling: $600,000.

High expectations awaited Wajima, who was named after a popular Japanese sumo wrestler of the time. He was favored in ten (odds-on eight times) of his sixteen career starts. Racing just four times at two, he won two races and finished second in the grade I Laurel Futurity.

A minor injury kept him out of the classics, but he quickly made up for it. Wajima reeled off five consecutive wins as a three-year-old, including the grade I Travers and Monmouth Invitational. Perhaps more impressively, he met five-year-old Forego on three occasions, and in two of those, the grade I Governor and Marlboro Cup, he defeated the handicap star.

After second-place finishes in the grade I Woodward and Jockey Club Gold Cup, Wajima was syndicated for a world-record price of $7.2 million (besting Secretariat's record of $6.08 million) and was whisked off to stud. His record at three of seven wins in twelve starts earned him three-year-old colt championship honors.

He arrived at Spendthrift Farm in Kentucky to much fanfare, including the presentation of a Governor's Citation, but his stud career was not impressive. His best offspring included stakes winners Excitable Lady and Polite Rebuff and Canadian grade I winner Key to the Moon.

When Spendthrift began to crumble financially, an equine exodus ensued, and Wajima was moved to Stone Farm in 1987. When his fertility became an issue, it was

not a huge loss to the breeding industry. Wajima was pensioned in 1992.

Wajima lived in relative anonymity, for years occupying a back paddock not part of the Stone Farm stallion tour. He grew a noticeable goiter on his throat and no longer had the thick, sleek look that caused such a fuss in the mid-1970s. But with his unusual eyes and finely tapered nose, he was still instantly recognizable.

The staff noticed Wajima wasn't doing well, and trying to lift the old horse's spirits, they moved him to a front paddock in autumn of 2000. For a horse who must have seen many things, he was kind and quite curious about the world. Before Halo's death, Wajima often spent moments staring quietly at that grand black horse in his adjacent paddock.

Finally, his infirmities became insurmountable and at twenty-nine years of age, Wajima was euthanized on August 27, 2001. He was buried on the farm.

Although Wajima perhaps didn't make his mark in the breeding shed, he sired twenty-six stakes winners and is the broodmare sire of twenty-four more. Many mares will carry on his beautiful blood.

He certainly was memorable, and no one can take away from all that he accomplished. From the final crop of the immortal Bold Ruler, this stunning bay stallion brought world-record prices both as a yearling and upon retirement, won four grade Is, and beat the remarkable Forego in two of three meetings.

He was a star.

Waya (Fr)

B. M. 1974-2001, BY FARAWAY SON—WAR PATH III, BY BLUE PRINCE

*A*s a race mare, she was a fierce competitor, full of fire and determination. She was so difficult that her racetrack groom was paid double wages. She was so headstrong that starters learned to back her into the starting gate, as she caused less of a fuss that way. But Waya could flat-out *run*.

Her career began in 1977 in France, where she won three of eight starts, including two group stakes. The next year Waya was brought to America, and owner Daniel Wildenstein turned her over to trainer Angel Penna. She won two allowance tests and finished second in two stakes, then reeled off four consecutive stakes victories. In the Man o' War Stakes and Turf Classic, both against males, she defeated such top performers as Tiller, Trillion, and Mac Diarmida.

In her 1978 finale, Waya finished third behind Mac Diarmida in the Washington, D.C., International. Mac Diarmida was crowned turf champion. As there was no Eclipse Award given specifically to turf fillies or mares, Waya — who had split victories with Mac Diarmida in their two meetings — would have to wait.

In 1979, for new owners Peter Brant and George Strawbridge Jr., Waya earned her own Eclipse Award.

Running in Peter Brant's colors and trained by David Whiteley, Waya won five stakes, including the grade I Santa Barbara and Top Flight handicaps and Beldame Stakes, and the Santa Ana Handicap. While she lost more races than she won that year, her dominance in her wins, including a rousing score under 131 pounds in the Santa Barbara, earned her the coveted statuette for champion handicap mare. Waya was retired with a record of twenty-nine starts, fourteen wins, six seconds, four thirds, and earnings of $822,948.

As a broodmare, Waya was quite successful, despite her offspring's inheriting perhaps too much of her attitude. Among her twelve foals were three stakes winners, including the handsome stallion De Niro and two additional stakes-placed runners. Her filly Seattle Way gained a moment of unwanted fame when she clipped heels at Saratoga in 1993, tossing Julie Krone to the turf. Eight

years later, Seattle Way made much happier headlines when her Kingmambo colt sold at Saratoga's Fasig-Tipton yearling sale for three million dollars.

When I wrote to George Strawbridge about visiting Waya at her Pennsylvania home, his reply mentioned she was still the strong-willed mare she'd been on the track more than twenty years earlier. He proudly noted that, while a pensioner, Waya still has strong motherly instincts and stringently guards her favorite in-foal pasture companion.

We arrived at Derry Meeting Farm and wandered into the barn. On the door of the first stall a small chalkboard was mounted, with "WAYA" written in large capital letters. In the back of the stall, the mare's eyes and trademark star glowed through the darkness.

Waya was none too happy with the visit, as she had no desire to break from her routine. While she carried a thick winter coat and a beautiful small splash of white across her temples, her body was still long and attractive, and she had little sway to her back.

She fought in childlike irritation with farm manager Bob Goodyear as he led her outside, and her large glowing eyes viewed me almost constantly no matter where we tried to make her look. Bob had infinite patience with his noble model, proud of the old champion.

When we finally gave up attempts for a perfect portrait after perhaps fifteen minutes, she swished her tail and was led — still arguing — back into the barn. There, she quickly settled back into her stall, content that we were leaving and happy to return to her unharried retirement.

* * *

Ten months later, on December 12, 2001, twenty-seven-year-old Waya was euthanized due to the debilitating effects of laminitis. Bob Goodyear could not bring himself to be present.

Wayward Lass

DK. B/BR. M. 1978, BY HAIL THE PIRATES—YOUNG MISTRESS,
BY THIRD MARTINI

*S*he's a great mother," Gus Schoenborn Jr. said, leaning forward in his chair. "She really loves her babies." But while Wayward Lass has loving maternal instincts, she has not yet come close to duplicating herself. Of her thirteen foals to race, eleven have won — an impressive statistic. But none have won or placed in a stakes race, and their earnings have not been overly impressive. But now with a new owner and a new plan, she'll have another chance.

Gus tends to Wayward Lass at his Contemporary Stallions in upstate New York, featuring a Catskill Mountains backdrop and brilliant sunsets. When Dr. Zacaries Aragon studied Wayward Lass' catalog page at the 1999 Fasig-Tipton Kentucky December sale, something caught his eye.

"Dr. Aragon thought she'd never really gotten a shot with a speed sire," Gus said. "She's been bred to horses like Dancing Brave, so he decided to try something different." Indeed, the stallions she has been bred to are among the finest in the world — Shareef Dancer, Lyphard, Dancing Brave, Last Tycoon — but most were not speed-oriented.

Dr. Aragon and his daughter Liz contacted Gus, who was promoting his new sire Rodeo. A brilliantly fast son of Gone West, Rodeo had just entered stud. Wayward Lass was shipped there, and in 2001 her Rodeo filly was born. Perhaps she'll be the one…

While many hopes ride on the new foal, anything else that Wayward Lass does for racing is simply a bonus. She has more than made her mark.

She raced primarily in New York for Flying Zee Stables and trainer Jose Martin, at a time when good race fillies were abundant. Looking at her charts sets an old-timer to remembering: Heavenly Cause, Dame Mysterieuse, Real Prize, De La Rose, Truly Bound…That she won nine of her twenty-five starts is a testament to the quality of her competition.

Wayward Lass won her share, including a neck score

in the grade I Mother Goose (over Heavenly Cause) and a win via disqualification in the grade I Coaching Club American Oaks. In addition, she dominated the competition at Aqueduct's inner track during the winter months of early 1981, prevailing in the Busanda by seven lengths, the Searching by twelve, and the Ruthless by eleven.

Those races, combined with placings in the Ashland, Fantasy Stakes, Kentucky Oaks, and Black-Eyed Susan, were enough to earn Wayward Lass the Eclipse Award for three-year-old filly.

Wayward Lass produced one foal for Flying Zee owner Carl Lizza Jr. before being sold at the 1983 Keeneland November sale for $2.35 million. Wayward Lass eventually made her way to Great Britain. For nearly a decade her foals were bred in the name of Sheikh Mohammed or the affiliated Darley Stud.

But royal breedings were not enough, and in 1994 she went through the same November sales ring for only seven thousand dollars. Five years later at Fasig-Tipton December, she brought $8,500 and was shipped to New York.

Wayward Lass' foal was just days away from weaning when I visited in late 2001. The filly no longer clung to her mother, wandering with the other foals as their dams grazed peacefully in the large paddock. Hudson River painter Frederick Church picked the Catskill region for a reason, and Wayward Lass and her friends painted a beautiful scene there as well.

A lovely, kind mare, Wayward Lass has both a trusting nature and a world of class. She still looks the part of a champion. Even now at twenty-four, she looks like two million bucks.

WAYWARD LASS WITH HER 2001 RODEO FILLY

Zuppardo's Prince

DK. B/BR. H. 1976, BY CORNISH PRINCE—PRIM LADY,
BY PRIMATE

 ew stallions have dominated a region as Zuppardo's Prince has. Through 2001, the sturdy dark bay stallion has been Louisiana's leading sire for eight of the past twelve years.

In four years of competition, the horse with the memorable name won back-to-back Phoenix Handicaps at Keeneland, ran second in the Derby Trial, and placed in consecutive Pelleteri handicaps. He won twelve of twenty-eight starts, placed in nine more, and earned $181,547.

Zuppardo's Prince was owned by Tony and Frances Zuppardo, and upon his retirement, Jack Lohman syndicated the stallion to stand at his Clear Creek Stud.

Lohman began the Folsom, Louisiana, farm in 1969, and two impressive names stood there in the early years: Assagai and Gran Zar. Zuppardo's Prince was a natural addition, as he not only had a strong race record but also solid bloodlines.

His third dam, Top Flight, was champion two-year-old and three-year-old filly. The blazed-faced filly earned an impressive $275,900 in the early 1930s. Among Top Flight's five winners was White Lady. White Lady produced nine foals, each of which won, including stakes-winning Prim Lady. Of Prim Lady's four winners, Zuppardo's Prince was the finest.

Zuppardo's Prince's first foals arrived in 1983, and although none won a stakes, twenty-three of his twenty-five foals raced. Twenty-one won. From his next crop came the hard-knocking One Tough Cat, who earned nearly $200,000. He won the Louisiana Stallion Stakes, the Lecomte, and the Lakefront Futurity.

Zuppardo's Prince's richest earner is one of the few horses to carry his name. Zuppardo Ardo, a long bay filly with a blaze, earned $667,886 in five seasons. Among her ten stakes wins was Churchill Downs' grade II Humana Distaff.

Astas Foxy Lady was perhaps Zuppardo's Prince's most popular runner. The diminutive chestnut lass romped in Saratoga's grade II Adirondack Stakes and ran second in the Spinaway, Schuylerville, Matron, all graded races, and the Kentucky Breeders' Cup.

* * *

Zuppardo's Prince just keeps chugging along. When I visited in 2000, the stallion's class glowed through. He

wasn't easy to photograph, as he enjoys visitors and likes being up close and personal. It's obvious that he's received loving care in abundance.

Val Murrell, part of a group that bought Clear Creek Stud, is justifiably proud of Zuppardo's Prince's accomplishments.

"He still gets them in foal, and we just kind of pamper him along," Murrell said. "He's a real class act.

"It's funny, but when you watch him out there grazing in his field he kind of looks like, you know, a twenty-six-year-old horse. But then you put the shank on him to take him to the breeding shed, and he looks like an eight-year-old."

After leaving Zuppardo's Prince, we passed through several small stallion barns. The groom pointed to a stallion named Malagra, whose ears were pinned. Malagra is the sire of a filly who was just then making a name for herself. The Louisiana-based Hallowed Dreams had won eleven straight, on her way to tying Citation's and Cigar's record of sixteen wins in a row.

In a paddock on the left, Bayou Hebert walked eagerly to us. It was hard to believe, but this consistent sire was even sweeter than Zuppardo's Prince.

A nearby area was splashed in dancing light — green, yellow, and brown. As with much of Louisiana, the plant life is thick, and far off trees hung heavy and protectively over two simple headstones. As I moved closer in hushed silence, the names came into focus: Assagai and Gran Zar. These two early Clear Creek stallions, both classic old champions, were interred in this idyllic, quiet haven.

When Zuppardo's Prince's days on earth are over, Murrell plans to lay his dark bay stallion beside them.

"He'll be right there," Murrell said. "He has to be. He's been such a major part of the farm."

Acknowledgments

For their help with this project, I am indebted to: Tom Gilcoyne of the National Museum of Racing and Hall of Fame, Kathy Machesky, Tom Hall, Judy Marchman, Rena Baer, Tom Keyser, Nancy Ross, and Keeneland Library's Cathy Schenck and Phyllis Rogers; Laura Darcy and Colleen Izzo for their photographic printing; Lyrical Ballad Bookstore in Saratoga Springs, N.Y.; and Sue Rosenbach, for her lovely photograph of Our Mims with Plush Dish.

Also, a most heartfelt thank you to everyone who allowed me the honor of photographing their senior Thoroughbreds.

About the Author

Barbara D. Livingston's photographs are among the most recognizable in Thoroughbred racing. The clarity, mood, and uniqueness of each moment she captures have made her a regular contributor to many publications, including *The Blood-Horse*. She has won two Eclipse Awards for outstand-

ing photography and numerous other awards. Livingston's work also has appeared in *Newsweek*, *People*, *Cigar Aficionado*, *GQ*, and on the cover of *TV Guide*. In addition, Livingston's work has appeared on many major book covers, including ones for Bantam, Doubleday, and Little, Brown and Company; a Mastercard and Visa campaign for the Adirondack Trust Company; and the Kentucky Tavern Kentucky Derby souvenir mirrors.

Her first book of photographs, *Four Seasons of Racing*, was published in 1998.

The upstate New York native first began photographing Thoroughbred racing in the early 1970s when she visited Saratoga Race Course. Over the past three decades her lens has captured scores of champions and classic racing scenes.

Livingston is a graduate of Syracuse University with a degree in fine arts.